WEST ACADE
EMERITUS /

COLLEGE SPORTS LAW

IN A NUTSHELL®

WILLIAM W. BERRY III
University of Mississippi School of Law

DANIEL E. LUST
New York Law School
Moritt Hock & Hamroff LLP

Nutshell Series, In a Nutshell and the Nutshell Logo are trademarks registered in the U.S. Patent and Trademark Office.

© 2024 LEG, Inc. d/b/a West Academic
      860 Blue Gentian Road, Suite 350
      Eagan, MN 55121
      1-877-888-1330

West, West Academic Publishing, and West Academic are trademarks of West Publishing Corporation, used under license.

Published in the United States of America

ISBN: 979-8-88786-542-3

OUTLINE

TABLE OF CASES VII

TABLE OF STATUTES AND REGULATIONS IX

TABLE OF NCAA RULES XI

TABLE OF NCAA INFRACTIONS CASES XIII

Prologue 1

Chapter One. The NCAA, the Student-Athlete, and the University 7
1. The NCAA 11
2. The Student-Athlete 12
3. NCAA Eligibility Requirements 14
4. Remuneration Before College 19
5. Progress Toward a Degree and the APR 21
6. The University-Athlete Contractual Relationship 26

Chapter Two. NCAA Enforcement 35
1. The NCAA Enforcement Staff 35
2. NCAA v. Tarkanian 39
3. Impermissible Benefits and Other Rules Violations 46
4. The Death Penalty 62
5. Criminal Activity 66

Chapter Three. The Evolution of Amateurism 75
1. The Board of Regents Case 77
2. Television Revenue 85

3. Antitrust and Amateurism 90
4. The College Basketball FBI Investigation.... 102
5. Agents and Drafts 103

**Chapter Four. Name, Image, and
Likeness** **107**
1. EA Sports, Video Games, and O'Bannon 108
2. The Fair Pay to Play Act and Alston............. 113
3. The NCAA's Interim NIL Policy.................... 117
4. State Collegiate NIL Laws............................. 119
   a. California: Senate Bill 206 (Fair Pay to
      Play Act).. 125
   b. Florida: SB 646 (Intercollegiate Athlete
      Compensation and Rights)...................... 127
5. University NIL Policies................................... 131
6. Collectives... 136
7. Boosters.. 144
8. Compliance after NIL...................................... 148
9. The Question of University Involvement...... 154
10. The Charlie Baker Era.................................... 158
11. Non-Scholarship Ivy League Athletes 161
12. Health Benefits and Insurance 163
13. EA v. Brandr.. 164
14. High School NIL Laws 165
15. High School NIL and NCAA Eligibility 177
16. Evaluating the Value of NIL 179

Chapter Five. The Transfer Portal................. **191**
1. The Evolution of NCAA Transfer Rules........ 191
2. The Application of Transfer Portal Rules 194
3. Impact of the Transfer Portal......................... 197

Chapter Six. The Change Agents of Antitrust and Employment Law 207
1. The Change Agent of Antitrust Law 207
2. House v. Nat'l Collegiate Athletic Ass'n 215
3. Choh & Kirk v. Brown University 219
4. Ohio v. NCAA 221
5. Tennessee and Virginia v. NCAA 225
6. Employee Athletes? 230
7. College Athlete Unions? 235

Chapter Seven. The Change Agent of Conference Realignment 245
1. Conference Realignment 245
2. The ACC Litigation 251
3. The End of the Pac-12 254

Chapter Eight. Coaches 257
1. Antitrust Limits on Capping Coach Salaries 258
2. The DiNardo Case 260
3. Pepper Rodgers, Jim O'Brien, Mike Leach, and Todd McNair 261
4. Coaches Behaving Badly 268
5. Coach Prime, Lane Train, and the Transfer Portal 272

Chapter Nine. The Role of Title IX 275
1. Title IX's Requirements 275
2. Cheerleading and Dance 280
3. Title IX and the NCAA 284
4. Privatization as an Alternative to Title IX? 286

5. Conference Employment as an Alternative
    to Title IX? 287
6. Transgender Athletes and Title IX 288

Chapter Ten. Gambling and Concussions 291
1. Murphy v. NCAA 292
2. A History of Point Shaving 295
3. Recent Trends in College Athletics
    Involvement in Gambling 303
4. The Concussion Cases: Gee v. NCAA 311

**Concluding Thoughts and
    Acknowledgements 315**
INDEX 317

TABLE OF CASES

References are to Pages

ACC v. University of Maryland, 250
Agnew v. NCAA, 27, 94
Banks v. NCAA, 92
Berger v. NCAA, 232
Bewley v. NCAA, 178
Bloom v. NCAA, 2, 20, 177
Boucher v. Syracuse University, 279
Brentwood Academy v. TSSAA, 44
Brown University, 238
Brown v. Pro Football, Inc., 213
Butler v. NCAA, 18
Chicago Board of Trade v. United States, 81
Choh & Kirk v. Brown University, 162, 219
Clarett v. NFL, 104
Conard v. University of Washington, 33
Cureton v. NCAA, 17
Dawson v. NCAA, 233
Decision and Direction of Election, Trustees of Dartmouth College, 162, 240
Deppe v. NCAA, 95
Dexter v. Big League Advance Fund II, 124
Doe 1 v. Baylor University, 72
Federal Baseball Club v. National League, 207
Gaines v. NCAA, 94
Ganden v. NCAA, 18
Gatto, United States v., 103, 123, 227
Glatt v. Fox Searchlight Pictures, Inc., 234
Grove City College v. Bell, 276
House v. NCAA, 215
Hutcheson, United States v., 105
Hysaw v. Washburn University of Topeka, 31
Jackson v. Drake University, 30
Johnson v. NCAA, 233
Law v. NCAA, 258
Leach v. Texas Tech University, 265
McCormack v. NCAA, 93

McNair v. NCAA, 267

Murphy v. NCAA, 160, 294

National Collegiate Athletic Association Student-Athlete Concussion Injury Litigation, In re, 311

NCAA v. Alston, 10, 85, 100, 209

NCAA v. Board of Regents of University of Oklahoma, 77, 84, 208

NCAA v. Lasege, 19, 177

NCAA v. Miller, 45

NCAA v. Smith, 212, 284

NCAA v. Tarkanian, 42

New York v. United States, 294

Northwestern University, 236, 237

O'Bannon v. NCAA, 9, 112

O'Brien v. Ohio State University, 263

Ohio v. NCAA, 193, 221

Parish v. NCAA, 15

Pederson v. Louisiana State University, 280

Printz v. United States, 294

Rodgers v. Ga. Tech. Athletic Assn., 261

Ross v. Creighton Univ., 23

Soule v. Connecticut Interscholastic Athletic Conference, 290

Standard Oil Company of New Jersey v. United States, 80

Taylor v. Wake Forest, 30

Tennessee & Virginia v. NCAA, 62, 122, 140, 152, 228

Trustees of Columbia University in the City of New York, The, 238

TSSAA v. Brentwood Academy, 44

Vanderbilt University v. DiNardo, 260

Waldrep v. Texas Employers Insurance Association, 231

TABLE OF STATUTES AND REGULATIONS

References are to Pages

---

20 U.S.C. § 1681.. 275
20 U.S.C. §§ 1681 et seq. 276
28 U.S.C. §§ 3701–3704.. 292
29 U.S.C. § 152(3) 235
29 U.S.C. § 203(e)(1) 231
29 U.S.C. § 203(g) 231
29 U.S.C. § 206(a) 231
29 U.S.C. § 207(a)(1) 231
42 U.S.C. § 1981.. 32
42 U.S.C. § 1983.. 31, 32
P.L. 93–380 276
34 C.F.R. § 106.41(c).................................... 276, 277, 278

TABLE OF NCAA RULES

References are to Pages

1990–91 NCAA Division I Manual, Bylaw 12.2.4.2 92
1990–91 NCAA Division I Manual, Bylaw 12.3.1 91
1993–94 NCAA Division I Manual, Bylaw 14.1.8.2 284
2002–03 NCAA Division I Manual, Bylaw 12.1.2 2
2002–03 NCAA Division I Manual, Bylaw 12.5.1.3 2
2009–10 NCAA Division I Manual, Bylaw 15.3.3.1 94
2009–10 NCAA Division I Manual, Bylaw 15.5.4 94
2017–18 NCAA Division I Manual, Bylaw 14.5 191
2017–18 NCAA Division I Manual, Bylaw 14.5.5.1 191
2018–19 NCAA Division I Manual, Bylaw 14.5.5.1 95
2023–24 NCAA Division I Manual, Const. art. 2.9 13
2023–24 NCAA Division I Manual, Bylaw 6.01.1 37
2023–24 NCAA Division I Manual, Bylaw 6.1.3 39
2023–24 NCAA Division I Manual, Bylaw 12.2.4 104
2023–24 NCAA Division I Manual, Bylaw 12.2.5 .... 19, 21, 177
2023–24 NCAA Division I Manual, Bylaw 12.3 104
2023–24 NCAA Division I Manual, Bylaw 12.4.1 215
2023–24 NCAA Division I Manual, Bylaw 12.4.1.1 215
2023–24 NCAA Division I Manual, Bylaw 12.4.2.3 215
2023–24 NCAA Division I Manual, Bylaw 12.4.4 215
2023–24 NCAA Division I Manual, Bylaw 12.5.1.1(f)... 154
2023–24 NCAA Division I Manual, Bylaw 12.5.2.1 215
2023–24 NCAA Division I Manual, Bylaw 12.11.4.2 ... 193, 222
2023–24 NCAA Division I Manual, Bylaw 14.5 ... 192, 193, 222
2023–24 NCAA Division I Manual, Bylaw 16.02.3 154
2023–24 NCAA Division I Manual, Bylaw 16.3 154
2023–24 NCAA Division I Manual, Bylaw 19 et seq....... 37

TABLE OF NCAA INFRACTIONS CASES

References are to Pages

Baylor University, Public Infractions Decision, August 11, 2021, 72

Florida State University, Negotiated Resolution, Case No. 020169, January 12, 2024, 61, 140, 227

Mississippi State University Public Infractions Report, June 7, 2013, 52

Mississippi State University, Negotiated Resolution, Case No. 01001, August 23, 2019, 25

Oklahoma State University Public Infractions Decision, April 24, 2015, 53

Southern Methodist University Placed on NCAA Probation, August 16, 1985, 63

Syracuse University Public Infractions Decision, March 6, 2015, 53

The Ohio State University Public Infractions Decision, April 19, 2022, 59

United States Air Force Academy, Negotiated Resolution, Case No. 020232, September 28, 2023, 308

University of Alabama, Negotiated Resolution, Case No. 020261, February 1, 2024, 310

University of Alabama, Tuscaloosa Public Infractions Report, February 1, 2002, 63

University of Georgia Public Infractions Report, August 5, 2004, 49

University of Louisville Public Infractions Decision, June 15, 2017, 56

University of Louisville, Decision of the NCAA Division I Infractions Appeals Committee, No. 473, February 20, 2018, 56

University of Miami (Florida) Public Infractions Report, October 22, 2013, 65

University of Miami (Florida), Negotiated Resolution, Case No. 020161, February 24, 2023, 61, 149, 227

University of Mississippi Public Infractions Decision,
  December 1, 2017, 58
University of Missouri, Columbia Decision of the NCAA
  Division I Infractions Appeals Committee, Nov. 16,
  2019, 25
University of Missouri, Columbia Public Infractions
  Decision, August 2, 2016, 54
University of Nevada Las Vegas, Placed on NCAA
  Probation, August 26, 1977, 41
University of North Carolina at Chapel Hill Public
  Infractions Decision, 2017, 24
University of Notre Dame Public Infractions Decision,
  November 22, 2016, 55
University of Notre Dame, Decision of the NCAA Division
  I Infractions Appeals Committee, No. 453, February 13,
  2018, 55
University of Southern California Public Infractions
  Report, June 10, 2010, 266
University of Tennessee, Knoxville, Public Infractions
  Report, August 24, 2011, 50

COLLEGE
SPORTS LAW
IN A NUTSHELL®

PROLOGUE

Intercollegiate Sports Law is the study of the application of legal and administrative rules to college athletics by the NCAA and courts. It is currently undergoing a shift from its historical model to an unsettled, emerging one.

The career of Jeremy Bloom illustrates the sea change occurring in intercollegiate sports. The NCAA blocked him from receiving endorsements because he was a student-athlete. State laws now allow college athletes to monetize their name, image, and likeness (NIL). And recent changes would also have allowed him to share the revenue generated by the University of Colorado football team.

As a teenager, Bloom enjoyed a successful career as a freestyle skier. He won a gold and a silver medal at the 2003 World Championships and a bronze medal at the same competition in 2005. In the 2002 Winter Olympics in Salt Lake City, Bloom finished ninth in the mogul competition. An appearance on MTV made him a household name. Bloom possessed a flair for competition and Hollywood-level appearance. Endorsement opportunities abounded, especially with ski equipment companies. Bloom received an offer to host a show on Nickelodeon. And he had a contract to model clothing for Tommy Hilfiger.

In the fall of 2002, Bloom discontinued his endorsement, modeling, and media activities. Bloom had signed a letter of intent to play football for the University of Colorado. He feared the endorsements

would interfere with his eligibility to play football.
Bloom wanted to be a professional skier and an
amateur football player. NCAA Bylaw 12.1.2
provided that a pro athlete may represent an
institution as an amateur in a different sport. As a
result, Bloom asked the NCAA to allow him to profit
off of his name, image and likeness.

The NCAA rejected Bloom's request because of its
principle of amateurism. As an amateur, Bloom could
only receive tuition, room, board, and books. If the
NCAA allowed him to receive endorsements, it
concluded that he would no longer be an amateur.
Bloom sued the NCAA in state court before the start
of the football season. *Bloom v. NCAA*, 93 P. 3d 621
(Colo. Ct. App. 2004). He sought an injunction that
would allow him to receive endorsements. Bloom
argued that (1) Bylaw 12.1.2 allowed pro skiers to
play amateur football; (2) the normal way to pay
skiers was NIL; and therefore (3) pro skiers could
receive NIL money while playing amateur football.

The Colorado Court of Appeals disagreed. It
deferred to the NCAA's interpretation of the rules.
NCAA bylaws "prohibit every student-athlete from
receiving   money   for   advertisements   and
endorsements." Bylaw 12.5.1.3 stated that an athlete
who accepts payment for NIL is ineligible to play.
Under the law of the association, courts usually defer
to associations. And the court found that the NCAA's
interpretation was not arbitrary or capricious. It did
not matter why a company was paying Bloom for his
NIL. Whether for athletic ability or good looks, NIL
payments made athletes ineligible.

The NCAA's amateurism rule cost Bloom a significant amount of money and career opportunity. Even so, Bloom went on to star as a Colorado receiver, making the freshman All-America team. He then played in the NFL briefly for the Philadelphia Eagles and the Pittsburgh Steelers. Bloom concluded his athletic career by returning to the slopes. He was unable to replicate his earlier successes.

As explored in Chapter One, the amateurism principle that the NCAA defended in *Bloom* has a long history. The concept of student-athlete rests at the heart of the modern NCAA. The NCAA has justified its principle as a form of protection against exploitation. In many situations, the NCAA has fought for this principle in the name of protecting athletes. Increasingly, public opinion has questioned whether the same principle likewise harmed athletes. And in May, 2024, the NCAA finally abandoned its prohibition of pay-for-play, approving a model to allow athletes to share in revenue generated by athletics.

Chapter Two recounts a number of the NCAA's efforts to enforce its amateurism rules against universities, athletes, and boosters. This chapter discusses the challenges inherent in enforcing NCAA rules and the sometimes draconian approach it has taken to punishing violations.

Chapter Three then examines the recent shift away from amateurism. Not only has the scope of athlete remuneration broadened in recent years to include cost of attendance and other compensation related to education, but also now allows basketball players to hire agents and enter the NBA draft without losing eligibility.

Chapter Four explores the heart of the current athlete compensation landscape—the monetization of athlete name, image, and likenesses. Under this new model, athletes can receive NIL compensation from third parties, but universities can only pay athletes education-related costs.

Chapter Five describes the major change that has paralleled the rise of NIL—the opening of the transfer portal and the loosening of restrictions on transferring schools. These changes together have been most responsible for the shift in college sports since July, 2021, especially the revenue sports of football and basketball.

Chapters Six and Seven consider the tripartite change agents to the prior status quo—antitrust litigation, according employee status to athletes, and conference realignment. A recent antitrust settlement will allow revenue sharing for the first time. A shift from student-athlete to employee-athlete would similarly amount to a significant change in the relationship between athlete and university, including the receipt of various employee benefits and the right to form unions in some places. Finally, the ongoing reshuffling of universities in the major conferences also threatens to narrow the number of schools participating in elite college football as an NFL-like model seems to be emerging.

Chapter Eight explores the role of coaches in intercollegiate athletics. Coaches enjoy lucrative contracts, but such contracts can give rise to litigation. Coaches also play an increasingly important role in college athletics given the rise of NIL and the complexities of the transfer portal.

Chapter Nine discusses the important role of Title IX in intercollegiate athletics. Title IX serves as a tool to promote and preserve gender equity. It also may play a role in preserving non-revenue sports amidst increasing commercialization in intercollegiate athletics.

Finally, Chapter Ten considers the intersection of gambling and college athletics. After explaining how the Supreme Court opened the door to growth in this area, the chapter explores how gambling might influence the future of college athletics.

This first edition of this book covers changes through the end of May, 2024, when the book went to press. In the interim before a future edition, we plan to cover major developments to college sports law on Professor Lust's podcast, *Conduct Detrimental: The Sports Law Podcast, and website*, https://www.conductdetrimental.com/.

CHAPTER ONE

THE NCAA, THE STUDENT-ATHLETE, AND THE UNIVERSITY

The story of college sports law begins with the story of the founding of the National Collegiate Athletic Association (NCAA). At least for now, the NCAA controls and oversees much of intercollegiate athletics.

In its infant stages, football was a brutal sport. During the 1904 season, 18 athletes died and another 159 received serious injuries. Some universities stopped football on their campuses. Many called for reform or abolition. At the urging of President Theodore Roosevelt, a group of Ivy League administrators met in December of 1905. On March 31, 1906, sixty-two schools founded the Intercollegiate Athletic Association of the United States (IAAUS). In 1910, the IAAUS changed its name to the National Collegiate Athletic Association (NCAA).

From the beginning, college football players received financial benefits, including scholarships and other forms of remuneration. Walter Camp, the coach at Yale, awarded the team captain James Hogan a ten day paid vacation in Cuba and a monopoly on the sale of American Tobacco Company products on campus in addition to tuition, a swanky apartment, and a stipend. Similar payments to athletes occurred throughout college football.

After World War II, the NCAA adopted the "Sanity Code," designed to impose uniform rules on college athletes and define the scope of amateurism. This 1948 code permitted the awarding of scholarships and jobs, with the caveat that athletes had to demonstrate financial neediness. In 1956, the NCAA sanctioned the awarding of athletic scholarships without regard to an athlete's promise or economic hardships.

Under the leadership of Walter Byers, the NCAA standardized its definition of amateurism and increasingly monitored athletic programs to ensure their compliance. During his tenure, the NCAA coined the phrase "student-athlete" to both emphasize the educational mission of intercollegiate athletics and to shield the NCAA and its members from workers' compensation lawsuits stemming from sports-related injuries. Student-athletes could receive tuition, room, board, and books, but those costs were educational in nature. Covering these expenses did not make athletes into university employees, at least from the perspective of the NCAA. Benefits provided to athletes beyond these categories violated NCAA rules and resulted in the athlete permanently losing eligibility to compete in college sports. The NCAA also regularly imposed sanctions imposed on universities, even if third parties provided the benefits.

A 1955 lawsuit in which the NCAA prevailed over deceased football player Ray Dennison, demonstrated the litigation value of the student-athlete concept. Dennison was a Fort Lewis A&M

lineman who suffered a shattered skull during a game. In that case, the court denied Dennison workmen's compensation because he was a student-athlete. Interestingly, Byers disavowed the use of the term student-athlete forty years later in his 1995 memoir, *Unsportsmanlike Conduct: Exploiting College Athletes.*

For decades, playing varsity NCAA sports was a three-year experience, as freshman were ineligible to play on the varsity team, even if they were better than the varsity athletes. Famously, UCLA's 1965–66 freshman team with Lew Alcindor (who later changed his name to Kareem Abdul-Jabbar) defeated the number one ranked varsity team. Beginning in 1972, the NCAA allowed freshmen to participate in varsity football and basketball.

The amateurism limit of tuition, room, board, and books remained static until 2015. In *O'Bannon v. NCAA* (see Chapter Four), the United States Court of Appeals for the Ninth Circuit held that the NCAA's amateurism rules violated antitrust law because they prevented universities from covering the full cost of attendance of college athletes. *O'Bannon v. NCAA*, 802 F.3d 1049 (9th Cir. 2015). The cost of attendance is an additional amount, above tuition, room, board, and books, that students incur through attending college, including travel, transportation, and other incidental expenses. The cost of attendance amount at most universities ranges from $5,000 to $10,000 above tuition, room, board, and books. The *O'Bannon* court considered the cost of attendance amount to be an additional educational cost protected by antitrust law.

In 2021, the Supreme Court decided *NCAA v. Alston* (see Chapter Four), which further expanded the definition of amateurism to include "all costs related to education" beyond tuition, room, board, books, and cost of attendance. *NCAA v. Alston*, 594 U.S. 69 (2021). According to the Court's decision, these costs can include computers, science equipment, musical instruments, summer abroad programs, and graduate school tuition. They also include an annual stipend of $5,980, known as "Alston money." The $5,980 amount related to the most compensation an individual student could receive in an academic year in participation, championship, or special achievement awards. The NCAA adopted this rule in 2020 in response to an injunction in the *Alston* case.

State laws becoming effective on July 1, 2021 and after also allowed college athletes to receive money from third parties to compensate them for use of their respective names, images, and likenesses. As explored in Chapter Four, the NCAA has struggled to place any limits on such compensation. According to its rules, NIL compensation must reflect services performed by an athlete and cannot serve as an inducement for an athlete to enroll at a particular school.

The current step in the expansion of the concept of amateurism is revenue sharing. Revenue sharing would constitute universities paying athletes some of the money received from television revenue. The settlement in the *House* lawsuit (see Chapter Six) make such arrangements possible.

1. THE NCAA

The modern NCAA regulates intercollegiate athletics. Comprised of approximately 1,120 member institutions, the NCAA has three divisions, with teams allocated in roughly 100 athletics conferences. Collectively, this includes over 500,000 athletes on 19,500 teams, with 90 championships in 24 sports. In 2023–24, Division I includes 37% of the athletes with 57% receiving athletics aid usually in the form of multi-year cost-of-attendance athletics scholarships. Division II includes 25% of athletes with 60% receiving athletics aid usually in the form of partial athletics scholarships. And Division III includes 39% of NCAA athletes, with 80% receiving non-athletics financial aid.

The NCAA, though, is just the compilation of its member institutions at its core. The NCAA staff works in conjunction with its member institutions, not independent of them. Critics that decry the NCAA should remember that college presidents are the ones who make the decisions with respect to college athletics. All faculty, staff, and students of these institutions thus "are the NCAA," represented by their respective college president or chancellor.

For much of the NCAA's history, its member institutions operated as a large democratic legislative body. The legislative model has had its challenges, with the interests of most of the universities being contrary to the Power conference schools (Southeastern Conference (SEC), Atlantic Coast Conference (ACC), Big Ten Conference (Big Ten), Big 12 Conference (Big 12), and the recently collapsed Pac-12 Conference (Pac-12). These schools make up around 65 of the over 1,000 NCAA member institutions.

For decades, the smaller programs controlled the rule-making process and limited athlete benefits to the historical tuition, room, board, and books. In 2014, Power conference schools pressured the NCAA membership into granting their conference members legislative autonomy with respect to certain rules. These autonomy rules included offering athletes multi-year scholarships and covering the cost of attendance.

This splintering continued in 2022 with the adoption of a new NCAA Constitution. The new Constitution decentralizes the NCAA's authority, delegating to each division the task of setting its own rules and shifting power to schools and conferences. This delegation includes the ability of the divisions to establish and enforce eligibility and academic standards.

2.   THE STUDENT-ATHLETE

The concept of student-athlete defines the relationship of the athlete to the university in terms of education. Under the NCAA's model, athletes attend college to receive an education, with athletic participation simply being part of that education. The NCAA's long-held "Principle of Amateurism" underscores this point. The Principle of Amateurism provides:

> Student-athletes shall be amateurs in an intercollegiate sport, and their participation should be motivated primarily by education and by the physical, mental and social benefits to be derived. Student participation in intercollegiate athletics is an avocation, and student-athletes should be protected from exploitation by professional and commercial enterprises.

2023–24 NCAA Division I Manual, Const. art. 2.9.

As such, when athletes are practicing or competing in athletic contests, they engage in an "avocation"— a recreational activity which is part of their education. The NCAA has long celebrated this idea in its advertising, emphasizing that the vast majority of its athletes "go pro" in something besides sports.

Further, the role of the NCAA is to protect college athletes from "exploitation by professional and commercial enterprises." The NCAA has used this idea to advance the notion that paying college athletes for their athletic efforts somehow corrupts the integrity of the game. Defending its ideals of amateurism remains at the heart of the NCAA's attempt to "protect" its athletes from third party interference and "exploitation."

To be sure, the application of the student-athlete concept in the context of non-revenue sports has been highly successful. In the revenue sport of football, however, the increase in revenue over time has complicated the picture.

As intercollegiate athletics has grown to a multi-billion dollar business annually, critics have questioned the legitimacy of the NCAA's athlete protection rhetoric. Specifically, some suggest that this rhetoric, as well as the conception of student-athlete, serves as a tool by which to block college athletes in revenue sports from sharing in the money beyond the education-related compensation they currently receive.

Over time, the NCAA and its member institutions have doubled-down on the student-athlete concept. The NCAA has increased both the academic prerequisites to participate as well as mandated that athletic programs achieve a certain level of graduation rate to participate in postseason competitions.

 After the *House* settlement, it seems likely that the NCAA will either change the definition of amateur or abandon it altogether.

3. NCAA ELIGIBILITY REQUIREMENTS

In its early days, the NCAA employed a "home rule" policy to determine athlete eligibility. Under this rule, schools decided whether to admit athletes. In 1964, the NCAA adopted the 1.6 Predictor Rule that conditioned eligibility on the perceived likelihood that a student would receive a minimum of a 1.6 GPA in college. This predictor combined the student's high school GPA with the student's standardized test scores.

Centenary College basketball star (and future Boston Celtic) Robert Parish challenged this rule in 1973. The NCAA had suspended Parish from playing based on his ACT score of 8, despite his college GPA being above 1.6. Interestingly, Parish's academic performance was defying the prediction applied to him.

Parish argued that the rule violated the Equal Protection clause of the Constitution because it had a disparate impact on black athletes. A disparate impact occurs when a rule impacts one group in a detrimental way as compared to another group. The Fifth Circuit Court of Appeals rejected Parish's claim. The court found that the rule was facially neutral despite its disparate racial impact—the rule applied the same to everyone on its face. Because the rule did not concern race or gender on its face, the court applied a rational basis test. Under this test, the court found that the rule had a rational basis—it promoted minimum academic standards. It thus rejected Parish's claim. *Parish v. NCAA*, 361 F. Supp. 1220 (W.D. La. 1973).

The NCAA nonetheless modified its rule after *Parish*, requiring a minimum high school GPA of 2.0 to be eligible to participate in intercollegiate athletics. In 1983, the NCAA changed its rule again, adopting Proposition 48. Proposition 48 required the same minimum 2.0 GPA but mandated a core group of 11 academic courses. It also required a minimum score of 700 on the SAT or 15 on the ACT. Proposition 48, though, did not serve as an absolute bar. Athletes who could meet either the GPA or test score criterion but not the other could receive "partial qualifier" status and enroll with an athletic scholarship. Partial qualifiers, however, could not participate in athletics in their freshman year and only became eligible after demonstrating satisfactory academic progress.

In 1992, the NCAA adopted Proposition 16, which raised the minimum high school GPA to 2.5 in 13 core courses. Proposition 16 also introduced a sliding scale in which a student could compensate for a lower GPA with a higher test score and vice versa. The sliding scale, though, was only partial. The NCAA still required a minimum 2.0 GPA and a minimum SAT of 820.

During the late 1980s and early 1990s, basketball coaches John Cheney of Temple and John Thompson of Georgetown, among others, were highly critical of Propositions 48 and 16 because of their effect on black athletes. Two athletes challenged the legality of Proposition 16 in 1996. Tai Kwan Cureton, who ranked 27/305 in his class, and Leatrice Shaw, who ranked 5/305 in her class, each challenged the rule after failing to qualify for a Division I scholarship. Like over a quarter of black athletes at the time, Cureton and Shaw failed to meet the minimum SAT score of 820. Two other similarly situated black athletes, Andrea Gardner, and Andrew Wesby, subsequently joined the lawsuit.

Unlike *Parish*, the plaintiffs' challenge in *Cureton* was a statutory one, not a constitutional one. They argued that Proposition 16 and its disparate impact on black athletes violated Title VI of the Civil Rights

Act of 1964. Title VI bars racial discrimination in the formation of contracts. As in *Parish*, the plaintiffs in *Cureton* argued that despite the Proposition 16 rule being facially neutral, it had a disparate impact based on race.

The district court found for the plaintiffs, holding that the disparate impact of Proposition 16 violated Title VI. The Third Circuit Court of Appeals reversed, however, finding that Title VI did not apply to the NCAA because it was not an institution receiving federal funds. *Cureton v. NCAA*, 252 F.3d 267 (3d Cir. 2001). The plaintiffs thus had demonstrated that the rule violated federal law, but had sued the wrong defendant—the NCAA, not the universities.

The NCAA responded to *Cureton* by again changing its rules. It raised the number of required courses to 16 (4 years of English, 3 years of Math, 2 years of Science, 1 additional course in English, Math, or Science, 2 years of social science, and 4 years of additional academic coursework). The minimum required GPA in these courses was an average of 2.0. The NCAA also modified its sliding scale to eliminate the minimum standardized test score. These changes did not change until the Covid-19 pandemic.

During the Covid-19 pandemic, the NCAA suspended standardized testing requirements altogether. In 2023, the NCAA permanently dropped the standardized test requirement for eligibility. Athletes no longer have to take the SAT or the ACT.

[handwritten note: No more standardized test requirement since Covid-19.]

One other question concerning NCAA eligibility relates to learning disabilities. Historically, the NCAA did not make exceptions for athletes with learning disabilities with respect to its core academic requirements. In the late 1990s, Michigan State swimming recruit Chad Ganden challenged the lack of an exception for learning disabilities in the NCAA bylaws. Ganden was one of the fastest young swimmers in the United States. Ganden also suffered from a learning disability—a "decoding" problem that affected his reading and writing skills.

Ganden was only a partial qualifier under NCAA academic standards. His ACT score meant that he needed a 2.275 GPA in the 13 core courses required at the time, but Ganden's GPA was a 2.136 in those courses. To avoid sitting out a year, Ganden sued the NCAA under the Americans with Disabilities Act (ADA). *Ganden v. NCAA*, 1996 WL 680000 (N.D. Ill. 1996). The district court found that the ADA applied to the NCAA. It also found that the eligibility denial related to Ganden's learning disability. But the court denied Ganden relief. Providing Ganden a waiver constituted an undue burden under the ADA because it would fundamentally alter the NCAA's academic requirements.

A similar case involving University of Washington football player Touré Butler resulted in the opposite outcome. In an unpublished opinion, the U.S. Court of Appeals for the Ninth Circuit found that the NCAA had violated Butler's rights under the ADA and required it to give him an academic waiver. *Butler v. NCAA*, 2 F. App'x 729 (9th Cir. 2001)(unpublished).

The NCAA subsequently entered a consent decree with the Department of Justice in 2001. The NCAA now provides academic waivers for students with learning disabilities on a case-by-case basis.

4.   REMUNERATION BEFORE COLLEGE

Under NCAA rules, athletes cannot play college sports in a sport that they have previously played as a professional. 2023–24 NCAA Division I Manual, Bylaw 12.2.5. One example of the NCAA enforcing this rule was the case of Muhammed Lasege. *NCAA v. Lasege*, 53 S.W.3d 77 (Ky. 2001). Lasege, a citizen of Nigeria, enrolled at the University of Louisville during the 1999–2000 academic year with the intention of playing for its men's basketball team. In March 2000, Louisville declared Lasege ineligible to play intercollegiate basketball because he had previously entered into professional basketball contracts. Specifically, Lasege had received preferential benefits which compromised his amateur status.

Prior to enrollment at Louisville, Lasege left Nigeria to go to Russia, seeking ultimately to obtain a visa to the United States. Lasege received remuneration for his expenses from New Sport, a Russian Sports Agency. He also signed two contracts to play on junior teams in Russia which covered his living expenses.

Lasege sued the NCAA and a temporary injunction allowed him to play for Louisville during the 2000–01 season. The NCAA appealed and the Kentucky Supreme Court reversed. Following the law of the association, the court held that the NCAA had not acted arbitrarily or capriciously in abiding by its own rules to find Lasege ineligible. A voluntary association, like the NCAA, has the power to impose its own rules upon those that agree to be its members.

The decision ended Lasege's college basketball career. Lasege, however, was an excellent student. He had a 3.9 GPA at Louisville, and eventually received an MBA from the Wharton School of Business at the University of Pennsylvania. By all accounts, Lasege was the quintessential student-athlete, and yet, the lack of flexibility of the NCAA's amateurism rules denied him a college athletic career.

The situation becomes slightly different when the athlete in question receives money from participation in one sport but wants to compete in college athletics in a different sport. In those cases, the athlete remains eligible in the new sport.

This was the situation of Jeremy Bloom described in the Prologue. Bloom was eligible to play football at Colorado, even though he had received compensation related to his skiing. The Colorado court upheld the NCAA's proscription against Bloom receiving skiing and modeling endorsements while playing college football. *Bloom v. NCAA*, 93 P.3d 621 (Colo. Ct. App. 2004).

As explored in Chapter Four, states have increasingly passed laws allowing high school athletes to receive compensation for uses of their

NILs. Unlike in Lasege's situation, receiving this compensation would not make the athletes ineligible, even under Bylaw 12.2.5. The distinction here would be two-fold. First, the athlete would not be receiving a contract to play the sport in question. The NIL contract might arise out of the participation in sports, but would not be compensation for participation. It would be compensation for NIL use. Second, many of the state laws in question would bar the NCAA from punishing the high school athlete for monetizing their NIL pursuant to state law.

Again, after the *House* settlement, one wonders whether restrictions like this one will remain or the NCAA will abandon them.

5. PROGRESS TOWARD A DEGREE AND THE APR

The NCAA currently requires athletes to make reasonable progress toward a degree to maintain their athletic eligibility. For Division I athletes, this means that athletes must complete forty percent of the required coursework for a degree by the end of the second year, sixty percent by the end of the third year, and eighty percent by the end of the fourth year. Division I athletes have five academic years to complete four years of athletic eligibility. Division I athletes also must earn at least six credit hours each term to be eligible for the following term, as well as meet the minimum GPA requirements related to the school's GPA standards for graduation.

In 2005, the NCAA adopted a formal tool, the academic progress rate (APR), to measure academic progress and improve graduation rates, particularly in the revenue sports. Schools calculate an APR rate for each sport. One half of the APR score relates to graduation rate; the other half relates to eligibility. Each athlete receiving athletically-related financial aid earns one point for staying in school and one point for being academically eligible. The NCAA divides a team's total points by total possible points and multiplies by 1,000 to calculate the team's APR. The NCAA uses both a team's current year APR and its rolling four-year APR to determine accountability.

To compete in championships, teams must earn a four-year average APR of 930. The NCAA demonstrated its seriousness about the APR standard in 2012–13, when it banned the defending national champion University of Connecticut men's basketball team from the NCAA tournament because of its non-compliant APR score. Other consequences for a low APR also include loss of allowable time to spend on sports and loss of scholarships.

The broader philosophical question behind the NCAA's regulation of academic progress relates to whether graduation is a good measure of education quality. Problems in recent years with athlete clustering—athletes taking the "easy" majors at a particular school—underscore this issue.

Perhaps the most egregious story of university malfeasance toward the education of its athletes is the case of Kevin Ross. Ross was a basketball star at Creighton University despite being unable to read above a seventh-grade level and having overall language skills of a fourth-grader. After four years of playing basketball for Creighton, Ross had a D average with 96 of 128 credits completed, even though he had done almost none of the academic work.

Ross sued Creighton, alleging the torts of negligent admission and educational malpractice, as well as breach of contract for failing to provide him an education. The court did not recognize either tort based on the chilling effects both could have. Students certainly would not support the idea that admitting lesser qualified students could be tortious; faculty likewise would not support the idea that poor teaching could be tortious. The court did find for Ross on the contract claim. It held that Creighton had not just failed to provide a quality education; it had failed to provide Ross any education at all. *Ross v. Creighton Univ.*, 957 F.2d 410 (7th Cir. 1992). To Ross' credit, he restarted his education in fourth grade and continued until he had graduated from Creighton.

Some critics question whether the NCAA should have any role in regulating academics at its member institutions. A 2017 NCAA infractions case involving an academic scandal at the University of North Carolina at Chapel Hill (UNC) demonstrated this tension. For over two decades, UNC's Department of African and Afro-American Studies offered "paper courses." The courses involved no class attendance; limited, if any, faculty oversight; and liberal grading. The paper courses included both independent studies and courses listed as standard lectures but taught as independent studies. Although the exact number of paper courses is unknown, a report following an independent investigation by a national law firm (the Cadwalader Report) conservatively estimated 3,100 students, including athletes, took a paper course involving irregular instruction. These so-called classes never met and rarely involved a faculty member. They typically required the submission of a paper, or two shorter papers. The secretary often graded the papers, and she admitted she did not read every word and occasionally did not read every page. The papers consistently received high grades.

Despite the NCAA's emphasis on the concept of student-athlete and education more generally, its Committee on Infractions (COI) found that UNC had not violated NCAA rules. *University of North Carolina at Chapel Hill Public Infractions Decision*, 2017. Specifically, the COI concluded that UNC's academic fraud involved both athletes and non-athletes alike. As a result, the university was not providing a benefit to athletes unavailable to other students. It did report its findings to the Southern Association of Colleges and Schools (SACS), UNC's accrediting agency, but otherwise did not take any formal action against UNC.

Two more recent examples, however, demonstrate the willingness of the NCAA to impose sanctions for academic misconduct. At Mississippi State University, a part-time athletics department tutor committed academic misconduct in an online general chemistry course by aiding ten football players and one basketball player. The tutor, who had previously studied at Mississippi State, completed multiple assignments, exams, and in some instances, nearly the entire course for the athletes. This meant that eight ineligible football players and one ineligible basketball player had competed for Mississippi State during the 2018–19 academic year.

After presenting the information concerning the cheating to the NCAA, Mississippi State entered into a negotiated resolution. *Mississippi State University, Negotiated Resolution,* Case No. 01001, August 23, 2019. Sanctions included scholarship reductions and reduction in recruiting opportunities, as well as three years of probation, but no limits on postseason participation.

A similar case around the same time from the University of Missouri led to harsher sanctions. In 2019, a Missouri athletics tutor violated NCAA rules by completing work in an online class for twelve athletes, including assignments, quizzes, and exams. This unauthorized help took place in two different university math courses, in math courses from other schools, and in the completion of a math placement exam at Missouri.

The COI found the conduct in question to be a Level I-Standard violation and imposed more serious sanctions than in the Mississippi State case. Specifically, the COI imposed one-year post-season bans in football, baseball, and softball, a five percent reduction in the number of scholarships in each of those sports, as well as additional recruiting restrictions. The Infractions Appeals Committee affirmed these penalties. *University of Missouri,*

Columbia Decision of the NCAA Division I Infractions Appeals Committee, Nov. 16, 2019.

A stated difference between the two cases related to the perceived difference in cooperation levels between Mississippi State and Missouri. Mississippi State allegedly reported immediately, while Missouri allegedly took longer. But cases like these with similar facts but disparate consequences raise questions about the fairness of the NCAA's enforcement process.

6. THE UNIVERSITY-ATHLETE CONTRACTUAL RELATIONSHIP

College athletes have a three part contractual relationship with universities. The first part of this agreement is the National Letter of Intent (NLI). High school athletes sign the NLI to secure their scholarship during the annual signing period. While the NCAA does not technically mandate the NLI, virtually all athletes sign it to make sure the university does not award the scholarship to another athlete.

The NCAA's NLI has a number of rules concerning its validity. Importantly, athletes cannot make any modifications to the text of the NLI. The NLI provides that it binds athletes to its terms, even if the coach leaves the institution. In addition, the coach and other representatives of the university cannot be present when the athlete signs the NLI. Once signed, the NLI blocks other schools from continuing to recruit the athlete and commits the athlete to one year of playing for the university. Some universities

Alston money = financial awards of #5,980/yr
to help w/academic expenses (musical instruments)

offer four year scholarships, others only offer one year.

The second part of the contractual relationship between the athlete and the university is the financial aid agreement. For scholarship athletes, agreement binds the university to cover the cost of tuition, room, board, books, and at most schools, cost of attendance. After *Alston*, this can also include other education-related expenses, including Alston money. The athlete agrees to enroll in the university, participate on the athletic team, and remain academically eligible.

The third part of the contractual relationship between the athlete and the university is the student handbook that sets out the rules and regulations for all university students. These handbooks specify both academic rules of the institution as well as conduct rules for students. Athletes that violate these rules, whether through academic misconduct or other inappropriate behavior, can jeopardize both their scholarships and their place at the university.

Historically, the NCAA prohibited multi-year scholarships. Scholarships were renewable annually, after a review by the financial aid office. Athletic department officials may not participate in such decisions, providing at least the appearance that athletic performance does not drive the renewal decision. In 2012, the NCAA adopted a new regulation permitting, but not requiring, multi-year scholarship contracts. This decision was concurrent with an antitrust lawsuit challenging the restriction on multi-year scholarships. *Agnew v. NCAA*, 683 F.3d

House = revenue sharing (+ ω)

328 (7th Cir. 2012)(discussed below in Chapter Three). Power conference schools now offer four-year scholarships.

One addition after the *House* settlement to the contracts between the athlete and university will presumably be a revenue sharing amount.

Irrespective of whether the scholarship is for one year or four years, the NCAA allows athletes four years of competition. Barring a waiver, athletes must complete this eligibility within five years of enrolling in a university. The NCAA extended this window in response to the Covid-19 pandemic and allowed students one extra year of eligibility. This allowed athletes who missed the opportunity to participate in NCAA championships in the spring of 2020 more opportunity, but also created a scholarship backlog. Kihei Clark, a freshman starter on the University of Virginia's 2018–19 national championship basketball team, took advantage of this rule to play five full seasons, ending his career in the 2022–23 season. Iowa basketball player Jordan Bohannon played six seasons as a result of this rule (one was a partial season with a redshirt) and holds the record for NCAA basketball games played—179, a record not likely to be broken soon.

It is also worth noting that not every sport offers full scholarships to its athletes. The revenue sports of football and basketball, known as headcount sports, award full scholarships (85 for football and 13 for basketball). Other sports like softball and baseball receive scholarships that are partial or do not cover the entire team. Baseball, for instance, receives 11.7 scholarships divided among a maximum of 27 players on a 35-player roster.

Several lawsuits have further defined the parameters of the athlete-university relationship. In 1972, Gregg Taylor sued Wake Forest for terminating his athletic scholarship. Taylor played for Wake Forest's football team in his freshman year. During the fall semester he compiled a grade point average of 1.0 (out of 4.0), far below the 1.35 the school required all students to have at the end of the freshman year. Taylor did not attend the spring football practices, and his GPA for the spring semester rose to 1.9. He then decided not to play football in the fall of his sophomore year; his GPA rose again, to 2.4.

Because of his refusal to play football, Wake Forest's Scholarship Committee, on the recommendation of the Faculty Athletic Committee, revoked his scholarship as of the end of his sophomore year. Taylor nevertheless remained at Wake Forest and graduated on time. He sued to recover $5,500 in expenses incurred during his last two years because he had lost his scholarship.

Taylor argued that the university had violated an oral contract he had made with the football coach, who had promised him that in the event of any conflict between educational achievement and athletic involvement, the university would be willing to limit or even eliminate his participation in athletic activities to assure reasonable academic progress.

The court, however, did not recognize the oral contract, finding that the written contract controlled. This meant that in order to receive his scholarship, Taylor had to play football and remain academically eligible. *Taylor v. Wake Forest*, 191 S.E.2d 379 (N.C. Ct. App. 1972).

Terrell Jackson of Drake University raised similar challenges based on the oral promises of his basketball coach. Jackson claimed that when Drake recruited him, basketball coach Tom Abatemarco promised him both the right to play basketball and an environment conducive to high academic achievement. When Jackson got to Drake, the coaches allegedly pressured him to take easy courses and submit plagiarized papers, and denied him adequate study time. When Jackson complained about the situation, Abatemarco allegedly harassed him at practice, called him foul names, and made him run extra drills and do extra exercises. In the middle of his sophomore year, Jackson quit the team.

Jackson's lawsuit alleged breach of contract, educational malpractice, negligent misrepresentation in recruiting, and fraud. The court dismissed the contract claim because Jackson's scholarship documents (the contract) did not expressly contain the entitlements Jackson claimed, including the right to play basketball. *Jackson v. Drake University*, 778 F. Supp. 1490 (S.D. Iowa 1991). While an athlete does have to attempt to play to receive a scholarship, the university does not violate the athlete's contractual rights (or constitutional rights) by kicking the athlete off of the team, as long as it continues to allow the student to pursue an education and pays the cost of the grant-in-aid. The court allowed Jackson's negligent misrepresentation and fraud claims to go forward, but the parties subsequently settled.

Another question concerning the contractual relationship between university and athlete is whether it gives rise to constitutional liberty or property interests. Under 42 U.S.C. § 1983, individuals can challenge deprivations of constitutional rights, privileges, or immunities, including property and liberty rights emerging from contractual relationships or other state law sources.

In *Hysaw v. Washburn University*, several black football players—Neils Chapman, Vernon Hysaw, and Eugene Battle—alleged that Washburn had violated their civil rights and breached their athlete-university contracts. *Hysaw v. Washburn University of Topeka*, 690 F. Supp. 940 (D. Kan. 1987). The athletes challenged the alleged preferential treatment of white football players over black football players by the coaching staff, particularly with decisions to award some white players full scholarships and black players only partial scholarships. The players complained to the administration and subsequently boycotted practice. After the boycott, the administration issued its own demands, including an apology by the players and a one game suspension. When the players did not agree to these demands, the coach dismissed the players from the team.

The players first alleged that the decision to prefer white players over black players violated 42 U.S.C. § 1981, the same statute at issue in *Cureton*. That statute bars discrimination in the execution of contracts. While not deciding the merits, the court denied summary judgment on that issue because the players had alleged a legitimate cause of action.

The players also claimed that Washburn had violated their rights under 42 U.S.C. § 1983 by infringing on their property, liberty, and free speech rights. With respect to the property rights, the court explained that the players only had a property interest in the right to scholarship funds under their contract. The contract did not give rise to a property interest in playing football or even being on the team. With respect to liberty interests, the court did not find that a liberty interest existed to pursue a college football career. As a result, Washburn had not violated the players rights by poisoning their chances of receiving a subsequent scholarship at Emporia State in speaking poorly of them to the Emporia coaches. As a result, the court granted summary judgment to the defendants on the property and liberty interest claims, as well as the breach of contract claim. Finally, the court found that the players had demonstrated a factual question as to whether the discipline imposed was a direct response to the players speaking out at their boycott. As a result, Washburn may have infringed upon the First Amendment rights of the athletes by punishing a boycott that did not cause any real disruption to the football team.

Sua sponte = on ~~one's~~ own accord
one's

Five years later, two University of Washington football players, Kevin Conard and Vincent Fudzie, sued to challenge the decision not to renew their athletic scholarships after one year. *Conard v. University of Washington*, 834 P.2d 17 (Wash. 1992) (en banc). The plaintiffs' cause of action concerned breach of contract and interference with contract by Coach Don James and his wife, but the Washington Court of Appeals held *sua sponte* that the failure to renew violated the plaintiffs' constitutional property interest in the renewal of their contracts.

The Washington Supreme Court, sitting *en banc*, reversed, finding that the plaintiffs did not have a protected property interest in the renewal of their athletic scholarships. The court explained that the terms of the contract only indicated that the university would consider the contracts for renewal, that there was no mutually explicit understanding that the university would renew the contract for four years, and the contract did not give rise to a particular procedure outside of the financial aid hearing already provided.

This chapter has provided an overview of the university-athlete relationship, circa 2023–2024. As explored in later chapters, imminent change in aspects of this relationship seem likely.

en banc = on the bench

CHAPTER TWO
NCAA ENFORCEMENT

The NCAA's rules are extensive with respect to college athletes and college athletics. This chapter explores how the NCAA has historically enforced its rules.

1. THE NCAA ENFORCEMENT STAFF

The NCAA Enforcement Staff investigates violations of NCAA rules. With respect to university employees and current athletes, there is some leverage for cooperation, but with respect to third party boosters and graduated athletes, there is no power to require participation. Unlike state and federal prosecutors, NCAA investigators lack subpoena power. This means that third parties can often avoid participating in NCAA investigations.

Once investigators find information that they believe rises to the level of one or more violations of NCAA bylaws, the NCAA sends a Notice of Allegations to the university in question. The university then responds to the Notice of Allegations. The response addresses the factual question— whether the university violated the rules. The response also can address the proposed sanctions in the Notice of Allegations. If the university rejects either the findings or the sanctions in the Notice of Allegations, then the case proceeds to the Committee on Infractions (COI). In recent years, the NCAA has provided a process for a Negotiated Resolution, as in the Mississippi State case discussed in Chapter One.

These settlements happen in situations where the institution and the NCAA agree on the appropriate sanction. Unlike decisions of the COI, Negotiated Resolutions do not have any precedential value in future infractions cases.

The COI process is an administrative process. It lacks many of the protections that apply in both civil and criminal cases in state and federal courts. There is no limit on the introduction of hearsay evidence, there is no right to depose or cross-examine witnesses, and the standards for admission of evidence are minimal at best. Further, many of the participants in the COI process lack legal training, although several law professors have served on the COI over the years.

After the Committee of Infractions issues its decision, a university does have the option of appealing the case to the Infractions Appeals Committee (IAC). The IAC consists of five administrators who review the COI decision. The IAC can either uphold the decision or lower the sanction.

In response to the criminal prosecutions (see discussion below) related to college basketball, the NCAA created the Independent Accountability Resolution Process (IARP) in 2019. The idea of this process was to separate out complex cases and avoid appearance of conflict of interest by having individuals not associated with Division I athletic programs deciding these cases. In 2023, the NCAA announced that it was closing the IARP once the IARP completes its pending cases.

The NCAA has divided its sanctions into four levels, with Level I being the most serious. It describes the levels as follows:

- Severe Breach of Conduct (Level I violation): lack of institutional control, academic fraud, failure to cooperate with NCAA, unethical/ dishonest conduct, cash payment, third party involvement with university knowledge, intentional/reckless violations, collective Level II or III violations.

- Significant Breach of Conduct (Level II violation): failure to monitor; systemic violations; multiple recruiting violations; collective Level III violations.

- Breach of Conduct (Level III violation): inadvertent/isolated violations; extra benefits

- Incidental Infraction (Level IV violation): minor, technical violations.

Sanctions for NCAA violations can include: competition penalties, financial penalties, scholarship reductions, show-cause orders, head coach restrictions, recruiting restrictions, vacation of wins, and probation. 2023–24 NCAA Division I Manual, Bylaw 19 et seq.

Lack of institutional control is perhaps the most serious rule infraction. 2023–24 NCAA Division I Manual, Bylaw 6.01.1. This requirement has at least some connection to the lack of subpoena power of the Enforcement Staff. Failure to recognize violations internally and be able to report them—exhibiting a lack of institutional control—can be worse than the misconduct itself, at least with respect to the sanctions imposed.

The NCAA lists the following acts as examples of a lack of institutional control:

- A person with compliance responsibilities:
  - Fails to establish a proper system of compliance or fails to monitor that system of compliance.
  - Fails to take steps when system of compliance is not working.
- Compliance supervisor divides responsibilities such that no one is in charge.
- Compliance duties assigned to subordinate without authority to garner respect of others.
- The institution fails to make clear that the institution will discipline NCAA rules violators.
- The institution fails to make clear that any involved with intercollegiate athletics have a duty to report violations.
- Failure to investigate an alleged violation (particularly by the AD).
- Head coach fails to create atmosphere for compliance or monitor assistant coaches regarding compliance.

The NCAA thus requires athletic departments to monitor the conduct of their coaches, athletes, and employees to promote an atmosphere of compliance and self-reporting. As such, athletic departments must have compliance departments and set up systems to track the behavior of those involved in athletics to make sure the university does not violate the NCAA's amateurism rules and report to the NCAA if they do.

Another important role is that of the faculty athletics representative (FAR) who serves as a liaison between the academic departments of the university and the athletics department. The FAR must be a member of the faculty and not an employee of the athletics department. 2023–24 NCAA Division I Manual, Bylaw 6.1.3.

As mentioned, one important challenge that NCAA enforcement faces is the lack of subpoena power. As a result, the NCAA encourages universities to self-report infractions and even propose sanctions. In its cases, the COI both rewards prompt self-reporting and co-operation as well as increases punishment for a lack of co-operation or delay in reporting.

2.   NCAA V. TARKANIAN

The Bill of Rights of the United States Constitution protects individuals, at least to some degree, from legislative infringements upon certain core rights. These rights include free speech, freedom of religion, the right to bear arms, the right to due process, and the right to be free from cruel and unusual punishments, among others. These protections relate to actions by representatives of government, known as state actors. If the interference with the right in question is not by a government actor, there is no constitutional violation.

NCAA athletes in different contexts have argued that NCAA policies violate their constitutional rights. But, as explained below, the Constitution does not apply to the NCAA's regulations because the NCAA is not a state actor.

Jerry Tarkanian became the head basketball coach at the University of Nevada at Las Vegas (UNLV) beginning in 1973. Tarkanian had served as the head coach at Long Beach State for four years, where his teams went 122–20. Long Beach State almost made the Final Four in 1971, when they lost 57–55 to UCLA in the Western Regional Final of the NCAA tournament.

Known as "Tark the Shark," Tarkanian had the habit of sucking on wet towels during games because they were so stressful to him. An accomplished coach, Tarkanian recruited stellar basketball players to his teams and continued his success at UNLV, winning the 1991 NCAA championship.

From early in his career as a coach at Long Beach State, Tarkanian's programs were consistent targets of the NCAA's Enforcement Staff. In 1976, after a four-year investigation, the NCAA Committee on Infractions (COI) found that the UNLV basketball program had committed 38 violations of NCAA rules, including 10 by Tarkanian.

Importantly, the COI found that Tarkanian had violated the University's obligation to provide full cooperation with the NCAA investigation. Because the COI lacks subpoena power, it relies on employees and athletes of its member institutions to disclose violations, and failure to do so incurs additional punishment.

The COI proposed a series of sanctions against UNLV, including a two-year period of probation with no television or post-season appearances. *University of Nevada Las Vegas, Placed on NCAA Probation*, August 26, 1977. The COI also issued a two-year "show cause" order with respect to Coach Tarkanian. This meant that UNLV had to discipline Tarkanian by removing him from UNLV's athletic program for two years or face additional sanctions. UNLV appealed this sanction to the NCAA Council (which predated the IAC), but the committee upheld the COI's decision.

UNLV had a disciplinary hearing for Tarkanian. The university president did not want to impose any sanction against Tarkanian but decided to follow the NCAA's disciplinary sanction and sever Tarkanian from all relations with the athletic department during the two-year probation period.

Tarkanian sued UNLV. He alleged that the university had deprived him of due process liberty and property rights inherent in his job. The trial court enjoined UNLV from disciplining Tarkanian. The Nevada courts subsequently concluded that the NCAA also were a proper party to the lawsuit. The trial court then extended the injunction to the NCAA prohibiting it from enforcing its show-cause order and from taking any other action against the University related to the NCAA's investigation.

The NCAA appealed the case to the United States Supreme Court. It argued that the Nevada Supreme Court had erred by applying the Constitution to its decisions. Specifically, the NCAA claimed that it is not a state actor.

The individual rights that arise under the Constitution's Bill of Rights, including the due process rights at issue in Tarkanian's case, are rights to be free from government intervention. In other words, these rights only pertain to government action and not actions by other private parties. The State of Nevada must respect Tarkanian's right to due process because it is a governmental entity—a state actor. The NCAA, though, is a private institution. Ordinarily, the bill of rights would not protect Tarkanian against the NCAA's action.

But Tarkanian argued that the NCAA was behaving as a state actor in his case. The Supreme Court's state action doctrine provides that private actors can be state actors where they act "under color of state law," with the authority or power of the state. Tarkanian specifically claimed that the Nevada delegated authority to the NCAA by allowing it to adopt and enforce rules on its behalf. He argued that by imposing discipline on Nevada and requiring it to discipline Tarkanian, the NCAA was in essence acting as the state of Nevada.

In a narrow 5–4 decision, the Supreme Court disagreed. *NCAA v. Tarkanian*, 488 U.S. 179 (1988).

It held that the NCAA was not a state actor and that the Constitution did not apply to its disciplinary decisions. UNLV, in the Court's view, had a choice of whether to discipline Tarkanian. And the NCAA had no power to discipline Tarkanian directly without UNLV's acquiescence.

The consequences of this decision are significant for college athletes. When NCAA rules infringe on athlete's constitutional rights, the athletes have no remedy against the NCAA. NCAA rules restricting free speech rights, gun possession rights, liberty rights, and property rights all do not violate the constitutional rights of athletes to the extent that the NCAA enforces them. The NCAA is not a state actor. Instead, athletes have to sue their respective institutions to challenge these kind of deprivations.

One subsequent Supreme Court decision explored the question of state action in connection with athletics. Brentwood Academy, a private high school in Nashville, Tennessee, sued the Tennessee Secondary School Athletic Association ("TSSAA") in the late 1990s. The TSSAA barred Brentwood Academy from postseason competition for one year after finding that it violated state recruiting rules in recruiting a middle school football player.

Brentwood Academy claimed that the TSSAA recruiting rule violated its First Amendment rights. Again, the question in the case was whether the TSSAA, a private athletic association, was a state actor.

The United States Supreme Court, unlike in the *Tarkanian* case, held that the TSSAA was a state actor by a 5–4 vote. *Brentwood Academy v. TSSAA*, 531 U.S. 288 (2001). Most of the justices voted similarly to *Tarkanian*, with Justice Stevens switching sides. The distinction between the cases related to the intra-state nature of the TSSAA as compared to the inter-state nature of the NCAA. While the NCAA's rules apply to institutions in all 50 states, the TSSAA's rules only apply to Tennessee high schools. As a result, it is easier to establish that the TSSAA controls Tennessee than that the NCAA controls Nevada.

Another important fact related to the membership of the TSSAA. Most of the TSSAA board served as administrators in public schools and were thus state employees. The Court thus found sufficient entwinement or "nexus" between the TSSAA and the State of Tennessee to make the TSSAA a state actor.

While Brentwood Academy won the battle, it lost the war. In a subsequent appeal, the Court held that the TSSAA had not violated Brentwood Academy's First Amendment rights. *TSSAA v. Brentwood Academy*, 551 U.S. 291 (2007). It was an unfortunate end to a decade of litigation for the high school.

Returning to Coach Tarkanian, the Supreme Court's decision on the state action question did not end the case. The litigation continued prior to the NCAA Committee on Infractions (COI)'s hearing to discipline Tarkanian. UNLV officials declined to participate in the hearing on grounds that the hearing violated Nevada state law. Specifically, the hearing did not require the NCAA to provide all materials thirty days prior to the hearing, to give each defendant the opportunity to confront all witnesses, to provide all exculpatory statements obtained by the NCAA, to have an open hearing, recorded and transcribed, as well as other procedural requirements of Nevada law.

The NCAA filed suit for a declaratory judgment and won in Nevada federal court. *NCAA v. Miller*, 795 F. Supp. 1476 (D. Nev. 1992). The court found that, to the extent it limited the ability of the NCAA to adjudicate its infractions cases, Nevada law violated the Commerce Clause and the Contracts Clause of the Constitution. As to the first point, the power of Congress to regulate interstate commerce means that states cannot interfere with such regulation without violating the Tenth Amendment.

Here, the court found that the NCAA's regulation of college sports was economic activity taking place in interstate commerce. This meant that the Nevada statute was unconstitutional because, even though it regulated an area of legitimate state concern, it placed an undue burden on interstate commerce. In other words, if the NCAA disciplinary procedure had to comply with each state's separate procedural prerequisites, the NCAA would be unable to regulate its economic activity across state lines.

Similarly, the Contract Clause bars states from passing laws that interfere with contractual obligations of private parties. The NCAA successfully argued that the Nevada law interfered with its contracts with its member institutions. Because the

NCAA's contract with Nevada public institutions predated the adoption of the Nevada statute in question, the statute was subject to the Contract Clause. The court here found that the interest in preventing interference into the NCAA contract outweighed the state interest in its statute. This was because the NCAA had a long history of regulating intercollegiate athletics while Nevada had never intended to regulate such behavior or apply the statute to such conduct.

One interesting point about *Miller* is that the NCAA did not rely on amateurism as it has in antitrust litigation dating to *Board of Regents*. Instead, the NCAA relied on the application of economic principles—constitutional protections of its commercial activity—to prevail in *Miller*.

3.   IMPERMISSIBLE BENEFITS AND OTHER RULES VIOLATIONS

The NCAA's amateurism rules, at least to some extent, have focused on punishing those providing athletes with impermissible benefits. Impermissible benefits constitute anything of value above tuition, room, board, and books. Historically, these rules applied irrespective of whether the university or a third-party booster provided the benefits. As explored in Chapter Four, these benefits now can include cost of attendance and other costs related to education when provided by the university. And there are no limits to compensation provided by third parties if made pursuant to an NIL contract.

Prior to the current NIL era, impermissible benefit violations have been widespread, if not rampant. A 2016 study by Doug Lederman of Inside Higher Ed found that almost half of schools in the Football Bowl Subdivision, including more than half of the Power conference schools, committed major violations in the ten-year period between January 2006 and December 2015. Sixteen schools received two separate sets of infractions sanctions, including Georgia Tech, Ohio State, and Tennessee. Oklahoma and West Virginia also had three major cases during that decade.

To understand the constant presence of NCAA infractions in recent college sports history, a brief survey of some of the many noteworthy cases is instructive. What is worth noting, in particular, are the number of prominent programs that have violated NCAA rules.

An infamous example of one such violation is the case of Reggie Bush. Bush, a star football player on the University of Southern California's (USC) 2004 National Championship team, had his Heisman Trophy revoked in 2010 because NCAA rules violations. From 2003 to 2005, Bush allegedly received unauthorized benefits from sports marketers and agents. These benefits included cash payments and free housing for his family.

In addition to punishing Bush by revoking his award and imposing a ten-year show-cause order against him, the NCAA imposed penalties against USC, including a postseason ban, scholarship reductions, and the vacation of wins. Bush voluntarily returned his Heisman Trophy to the

Heisman Trust. This marked the first instance in the award's history that the NCAA had stripped a recipient of the honor. With the kind of benefits Bush received from third parties now permissible under NCAA rules, Bush has asked that the NCAA return the trophy, and the NCAA finally acquiesced in the spring of 2024.

Around the same time, the NCAA imposed four years of probation against the men's basketball program of the University of Georgia as well as a scholarship reduction over four years and a vacation of wins during the 2001–02 and 2002–03 seasons. Georgia had hired head coach Jim Harrick, who had won a national championship at UCLA. Under Harrick's leadership, Georgia had enjoyed a resurgence, winning the regular season SEC championship in 2001–02 and making the NCAA tournament for two years in a row.

A disgruntled player, Tony Cole, accused Harrick's son, assistant coach Jim Harrick Jr., of paying Cole's bills and giving Cole an A in a class he never attended. After further investigation, Georgia's Athletic Director responded by firing Harrick Jr., suspending Harrick, and withdrawing Georgia from postseason play before the NCAA tournament. Harrick and Georgia agreed to part ways soon after, perhaps as a way to move beyond the scandal. Harrick Jr. had apparently taught a class on the subject of basketball and his final exam became publicly available in discovery. It included a question about how many points a three-pointer was worth. The NCAA imposed a seven-year show cause penalty against Harrick Jr. *University of Georgia Public Infractions Report*, August 5, 2004.

During the tenure of Jim Tressel, Ohio State celebrated nine years of sustained football success, including an 8–1 record against Michigan, six conference championships and a national championship in 2002. The Buckeyes' troubles with the NCAA began in 2002, when it suspended star running back Maurice Clarett for accepting $500 in cash and allowing a local caterer to pay thousands of dollars to cover Clarett's cell phone bills. Clarett subsequently sued the National Football League to enter the draft early, a case discussed in the next chapter.

In 2010, the NCAA sanctioned five Ohio State football players—Mike Adams, Daniel "Boom" Herron, DeVier Posey, star quarterback Terrelle Pryor, and Solomon Thomas—for selling memorabilia in exchange for cash and tattoos. The memorabilia sold included jerseys, championship rings, and awards. The NCAA allowed the players to play in the 2010 Sugar Bowl, a 31–26 win over the University of Arkansas, but suspended them for the first five games of the 2011 season. The NCAA required the players to repay the amount of money made by selling the memorabilia, which cost Pryor $2,500.

Initially, Jim Tressel did not receive any sanction, but Ohio State subsequently fined him $250,000 and suspended him two games for not informing the university and the NCAA that he knew about the benefits received by the players. The university then increased Tressel's suspension to five games to match that of the players. When Sports Illustrated reported that Ohio State players had been trading and selling memorabilia dating back to the 2002 season, Tressel abruptly resigned from his position as head coach.

Bruce Pearl had a highly successful tenure as the head basketball coach of the University of Tennessee. In six seasons, Pearl amassed a record of 145–61, with a regular season conference championship, two Sweet Sixteen appearances, one Elite Eight appearance, and two SEC coach of the year awards. Pearl and his staff, however, allegedly committed numerous NCAA recruiting violations. In particular, the NCAA obtained a photograph from social media of Pearl with a high school recruit Aaron Craft taken during a cookout Pearl hosted for several recruits at his home. According to the NCAA, Pearl subsequently lied to investigators about the photograph and the cookout. During the investigation, the SEC suspended Pearl from coaching eight league games during the 2010–11 season. Tennessee subsequently fired Pearl.

In 2011, the NCAA punished Pearl for unethical conduct, imposing a three-year show cause penalty, barring him from coaching for that period. Tennessee received a two-year probationary penalty along with a number of recruiting restrictions. *University of Tennessee, Knoxville, Public Infractions Report,* August 24, 2011.

Pearl, however, resuscitated his career. He spent the time during his ban as an ESPN analyst and then became the head coach of Auburn University, an SEC rival of Tennessee. He led Auburn to its first Final Four in 2019.

In 2013, the NCAA concluded its investigation into Oregon's football program. Under Coach Chip Kelly, the Ducks enjoyed trips to four consecutive BCS bowl games from 2010–13, including the 2011 BCS National Championship Game, which it lost to Auburn 22–19.

A mysterious $25,000 payment by Oregon to recruiting consultant Will Lyles was at the center of the investigation, with Lyles allegedly "delivering" star players to Oregon. The NCAA found that Oregon had violated NCAA bylaws with respect to the football program's use of multiple recruiting and scouting services over a three-year period.

The punishments, however, reflected a conclusion that the violations were not particularly serious. Sanctions included a public reprimand and censure; three years of probation; limits on official paid football recruiting visits to 37 (down from 65) for each of the 2013–14, 2014–15 and 2015–16 academic years; limits on the permissible number of football evaluation days to 36 (of 42) in the fall of 2013, 2014 and 2015; and a ban on the subscription to recruiting services during the period of probation. The NCAA also imposed an eighteen month show cause order on Coach Kelly for failing to monitor the recruiting activities. This punishment was of no consequence, however, as Kelly had left Oregon to become the coach of the Philadelphia Eagles.

In another 2013 infractions case, Mississippi State University demonstrated the value of quick cooperation with the NCAA enforcement committee. After discovering that boosters had given athletes recruiting inducements including cash, clothing and vehicle discounts, the University investigated and reported to the NCAA. The NCAA imposed a public reprimand and censure as well as two years of probation, but did not impose a bowl ban or recruiting restrictions. Assistant football coach Angelo Mirando, whom Mississippi State fired, received a one-year show cause order after he mislead investigators concerning his knowledge about the booster activity. *Mississippi State University Public Infractions Report*, June 7, 2013.

Also in 2013, Sports Illustrated released a five-part expose into the Oklahoma State University (OSU) football program. The expose alleged widespread NCAA violations including impermissible benefits, drug abuse, and inappropriate actions of the Orange Pride, the OSU hostess group. These hostesses would regularly entertain football recruits, with a small subset allegedly having sex with recruits to entice them to come to OSU.

The NCAA's findings did not quite match the salacious reporting. The NCAA found that Oklahoma State University did not follow its drug testing policy and the athletics department should not have allowed the Orange Pride student group to participate in hosting prospects which led to some recruiting violations. The penalties in the OSU case included one year of probation, $8,500 in fines, suspension of the Orange Pride program, and university-imposed recruiting restrictions. *Oklahoma State University Public Infractions Decision*, April 24, 2015.

In 2015, the NCAA ended a wide-ranging eight-year investigation into the football and men's basketball programs of Syracuse University. The NCAA found a lack of institutional control within the athletic program. Specifically, Syracuse discovered and self-reported ten violations including academic misconduct, extra benefits, the failure to follow its drug testing policy, and impermissible booster activity. The other violations found included impermissible academic assistance and services, the head basketball coach Jim Boeheim's failure to promote an atmosphere of compliance and monitor his staff, and the school's lack of control over its athletics program. *Syracuse University Public Infractions Decision*, March 6, 2015.

Penalties included five years of probation; financial penalties; reduction of three men's basketball scholarships per year for four years; vacation of wins in which ineligible students participated; a nine conference game suspension for the head basketball coach; and men's basketball recruiting restrictions for two years. Additionally, Syracuse self-imposed a one-year postseason ban in men's basketball.

Missouri announced in January 2016 that it had discovered major NCAA violations committed within its men's basketball program between 2011–14. Specifically, investigators found a donor provided impermissible benefits to four players—three active players and one recruit—by falsely categorizing them as summer intern employees. The donor provided cash, iPads, meals and other minor benefits that violated NCAA bylaws. Another donor allegedly gave eleven men's basketball student-athletes a reduced rate at a hotel, provided transportation to the facility and offered players access to a boat. Other minor violations included a donor illegally contacting a recruit, the payment of a meal for a coach and a former assistant helping a student-athlete's mother find housing by putting her in contact with a booster.

The NCAA agreed that the University of Missouri had failed to monitor its men's basketball program related to both boosters. The total amount of impermissible inducements and extra benefits provided by the two boosters totaled $11,402. *University of Missouri, Columbia Public Infractions Decision*, August 2, 2016.

The NCAA accepted the university's self-imposed penalties and added one year of probation. Penalties self-imposed by the school include a one-year postseason ban for the men's basketball team, completed during the 2015–16 season, scholarship reductions, recruiting restrictions, disassociation of the two boosters, a vacation of men's basketball wins and a fine.

In 2016, the NCAA imposed sanctions against the University of Notre Dame for impermissible benefits provided to football players. A former University of Notre Dame student athletic trainer violated NCAA ethical conduct rules. She committed academic misconduct on behalf of two football student-athletes by completing their coursework as well as providing six other football student-athletes with impermissible academic extra benefits in a total of eighteen classes. The players included KeiVarae Russell, DaVaris Daniels, Ishaq Williams, Kendall Moore and Eilar Hardy. Notre Dame had previously lost its starting quarterback in 2013, Everett Golson, whom the university dismissed for cheating on a test. *University of Notre Dame Public Infractions Decision*, November 22, 2016.

The NCAA levied sanctions of one year of probation, a two-year show-cause order and disassociation for the former student trainer, and a $5,000 fine for the university. The NCAA also vacated Notre Dame's wins from the 2012 season, in which it lost in the national championship game to Alabama, and the 2013 season. Notre Dame appealed, but the Infractions Appeals Committee upheld the sanctions. *University of Notre Dame, Decision of the NCAA Division I Infractions Appeals Committee*, No. 453, February 13, 2018.

Another serious scandal concerning an elite college basketball program happened at the University of Louisville for conduct during the 2012–15 seasons. Specifically, Louisville director of basketball operations Andre McGee arranged striptease dances and sex acts for prospects, student-athletes and others, and did not cooperate with the ensuing NCAA investigation. The head men's basketball coach, Rick Pitino, violated NCAA head coach responsibility rules when he did not monitor the activities of

McGee. *University of Louisville Public Infractions Decision*, June 15, 2017.

The NCAA imposed a number of sanctions against Louisville, including a suspension of Pitino for the first five Atlantic Coast Conference (ACC) games of the 2017–18 season, a ten-year show-cause order against McGee, a vacation of basketball records from 2012–15, including the 2013 national championship, and all of the revenue paid to Louisville through ACC conference revenue sharing from the 2012–15 NCAA basketball tournaments. The Infractions Appeals Committee upheld these sanctions on appeal. *University of Louisville, Decision of the NCAA Division I Infractions Appeals Committee*, No. 473, February 20, 2018.

A subsequent FBI investigation into benefits paid to the family of Louisville recruit Brian Bowen by Adidas executive James Gatto (discussed later in this chapter) led to the dismissal of Pitino in 2017. Pitino claimed not to know about either the adult entertainment activities or the payments to Bowen, but the second scandal in a three year period convinced Louisville to part ways with Pitino.

In 2017, the NCAA imposed sanctions against the University of Mississippi (Ole Miss) related to its football program. In 2013, Ole Miss had landed one of the best recruiting classes in the country, including defensive end Robert Nkemdeche (whose brother was already on the team), top receiver LaQuon Treadwell, and star offensive tackle Laremy Tunsil. This class proved its worth, being part of Ole Miss teams in 2014 and 2015 that defeated Alabama, went a

combined 19–7, and won the Sugar Bowl on January
1, 2016. The 2014 Alabama game, a 23–17 Ole Miss
win in Oxford, was the infamous "Katy Perry" game
in which the singer predicted the Ole Miss upset on
College Gameday and then "won the party" by
celebrating late into the evening on the Oxford
Square.

During the success of these teams, Coach Hugh
Freeze publicly challenged pundits and fans accusing
Ole Miss of violating NCAA rules to submit
information to the NCAA. The NCAA did begin
investigating Ole Miss, in part related to infractions
that happened during Houston Nutt's time as head
coach before Hugh Freeze arrived and in part related
to a minor infraction concerning Tunsil, who had
allegedly received the benefit a loaner car from a local
dealership. Some public reports indicated that the
university and the NCAA enforcement committee
were working toward a negotiated resolution.

The NFL draft, however, changed the tenor of the
investigation. As the draft commenced, an
anonymous third party circulated a photograph of
Tunsil smoking marijuana sitting in front of a
confederate flag. Tunsil dropped a number of spots in
the first round of the draft and subsequently
suggested that he had received financial benefits
from Ole Miss in the ensuing interview at the draft.
The optics of the draft coverage likely contributed to
the enforcement staff deciding to investigate further.

As the NCAA's investigation continued, it
uncovered alleged benefits paid to star Mississippi
State linebacker Leo Lewis. An Ole Miss assistant

coach had allegedly paid Lewis $10,000 during his recruitment. Sources reported that LSU and Mississippi State had also paid Lewis, but those allegations have not been part of any subsequent NCAA case.

Another part of the NCAA allegations related to Rebel Rags, an Oxford store that sells Ole Miss apparel, allegedly providing swag to Ole Miss recruits. Rebel Rags challenged the NCAA's account and sued. The NCAA and Rebel Rags settled their lawsuit on the eve of trial in August, 2023.

Ultimately, the NCAA found the Ole Miss lacked institutional control and fostered an unconstrained culture of booster involvement in football recruiting. Six football staff members and twelve boosters were involved in the violations, which included the provision of approximately $37,000 to prospects through cash payments, and the use of automobiles, lodging, transportation, meals, and apparel. Two staff members also helped arrange fraudulent standardized test scores for three prospects. The COI found that Coach Freeze failed to monitor the program, allowing his staff to knowingly commit a series of recruiting violations, submit false information on recruiting paperwork, and not report known violations. *University of Mississippi Public Infractions Decision*, December 1, 2017.

Penalties in the case were particularly stiff. They included three years of probation; a two-year postseason ban for the football team; a financial penalty; scholarship and recruiting restrictions; vacation of records; a two-conference-game suspension for Freeze; an eight-year show-cause order for the operations coordinator; five-year show-cause orders for an assistant coach and an assistant athletics director; and a two-year show-cause order for another assistant coach.

A final subtext to the case involved Coach Freeze. In its response to the NCAA, the Ole Miss athletic department highlighted the role of Coach Nutt in some of the violations. Coach Nutt sued Ole Miss, alleging that it was defaming him and also was violating his termination agreement. During discovery, the lawyer for Coach Nutt received Coach Freeze's phone records, which included calls to escort services on Freeze's university-issued cell phone. Once athletic director Ross Bjork became aware of these records, he terminated Coach Freeze. The university subsequently settled the case with Coach Nutt.

While most of the infractions described in this chapter relate to the revenue sports of football and men's basketball, other sports commonly violate NCAA amateurism rules as well. A recent example involves the Ohio State University.

Over the course of several years, multiple NCAA violations occurred in the Ohio State fencing, women's golf and women's basketball programs. The former fencing head coach and former women's golf head coach violated head coach responsibility rules, and the fencing coach and former women's basketball associate head coach violated ethical conduct rules when they did not meet their obligation to fully cooperate with an investigation. *The Ohio State*

University Public Infractions Decision, April 19, 2022.

NCAA sanctions included four years of probation, paying a small percentage of certain teams' budgets, recruiting restrictions, a vacation of records, show cause orders, and a one year post-season ban for each of the four programs at issue.

Most recently, the University of Michigan football team marched to an undefeated season and national championship in the 2023–24 season. The Wolverines capped off the final year of the NCAA's four team playoff era by defeating Alabama in the Rose Bowl and Washington in the national championship game in dramatic fashion. Coach Jim Harbaugh, however, suffered two suspensions during the season, both related to NCAA investigations. First, Michigan suspended Harbaugh for the first three games of the season as part of self-imposed sanction. The infractions case related to improper contact with recruits during a dead period during the Covid-19 pandemic. The investigation did not directly implicate Harbaugh, but his alleged lack of cooperation impeded the ability of Michigan to reach a negotiated resolution of the case.

Then, in October, 2023, the NCAA notified Michigan and the Big Ten that it had received allegations that Michigan was involved in a sign-stealing scheme. This scheme involved Michigan allegedly sending representatives to the games of future opponents to scout these opponents and record their use of play-calling signs during games. NCAA rules have, at least since 1994, barred such scouting, even though tens of thousands of fans attend such games and networks televise almost all of the games. At the center of the scandal was Connor Stalions, a Michigan off-field analyst. While it became clear that Stalions had regularly attended games of future Michigan opponents, Harbaugh nonetheless denied wrongdoing.

Late in the season, the Big Ten negotiated a settlement with Michigan regarding a punishment for its alleged rules violation. The Big Ten agreed to drop its investigation in exchange for Harbaugh agreeing to a three-game suspension for the final three games of the 2023 regular season, including games against rivals Penn State and Ohio State. At the time of this writing, the NCAA's investigation remains ongoing. In the meantime, Harbaugh has accepted a job as the head coach of the Los Angeles Chargers.

Finally, a new infractions front has emerged with respect to NIL deals. In January, 2024, the NCAA sanctioned Florida State University for using NIL deals as recruiting inducements. *Florida State University, Negotiated Resolution*, Case No. 020169, January 12, 2024. This was the first such case involving college football recruiting, following a similar case (see Chapter Four) involving the women's basketball team at Miami. *University of Miami (Florida), Negotiated Resolution*, Case No. 020161, February 24, 2023.

In April 2022, a Florida State assistant football coach violated NCAA rules when he facilitated an impermissible recruiting contact between a football transfer prospect and a booster. During that contact, the booster encouraged the prospect to enroll at Florida State and offered a name, image, and likeness deal as a recruiting inducement. The NIL opportunity was for approximately $15,000 per month. The assistant coach then violated ethical conduct rules when he provided false or misleading information to the NCAA about his involvement in the arranged meeting.

Florida State cooperated with the NCAA staff, and as a result was able to reach a negotiated resolution in the case. The sanctions imposed included two years of probation, a two-year show cause order for the assistant coach, a three-year disassociation from the booster, and additional limitations on recruiting.

As discussed in Chapters Four and Six, Tennessee has challenged a similar investigation on antitrust law grounds and received a preliminary injunction against enforcement of the anti-NIL inducement rule as of February 2024. *Tennessee & Virginia v. NCAA*, 2024 WL 755528 (E.D. Tenn. 2024).

4.   THE DEATH PENALTY

The most serious sanction that the NCAA COI has ever imposed is the death penalty. The death penalty requires a university to cease operation of a particular sport for a year. The consequence is severe because all of the athletes on the team will transfer and the program will have to start over from scratch.

The football program at Southern Methodist University (SMU) received the death penalty in 1987.

Southern Methodist University Placed on NCAA Probation, August 16, 1985. The NCAA required it to suspend its football program for the 1987–88 year. It is the only institution to ever receive this punishment. Because of transfers and difficulty in recruiting after receiving the death penalty, SMU was also unable to field a team for the 1988–89 season. After winning over 80% of its games between 1980 and 1984, SMU did not play in a bowl game after its penalty in 1987 until it won the 2009 Hawaii Bowl.

Prior to receiving the death penalty, SMU was already on NCAA probation for recruiting violations in 1985. The COI discovered that SMU had made approximately $61,000 in booster payments during 1985 and 1986. Indeed, a slush fund to pay athletes had been in existence since the mid-1970s, and athletic department officials had known about these payments at least since 1981. The blatant disregard of the NCAA's prior sanctions seemingly played a role in SMU receiving the death penalty.

The University of Alabama faced a similar situation when it came before the COI in 2002. At the time, Alabama had recently served a two-year probation in 1995 relating to payments made to All-American defensive back Antonio Langham after the school won the Sugar Bowl and national title in 1994. *University of Alabama, Tuscaloosa Public Infractions Report*, February 1, 2002.

Alabama booster Logan Young was at the center of the 2002 case which involved several allegations of misconduct. Young allegedly promised a Memphis high school coach $100,000 and two SUVs in exchange for directing star recruit Albert Means to attend Alabama. A second series of violations involved payments to a recruit and lodging for him and his family during a recruiting trip to Nashville.

Tennessee football coach Philip Fulmer was partially responsible for blowing the whistle after learning about the alleged payments while recruiting in Memphis. He sent an infamous memo labeled "for your eyes only" to then-SEC commissioner Roy Kramer suggesting that the league should investigate.

In total, Alabama received ten major violations and five minor ones. The chair of the COI, Thomas Yeager stated that "[t]hese violations are some of the worst, most serious that have ever occurred." The COI, however, elected not to give Alabama the death penalty. Instead, the COI placed Alabama on probation for five years, including a two-year bowl ban and significant reductions in the number of football scholarships the school could award (a loss of 21 over 3 years).

The COI explained that the cooperation provided by Alabama during in the investigation mitigated its punishment. The COI indicated that it seriously considered giving Alabama the death penalty but its cooperation dissuaded the COI from imposing this punishment.

Perhaps even more egregious was the conduct of booster Nevin Shapiro at the University of Miami. Shapiro engaged in rampant violations of NCAA rules for over a decade. Shapiro allegedly provided Miami football players cash, goods, prostitutes, and assorted favors. Shapiro subsequently received a twenty-year prison sentence for orchestrating a $930 million Ponzi scheme.

While in prison, Shapiro decided to reveal all of the NCAA violations he had participated in, which included paying a total of $2 million in benefits involving at least seventy-two Miami football players. In response to the allegations, the University of Miami imposed significant penalties on itself, including the suspension of eight football players, and removed itself from post-season bowl contention for one year.

On October 22, 2013, after a two-and-a-half year of investigation, the NCAA announced that the University of Miami football team would lose three scholarships in each of the next three seasons, a three-year probation, recruiting restrictions, a five-game suspension of the Miami Hurricanes men's basketball coach, and a two-year show-cause order for three former assistant football and basketball coaches. *University of Miami (Florida) Public Infractions Report*, October 22, 2013.

Before the NCAA announced its penalties, news outlets reported that NCAA enforcement staff paid Shapiro's lawyer $25,000 to call in University of Miami personnel during an unassociated legal deposition for Shapiro's bankruptcy, and ask a specific list of questions related to the university's scandal. Shapiro's attorney used her subpoena power in the bankruptcy case to question two witnesses who were crucial to the NCAA's case. The NCAA had no subpoena power, and neither witness had any obligation to talk to the association. The backlash from the revelations about the NCAA's ethically dubious activities, coupled with the university's unprecedented self-imposed sanctions, probably helped the Miami escape the death penalty.

After the COI's decisions in the Alabama and Miami cases, it seems unlikely that the COI will ever impose the death penalty again. This is particularly true now that NIL laws enable third party donors and collectives to pay athletes for use of their NILs.

5.   CRIMINAL ACTIVITY

The scandal at Pennsylvania State University (Penn State) involving former assistant football coach Jerry Sandusky in 2011 raised the issue of the NCAA's role related to criminal activity in athletic programs. Sandusky engaged in sexual abuse of minors over a fifteen year period, including many interactions inside Penn State athletics facilities.

In 2012, a jury found Sandusky guilty of 45 counts of sexual assault. The judge sentenced Sandusky to 30 to 60 years in prison. It also designated him as a violent sex offender. In 2013, Penn State reached a $59.7 million settlement with twenty-six victims of Sandusky.

In addition, Penn State's athletic director Tim Curley and vice president Gary Schultz pled guilty to child endangerment. Also, a jury convicted Penn State president Graham Spanier on the same charge (after an acquittal on more serious conspiracy allegations). All three began serving prison sentences of between 4 months and 2 years in 2018.

Any scrutiny of the involvement of Penn State's legendary football coach, Joe Paterno, ended with his death in January 2012, three months after the scandal broke. Shortly after the scandal erupted, the Penn State Board of Trustees commissioned an investigation of the entire episode by former FBI director Richard Freeh, who issued a lengthy report. It concluded that the Penn State officials noted above had failed to disclose information they knew concerning Sandusky's sexual abuse.

Relying primarily on the Freeh Report, NCAA President Mark Emmert announced on July 23, 2012 that the NCAA's Executive Committee was levying several sanctions against Penn State for fostering an unhealthy culture that allowed the Sandusky crimes to happen and go unreported. The sanctions included: (a) a fine of $60 million; (b) a five year post-season ban for the football team (through the 2016 season); (c) a reduction in the number of football scholarships Penn State could give from 2012 through 2015 to fifteen a year and a total of no more than sixty-five (the normal maximum for a Division I-A school is eighty-five); and (d) requiring Penn State retroactively to forfeit 112 wins earned from 1998 through 2011 (the years that Sandusky was committing his crimes). This forfeiture caused Coach Paterno to lose his status as the winningest Division I-A football coach of all time. At the same time as he announced the sanctions, Emmert stated that the

Penn State Board of Trustees had signed a consent form accepting the penalties and agreeing not to contest them.

In 2014, the NCAA began restoring some of the football scholarships so that Penn State was able to give twenty in 2014 (for a total of 75), and twenty-five (a full complement) thereafter so it would have a full allotment of eighty-five by the 2016 season. The stated reason for reducing this penalty was that the University had made strong good-faith efforts to change its culture by adopting many of the 119 recommendations the Freeh Report had made. In September 2014, the NCAA lifted the ban on post-season play two years earlier than originally imposed, allowing the Penn State football team to play and defeat Boston College by one point in overtime in the New Era Pinstripe Bowl in Yankee Stadium two days after Christmas in 2014.

In February 2013, a report commissioned by Joe Paterno's family found that the Freeh Report was in many respects factually wrong, speculative, and fundamentally flawed. Based on this Report, Coach Paterno's wife and children, his estate, and five members of the Penn State Board filed a lawsuit in Pennsylvania state court. They claimed that by rushing to judgment and falsely publicly accusing Joe Paterno of covering up Sandusky's criminal behavior, the NCAA and President Emmert had committed various torts and interfered with the NCAA's contract with the University. The plaintiffs sought an injunction setting aside the consent agreement between the NCAA and the Penn State trustees (that it claimed was the product of coercion) and several of the sanctions, including the one that vacated 112 of Coach Paterno's victories.

State Senator Jake Corman and Treasurer Rob McCord then filed suit against the NCAA in state court in Harrisburg seeking to require the NCAA to spend the $60 million in fines collected from Penn State exclusively in Pennsylvania. They made this claim not only because of the Endowment Act, but also because the monies are state funds legally under the oversight of the Senate Appropriations Committee that Corman chairs.

In January 2015, the NCAA settled these lawsuits by agreeing to restore the 112 wins it had previously struck from the records (thereby once again making Joe Paterno the winningest Division I-A football coach in history) and to spend the $60 million fine on child abuse prevention and treatment programs in Pennsylvania. Thus, by 2015, the NCAA had either lifted, substantially reduced, or modified all the sanctions imposed against Penn State. Most of the reforms Penn State introduced to persuade the NCAA to lift sanctions remain in place.

In 2018, another sex abuse scandal followed this sordid saga. It involved Larry Nassar, a Michigan State physician. Nassar, a team doctor for USA Gymnastics, molested hundreds of mostly female young athletes, as part of his "medical care." Nassar pleaded guilty to seven counts of criminal sexual conduct, admitting to sexually assaulting and abusing young girls under the guise of providing medical treatment. As part of his plea deal, 144 victims gave victim impact statements. In all, Nassar will be serving three prison sentences, two of 40–125 years for molestation and abuse, and another 60-year sentence for child pornography.

Nassar had been an associate professor at Michigan State since 1997. Questions immediately arose, as with the Penn State scandal, concerning whether the university knew about Nassar's criminal behavior. In the wake of the revelations about Nassar, both the Michigan State president and athletic director resigned. The NCAA sent a letter in January 2018 asking for more information concerning the scandal. Unlike Penn State, it did not commission a law firm to prepare an outside report. In May 2018, Michigan State reported that it did not find any NCAA rules violations in relation to the Larry Nassar case, and in August 2018, the NCAA's enforcement unit confirmed that conclusion. Michigan State agreed in 2018 to pay $500 million to settle claims with more than 300 women and girls allegedly assaulted by Nassar.

The University of Michigan had a similar issue with one of its doctors. Dr. Robert Anderson, a sports doctor, abused over 1,000 people, mostly men, during routine medical examinations over a four-decade career. Anderson died in 2003 before the allegations became public. but The University of Michigan agreed to pay victims $490 million in 2022. Many former Michigan football players were among Anderson's victims.

Another repugnant scandal involved Baylor University, with the ultimate consequences largely left to the criminal justice system. The scandal involved a series of sexual and non-sexual assaults committed by Baylor students, most of whom were football players. From 2012–16, school officials allegedly suppressed reports of rapes and sexual misconduct.

On January 23, 2014, a Texas court sentenced Tevin Elliott, a former Baylor linebacker to twenty years in prison for two sexual assaults committed against a Baylor student in 2012. In August 2015, Texas court also convicted defensive end Sam Ukwuachu for the sexual assault of a female Baylor soccer player. Ukwuachu has argued that the sexual encounter in question was consensual. He received a 180 day sentence and ten years of probation. His case has continued for almost a decade, bouncing between the Waco Court of Appeals and the Texas Court of Criminal Appeal.

On March 3, 2016, Jacob Anderson, the president of Phi Delta Theta, was charged with sexual assault. He pled no contest to a charge of unlawful restraint and received three years probation. On April 13, 2016, Shawn Oakman, a former All-America defensive end was charged with sexual assault against a female student. In February 2019, a jury found him not guilty of the charges against him.

In 2015, following the convictions of Elliott and Ukwuachu and in light of allegations against other players, Baylor commissioned the law firm of Pepper Hamilton to conduct an independent external investigation of Baylor's handing of sexual violence. Following the presentation of the report in May 2016,

Baylor fired head football coach Art Briles. Baylor president Ken Starr and athletic director Ian McCaw also resigned. Briles sued Baylor for wrongful termination but subsequently reached an out-of-court settlement.

In a 2017 lawsuit, fifteen victims suing the university alleged that from 2011 to 2014 at least thirty-one football players committed at least fifty-two rapes. *Doe 1 v. Baylor University*, 240 F.Supp.3d 646 (W.D. Tex. 2017). After the trial court denied Baylor's motion to dismiss, the parties settled the suit in September, 2023.

The NCAA, for its part, conducted a seven-year investigation into the Baylor athletics program. The NCAA, however, only imposed probation and relatively minor sanctions. Despite finding the behavior in question egregious, the "unacceptable" behavior at the heart of the case did not violate NCAA rules. *Baylor University, Public Infractions Decision*, August 11, 2021.

The Committee on Infractions noted that the allegations centered on conduct never before presented to the committee—that Baylor had "shielded football student-athletes from the institution's disciplinary process and failed to report allegations of abhorrent misconduct by football student-athletes, including instances of sexual and interpersonal violence." While recognizing the moral and ethical failings of Baylor, the panel found that these shortcomings fell outside of the scope of NCAA legislation.

As with Penn State, Michigan State, and Michigan, the Baylor saga raises interesting and important questions about the NCAA's role in responding to criminal activity within athletic programs. On the one hand, the criminal justice system exists to punish criminal behavior. And university officials typically face consequences for such actions happening on their campuses. But at the same time, to the degree that college athletics plays a role in such criminal activity, by creating a space or culture that enhances the likelihood of such criminal activity, one wonders whether more serious intervention by the NCAA is necessary. It remains unclear how the NCAA will handle future situations of criminality within college athletics, but its current approach seems to suggest deferring to the criminal justice system, at least as an initial matter.

CHAPTER THREE
THE EVOLUTION OF AMATEURISM

As a concept, amateurism in the playing of sports has an English heritage. Traditionally in the playing of sport, the idea of an amateur emerged from the principle that a gentleman never competes for money. In other words, wealthier individuals enjoyed a purity of participation of sorts because engaging in sports was a recreational activity not a profession. Athletes, then, performed for the love of the game and the inherent benefits found in playing the game as opposed to for the purpose of making money.

This concept of amateurism, however, was not the driving force behind the founding of the NCAA. As discussed in Chapter One, the motivation for the creation of the Inter-Collegiate Athletic Association in 1905, later renamed the NCAA in 1910, was the need to address safety concerns. In the early 1900s, the concept of amateurism gained prominence to uphold the educational integrity and social reputation of colleges. This era witnessed a concentrated effort to enhance safety in college sports, especially football, notorious for its violent nature.

As revenues increased in the mid-1900s, the NCAA introduced the Sanity Code, which aimed to preserve amateur sports while indirectly allowing institutions to provide athletes with amenities such as lodging, meals, and tuition covered by athletic scholarships. This marked the formal association of the term amateurism with college athletics. To uphold the amateur status, the NCAA placed restrictions on athletes receiving endorsements or payments from businesses, as well as engaging in paid activities related to their sport. The NCAA designed this framework to ensure that college athletes remained unpaid, thus maintaining their amateur standing.

For much of its history, the NCAA's definition of amateurism allowed universities to pay the tuition, room, board, and books of athletes. It generally barred any other benefit given by universities. It also prohibited, as explored in Chapter Two, benefits provided by third party boosters.

Two main reasons emerged for these limitations: (1) concerns that fan interest would decline if players were professionals, especially in lucrative sports like basketball and football, and (2) the belief that scholarship limits would integrate student-athletes into the campus community, thereby enhancing their education. For decades, the NCAA continued to prohibit athletes from receiving fees for endorsements or compensation related to their names and likenesses.

The term "student-athlete" plays a pivotal role in discussions about amateurism. Coined by the NCAA in the 1950s, it aimed to counter potential claims that college athletes were employees eligible to worker benefits such as compensation for game-related injuries. To date, this conception of the athlete as a student and not as an employee remains, but continues to face legal challenges, as explored in this chapter and Chapter Six.

The concept of amateurism with respect to the relationship of the athlete and university has finally collapsed as a result of antitrust challenges. The historical tuition, room, board, and books then also included the cost of attendance and costs "related to education." And with the settlement in the *House* case, it can also include revenue sharing. This chapter traces these antitrust cases.

The concept of amateurism with respect to third party payments is gone. The recent emergence of Name, Image, and Likeness (NIL) payments stemming from state laws that the NCAA must follow has provided a robust market used to compensate athletes. Chapter Four explores this new development and the many ways it is transforming college sports.

1.   THE BOARD OF REGENTS CASE

The conversation around the application of antitrust law to college sports centers around one landmark case—*NCAA v. Board of Regents of University of Oklahoma*, 468 U.S. 85 (1984). This case opened the door to the commercialization of college sports through television and also served, for three decades, as an antitrust defense of the NCAA's student-athlete model.

The University of Pennsylvania first televised a home college football game in 1938. From 1940 through 1950, Penn televised all of its home games. The NCAA became increasingly wary of televising of games as it worried that television would negatively impact attendance.

In 1951, the NCAA formed a committee to study the impact of televising games on attendance and formulate a television policy for member institutions. Its initial report found that "the television problem is truly a national one, and requires collective action by the colleges." As a result, the Television Committee adopted a plan for 1951. This plan allowed televising only one game per week in a particular area and a total blackout for areas on 3 of 10 Saturdays during the season. Further, a team could appear on television only twice during a season.

While almost all NCAA members accepted the plan, Penn challenged it. The NCAA council declared that Penn was a member in bad standing and Penn lost four games in 1951 because other teams would not play them. Penn subsequently agreed to follow the NCAA plan.

The annual television plans followed the same parameters for the next twenty-five years. In 1977, the NCAA decided to move from one year television contracts to four year contracts. It entered into an exclusive four year contract with American Broadcasting Companies (ABC) for the 1978–81 seasons. In 1981, the NCAA entered into similar contracts with ABC and the Columbia Broadcasting System (CBS) for the 1982–85 seasons. Each network would televise 14 games per season under the contract.

The five major football conferences, together with major football-playing independent institutions, organized the College Football Association (CFA) in 1977. The CFA decided to enter into its own contract with the National Broadcasting Company (NBC) in 1981. In response, the NCAA publicly announced that it would take disciplinary action against any CFA member that complied with the CFA-NBC contract. The NCAA made it clear that sanctions would not just apply to the football programs of CFA members, but also to other sports as well.

Two CFA members, the University of Oklahoma and the University of Georgia, filed a lawsuit in September 1981 alleging that the NCAA's actions violated § 1 of the Sherman Antitrust Act by unreasonably restraining trade in the televising of college football games.

Oklahoma and Georgia were keen on having their games televised as often as possible in part because they had outstanding football teams at the time. Georgia had just won the national championship in January 1981 after a 12–0 season in which they defeated Notre Dame in the Sugar Bowl. They had another successful season in the fall of 1982, again going undefeated in the SEC before losing in the Sugar Bowl to a stellar Pittsburgh Panthers team led by future NFL star quarterback Dan Marino. Georgia's star running back Herschel Walker won the Heisman Trophy in 1982, finishing his career as one of the greatest college football players of all-time.

Oklahoma similarly enjoyed success at the end of the 1970s, finishing the 1978, 1979, and 1980 seasons ranked third in the country, winning Big 8 conference championships and the Orange Bowl each year. Oklahoma had previously won the national championship in 1974 and 1975, with its star running back Billy Sims winning the Heisman Trophy in 1978. Led by coach Barry Switzer, Oklahoma dominated its opponents by running the wishbone offense, a triple option running game that amassed hundreds of yards of rushing each game while rarely passing the ball.

Section one of the Sherman Act provides, "Every contract, combination in the form of trust or otherwise, or conspiracy, in restraint of trade or commerce among the several States, or with foreign nations, is declared to be illegal." The Supreme Court has interpreted this language to apply to all contracts in interstate commerce that unreasonably restrain trade. *Standard Oil Company of New Jersey v. United States*, 221 U.S. 1 (1911). Contracts unreasonably restrain trade when they restrict economic competition in a particular market. The point of antitrust law in this context is to protect the consumer by ensuring that there is a competitive market where companies cannot collaborate to fix prices.

To determine whether a restraint is reasonable under the Sherman Act, the Court uses either a per se test or a rule of reason test. The Court uses per se test when assessing horizontal restraints of trade, that is, restraints that occur between entities operating at the same level of distribution in the market. Because horizontal restraints clearly interfere with economic competition without promoting competition in another market, these restraints are per se illegal and do not require further analysis by courts. For instance, if all of the gas stations in a college town decided to fix the price of gasoline at $25 per gallon during the weekend of the big football game, that would be a horizontal restraint on trade that would be per se illegal in violation of the Sherman Act.

The rule of reason is a three-part test established by the Supreme Court to determine if a particular restraint on trade is unreasonable and thus illegal. *Chicago Board of Trade v. United States*, 246 U.S. 231 (1918). To evaluate the effect of the behavior in question, the court must first define the applicable market. With respect to that market, the rule of reason assesses the justifications for the restraint in question. This three-part burden-shifting test works as follows: (1) the Plaintiff must show that the restraint in question creates anti-competitive effects; (2) the Defendant must show that the anti-competitive effects create pro-competitive benefits; and then (3) the Plaintiff must show that the restraint is not necessary to accomplish the stated goal—the company could achieve the same pro-competitive end through less competitive means.

Over time, the Court has also adopted a quick look test that falls between the per se and rule of reason tests. The quick look test engages in a rule of reason type analysis that is less thorough because the issue in question is one that could, in other contexts, be susceptible to a per se determination of unreasonableness.

The rule of reason test typically applies to vertical restraints, agreements between companies at different levels of the distribution chain, as well as joint ventures. Because college sports involve athletic competition, the Court has used the rule of reason in cases involving college and professional sports. Antitrust law applies to restrictions on economic competition. The likelihood of confusion and overlap between athletic and economic competition is another reason that the Court has used the rule of reason in sports cases.

Restraints on athletic competition, which do not trigger antitrust scrutiny, could include rules about allowable equipment, the number of games teams play, and the number of assistant coaches a team may have. All of these rules relate to the competition itself. Restraints on economic competition, by contrast, limit the ability of individuals or institutions to operate in a free market. These economic restraints do trigger antitrust scrutiny. Examples of economic restraints include the price teams can pay to other teams to play a game, the number of times the team is on television, and the amount institutions can pay coaches.

While discussions of antitrust law may appear boring at first glance, they are not. The consequences of winning an antitrust suit for a plaintiff can include an injunction against the actions of a defendant, treble damages—the court automatically triples the damages amount, and attorneys' fees.

In the Oklahoma-Georgia antitrust lawsuit against the NCAA, known as *Board of Regents*, the universities claimed that the NCAA violated the Sherman Act by limiting the number of football games the networks could televise. The market in question was the market for entertainment.

The NCAA's television plan and its threat to punish the universities for entering into their own contracts with the television networks constituted a clear restraint of trade. As the Court explained, the NCAA plan operated to both raise price and reduce output, both of which were unresponsive to consumer preference. In other words, the NCAA's plan ignored consumer demand, which likely would have wanted talented teams like Georgia and Oklahoma to have more than one or two games on television in a season.

The question in the case was whether the NCAA had a pro-competitive justification for this restraint. In other words, the NCAA had to show that its restraint, while anti-competitive in one market, promoted economic competition in another market.

In support of its claim under the rule of reason, the NCAA offered several justifications. The Court was not convinced that any of them were pro-competitive. First, the Court rejected the NCAA's proffered justification that it was a cooperative "joint venture" assisting in the marketing of broadcast rights. The Court found that the NCAA could market its football games just as effectively without the television plan in question.

Second, the NCAA claimed that its restraints were necessary to preserve live attendance at football games. According to the NCAA, the restriction in the television market increased the ability to compete in the market for game tickets. The Court rejected this claim because the rule of reason "does not support a defense based on the assumption that competition itself is unreasonable." In other words, one cannot just limit output as a way to compete in the market.

The Court's rejection of both of these NCAA arguments has survived the test of time. The televising of more games has increased attendance at games, as well as the overall popularity and revenue generating ability of college football. FBS football game attendance in 1983 was roughly 25.3 million per season, while FBS attendance was roughly 37.5 million in 2023 despite networks televising almost every FBS game.

Finally, the NCAA argued that restricting the televising of games was important to remain competitive balance in the sport of college football. But that benefit is not economically pro-competitive. It is athletically pro-competitive, which is not a defense under the Sherman Act. It is also not necessarily true that parity will draw more interest in sports than having dominant teams. *See* William W. Berry III, *Superstars, Super-Teams, and the Future of Player Movement*, 13 HARV. J. SPORTS & ENT. L. 199 (2022).

Thus, the Court held in the *Board of Regents* case that the NCAA's television plan and its restrictions on the ability of Georgia and Oklahoma to enter their own television contracts violated the Sherman Act. *NCAA v. Board of Regents of University of Oklahoma*, 468 U.S. 85 (1984). The Court enjoined the NCAA from placing restrictions on the ability of its member institutions to enter their own television contracts.

At the end of its opinion, the Court added a paragraph of dicta providing context for its decision:

> The NCAA plays a critical role in the maintenance of a revered tradition of amateurism in college sports. There can be no question but that it needs ample latitude to play that role, or that the preservation of the student athlete in higher education adds richness and diversity to intercollegiate athletics and is entirely consistent with the goals of the Sherman Act. But consistent with the Sherman Act, the role of the NCAA must be to preserve a tradition that might otherwise die; rules that restrict output are hardly consistent with this role.

Board of Regents, 468 U.S. at 120.

As explored below, the NCAA used this dicta for almost forty years to justify its freedom from antitrust scrutiny of its student-athlete amateurism model. The Supreme Court finally rejected the NCAA's reading of this language in 2021. *NCAA v. Alston*, 594 U.S. 69 (2021).

2. TELEVISION REVENUE

The consequences of the Court's decision in *Board of Regents* have been far-reaching. The current revenue for televising college football games is over $1 billion annually, and the NCAA does not receive any of that money. It also does not control the bowl games or the college football playoff, and has not been part of the development of that system, dating back to the Bowl Championship Series (BCS).

The immediate aftermath of the *Board of Regents* decision saw football conferences enter into lucrative deals with television networks. Setting the stage, ABC acquired ESPN from Texaco for $188 million. The CFA negotiated multiple deals with ABC, ESPN, and TBS, cumulatively worth $21.2 million. The non-CFA conferences, the Big Ten and the Pac-10, signed a one-year deal for $8 million with CBS, followed by a two-year deal in 1985 worth $24 million from ESPN and $31 million from ABC. The ACC also signed a contract with CBS for $3.5 million for the 1985–86 season, leaving the CFA. In 1987, CBS took over the rights to at least 15 games for $60 million. ESPN also signed a deal with CFA for the 1987–90 seasons worth $70 million. In 1991, the CFA signed two deals—one with ABC worth $210 million (through 1995) and one with ESPN for $110 million (through 1994).

In a move underscoring the same issues that have shaped conference realignment (explored in Chapter 7), Notre Dame left the CFA in 1991. It signed a five-year deal with NBC worth $38 million, a deal ultimately expanded to $185 million. From 1991–2000, Notre Dame received $7.6 million per season; from 2001–2010, $9 million per season. This amount increased to $15 million per season for the 2011–15 seasons, and $20 million in the current contract from 2016–25. The SEC and the Big East left the CFA in 1995, leading to its eventual ending of its operations in 1997.

In 1996, the SEC moved to CBS with a five-year deal worth $85 million and also signed an additional $30 million deal with ESPN. The SEC's subsequent deal with CBS and ESPN was worth $50 million per year from 2001 through 2008. This amount grew even more in 2009 when SEC and ESPN agreed to a 15-year deal worth $2.25 billion. After expanding to add Missouri and Texas A&M in 2012, the SEC Network launched in 2014, with a 20-year ESPN deal. ESPN will also take over the SEC-CBS deal in 2024 by paying the SEC $3 billion over ten years. Beginning in 2024, the SEC ten-year deal with ESPN will amount to a minimum of $5.25 billion and as high as $7 billion with the addition of Texas and Oklahoma that same year. One estimate of this payout will be roughly $710 million per year from 2024–33.

The Big Ten has likewise enjoyed lucrative increases in its television deals for college football. At the time of the CFA dissolution in the mid-1990s, the Big Ten entered into a ten year deal with ESPN for $100 million. In 2007, the Big Ten split its package with ESPN and Fox, with Fox launching the conference's own channel, the Big Ten network. This deal was worth $1 billion from ESPN and $1.5 billion from Fox over a decade. The original twenty year Big Ten network deal with Fox will net the Big Ten $3 billion over twenty years. The Big Ten subsequently signed a 6-year deal in 2017 worth $2.6 billion through 2022.

The ACC's first post-CFA deal was a five-year, $80 million agreement with ABC, ESPN, and Jefferson Pilot from 1996–2000. The ACC renewed that contract for another three years for $70 million. The addition of Miami and Virginia Tech to the league in 2004 and Boston College in 2005 accounted for the shorter contract and led to a $258 million contract from 2004–10. The ACC's ensuing contract, a $1.86 billion agreement for twelve years with ESPN was short-lived. The ACC renegotiated it one year later to account for the inclusion of Pittsburgh and Syracuse, along with Notre Dame in all sports except for football. The new contract was a fifteen-year contract worth $3.6 billion. The conference restructured the deal again in 2013 with the addition of Louisville and the loss of Maryland, for a total of $4.2 billion ($300 million per year) running through the 2026–27 season. The ACC and ESPN amended the deal a third time in July 2016, and agreed to a twenty-year deal worth $6 billion ($300 million per year). This deal included the addition of the ACC network and a Grant of Rights. The Grant of Rights was a tool designed to discourage schools from leaving the conference and assigned all of each university's media rights to ESPN. With a revenue amount locked in for two decades when other conferences are receiving increases on new contracts, ACC members Florida State and Clemson have expressed discontent with the current deal. The ACC expansion of 2023 (see Chapter Seven), adding Stanford, California, and SMU, has complicated the picture.

In addition to the television contracts, the college football playoff provides an additional source of revenue for Power conference schools. The first postseason college football television contract was for the Bowl Championship Series (BCS). The BCS contract covered the years from 1998–2005, with revenue of $550 million over the eight years paid by ABC. The BCS then moved to Fox for the 2006–09 seasons with a payout of $320 million over 4 years. The last four years of the BCS moved to ESPN for a payout of $500 million for the 2010–13 seasons.

The College Football Playoff (CFP) has been even more lucrative, with a payout of $470 million per year during the 2014–23 seasons. In 2019–20, the Power conferences received $67 million each from CFP, with the Group of Five conferences splitting another $92 million. The television revenue from CFP will increase significantly beginning in 2024 when the playoff expands from 4 to 12 teams. The estimated annual cost of televising the CFP games will be around $2 billion, almost double the annual amount the March Madness basketball tournament generates.

In March, 2024, the conferences reached a new deal on the college football playoff. Under the deal which extends the CFP through 2031–32, ESPN will pay an estimated $1.3 billion per year beginning in 2025–26. Unlike prior deals, the approach is one of revenue sharing, as opposed to based on the number of conference teams that make the playoff, with the Big Ten and SEC gaining the largest shares.

Locked in through 2026, the initial format is a twelve-team playoff with five automatic bids going to the conference champions of the SEC, Big Ten, ACC, Big 12, and highest-ranked Group of Five champion (from the American Athletic, Conference USA, Mid-American, Sun Belt, and Mountain West). The other seven spots in the playoff will be at-large spots based on ranking.

The deal anticipates a possible expansion to fourteen teams after 2026. The discussed breakdown of a fourteen team playoff would be $21 million annually per school for the SEC and Big Ten, $13 million for the ACC, $12 million for the Big 12, $12 million for Notre Dame, and the Group of Five conference schools each making almost $1.8 million annually. Washington State and Oregon State would earn $360,000 each as independents in the new contract.

3.   ANTITRUST AND AMATEURISM

On its face, the NCAA's historical student-athlete arrangement looks like a per se violation of antitrust law, at least with respect to the NCAA's amateurism rules. All of the employers in a particular industry, college athletics, have agreed upon a single set of rules that imposes a salary cap upon all athletes of tuition, room, board, and books. It restrains trade horizontally by fixing prices in the market—the amount of compensation college athletes can receive.

The NCAA's response rests on its concept of student-athlete. Its rhetoric categorizes athletes as students seeking to receive an education, of which athletics is a mere part. College sports are educational in nature, not economic, and as a result should fall outside the purview of antitrust law.

In its antitrust litigation, the NCAA long relied on the dicta from *Board of Regents* indicating that the

NCAA needs ample latitude to regulate intercollegiate athletics. Prior to 2015, this strategy worked and limited the NCAA's antitrust liability.

A case that perhaps best exemplifies the judicial deference toward the NCAA in early antitrust cases is *Banks v. NCAA*. Braxston Banks was a running back at the University of Notre Dame. As a freshman, Banks started in four games and played in all eleven contests. In the first game of his sophomore year, Banks injured his knee and, as a result of his injury, played in only seven games. Again, in his junior year, allegedly because of the knee injury, Banks played in only six games. Banks chose to sit out his senior year because he wanted to be sure that his knee had completely healed.

Having completed three years of college, Banks was eligible to enter the NFL draft in 1990. He hired an agent and entered the draft. No team selected Banks, and he did not receive a free agent contract, either. With one year of eligibility remaining, Banks decided to return to Notre Dame to play a final season. The NCAA, however, declared Banks ineligible under both its No-Agent Rule and its No-Draft Rule.

The No-Agent rule provided that "[a]n individual shall be ineligible for participation in an intercollegiate sport if he or she ever has agreed (orally or in writing) to be represented by an agent for the purpose of marketing his or her athletics ability or reputation in that sport." 1990–91 NCAA Division I Manual, Bylaw 12.3.1. The No-Draft rule provided that "[a]n individual loses amateur status in a particular sport when the individual asks to be placed on the draft list or supplemental draft list of a professional league in that sport." 1990–91 NCAA Division I Manual, Bylaw 12.2.4.2.

Banks argued that the No-Agent rule and the No-Draft rule both violated the Sherman Antitrust Act. Specifically, Banks claimed that each of these rules constituted an illegal restraint of trade. Under the rule of reason, Banks asserted, the NCAA could not justify the restraint as having pro-competitive benefits in another market.

The district court dismissed the case under a 12(b)(6) motion for failure to state a claim and the Seventh Circuit Court of Appeals affirmed. *Banks v. NCAA*, 977 F.2d 1081 (7th Cir. 1992). The court found that the rules did not constitute a restraint of trade. It explained that the purpose of the rules in question was to maintain amateur college athletics "as an integral part of the educational program and the athlete as an integral part of the student body and by doing so, retain a clear line of demarcation between intercollegiate athletics and professional sports. . . . The overriding purpose of the Eligibility Rules, thus, is not to provide the NCAA with commercial advantage, but rather the opposite extreme—to prevent commercializing influences from destroying the unique 'product' of NCAA college football." *Banks*, 977 F.2d at 1089.

Unlike the majority, which viewed the rules in question as part of an amateur student-athlete model, the dissent interpreted the issue through an economic lens. Judge Flaum found that the rules in question amounted to terms of employment, making them subject to antitrust scrutiny. In particular, he called into question the NCAA's characterization of its amateurism model.

> On a broader level, I am also concerned that today's decision . . . will provide comfort to the NCAA's incredulous assertion that its eligibility rules are "noncommercial." The NCAA would have us believe that intercollegiate athletic contests are about spirit, competition, camaraderie, sportsmanship, hard work (which they certainly are) . . . and nothing else. Players play for the fun of it, colleges get a kick out of entertaining the student body and alumni, but the relationship between players and colleges is positively noncommercial.

Banks, 977 F.2d at 1098–99 (Flaum, J., dissenting).

Other courts reached similar conclusions in antitrust cases both before and after *Banks*, until the *O'Bannon* case. In *McCormack v. NCAA*, 845 F.2d 1338 (5th Cir. 1988), a group of Southern Methodist University alumni, football players, and cheerleaders challenged the NCAA's decision to suspend SMU's football program for the 1987 season and impose other penalties (see Chapter Two). They contended that the NCAA violated the antitrust and civil rights laws by promulgating and enforcing rules restricting the benefits that universities and third parties may award to student athletes. The court found that the NCAA amateurism rules in question did not violate the Sherman Act under the rule of reason. The court did not engage in extensive analysis, but instead relied on the Court's dicta from *Board of Regents*.

In 1990, Vanderbilt University football player Brad Gaines sued the NCAA and Vanderbilt, alleging that the NCAA's no-draft rule violated antitrust law. *Gaines v. NCAA*, 746 F. Supp. 738 (M.D. Tenn. 1990). The court found that the rule in question was an eligibility rule, not a commercial rule. As a result, the court held that the rule was not subject to antitrust law.

In *Agnew v. NCAA*, 683 F. 3d 328 (7th Cir. 2012), plaintiffs Joseph Agnew and Patrick Courtney brought an antitrust suit against the NCAA. They challenged the NCAA rule that capped the number of athletic scholarships per team (2009–10 NCAA Division I Manual, Bylaw 15.3.3.1) and the NCAA rule that prohibited schools from awarding multi-year scholarships (2009–10 NCAA Division I Manual, Bylaw 15.5.4). Agnew and Courtney both were highly successful high school football players that had their college careers cut short by injury. Their respective schools, Rice University for Agnew and North Carolina A&T for Courtney, did not renew their scholarships.

Like in *Banks*, the court dismissed the case for failure to state a claim. It found that the plaintiffs had not identified the appropriate market—the market for student-athletes, but suggested that such a suit could have merit. The NCAA moved quickly in response to the case, changing its multi-year scholarship rule before the court decided the appeal.

In *Deppe v. NCAA*, 893 F.3d 498 (7th Cir. 2018), punter Peter Deppe challenged the NCAA's transfer rule year-in-residence requirement. 2018–19 NCAA Division I Manual, Bylaw 14.5.5.1. This rule required transfers to sit out a year after transferring from one school to another if the athlete played football, men's basketball, baseball, or hockey (see Chapter Five). Deppe argued that the transfer rule violated antitrust law as an unreasonable restraint of trade. Deppe wanted to transfer from Northern Illinois University to the University of Iowa but did not want to have to sit out a year before being able to play football, as required by the transfer rule.

The Seventh Circuit upheld the NCAA's motion to dismiss. It held that NCAA eligibility rules were presumptively pro-competitive. The court explained that the rule clearly meant to preserve the amateur character of college sport. As such, protecting the market for amateur sports thus justified any restraint the rule imposed on Deppe.

Finally, *White v. NCAA* involved a challenge by athletes to the NCAA's restrictions on the value of athletic scholarships. The NCAA limits athletic scholarships to tuition, mandatory fees, room, board, and required books. This is less than the cost of attendance which also includes optional fees, school supplies, and other miscellaneous expenses. The athletes in *White* argued that the NCAA's full grant-in-aid definition was a violation of the Sherman Antitrust Act.

Before trial, the NCAA settled the case. Under the settlement, schools could purchase health insurance for athletes. In addition, the NCAA combined two funds that provided benefits to athletes and allowed universities to use them for more purposes. The NCAA also set up a $10 million fund that past athletes could receive either a cash payment or additional money for further education.

The approach of the courts in all of these cases presumes that the NCAA's eligibility rules are non-commercial in nature. The amount of money in intercollegiate athletics, however, has exponentially increased over the past two decades. As a result, the argument that the NCAA's amateurism rules are necessary to preserve the character of the product of college sports in the market for entertainment has started to carry less weight. As college basketball and college football are multi-billion dollar industries, courts have grown less deferential to the NCAA in the antitrust context. In particular, the Ninth Circuit's decision in *O'Bannon* and the Supreme Court's decision in *Alston* demonstrate this shift.

After these cases, the question of whether some or even all of the NCAA's amateurism rules violate the Sherman Act remains an open one. Chapter Six explores a current challenge to these rules in *House v. NCAA*.

In 2008, Ed O'Bannon, a former All-American basketball player at UCLA, visited a friend's house, where his friend's son told O'Bannon that he was a character in a college basketball video game. Electronic Arts (EA) manufactured the game in question as well as other video games based on college football and men's basketball teams from the late 1990s until around 2013. The friend's son turned on the video game, and O'Bannon saw an avatar of himself—a virtual player who visually resembled O'Bannon. The avatar played for UCLA, wore O'Bannon's jersey number, 31, and moved on the court in a similar manner to O'Bannon. EA had used NCAA game footage to build the avatar, resulting in its recognizability as O'Bannon. To be sure, O'Bannon had never consented to the use of his likeness in the video game, and he had never received compensation for it.

Former Arizona State and Nebraska quarterback Sam Keller filed a similar lawsuit challenging the NCAA's sharing of game footage as an impermissible appropriation of Keller's name, image, and likeness (NIL). A California district court consolidated the *Keller* and *O'Bannon* cases and certified a class of plaintiffs that included all current and former college football and basketball Division I athletes included in game footage and/or the EA videogames. EA settled with the former athletes who appeared in its video games and ceased making college sports video games. The consolidated lawsuit that proceeded against the NCAA sought injunctive relief. Specifically, the plaintiff sought to bar the NCAA from enforcing its amateurism rules. These rules prohibited college athletes from receiving compensation for use of their NILs.

The plaintiffs' antitrust claim alleged improper restraints in two markets—the college education market and the group licensing market. The college education market refers to the market for recruiting college athletes. The group licensing market refers to the market for athletes to collectively license their NILs for video games. The court found that the NCAA's rules had an anti-competitive effect with respect to the college education market, but not the group licensing market.

Under the rule of reason, the next question was whether the NCAA had a pro-competitive justification for its restraint on the college education market. In other words, the NCAA had the burden of showing that its amateurism rules, which restricted the ability of athletes to receive compensation, including for their NILs, were necessary to allow it to compete in another market.

The NCAA argued that pro-competitive purpose of promoting amateurism justified the restraints in question. Promoting amateurism allows the NCAA to compete in the market for entertainment, the NCAA argued, because amateurism is inherent to the product of college sports it sells in the marketplace. The idea is that consumer demand for college sports depends on the unique nature of those sports, namely that its participants are amateurs.

Given the nature of a plausible pro-competitive justification, the court turned to the final part of the rule of reason inquiry—whether an alternative exists to the restraint in question. The court explained that the alternative must be virtually as effective in serving the pro-competitive purpose without significantly increasing cost.

The district court identified two plausible alternatives—(1) allowing NCAA-member schools to provide athletes grants-in-aid that covered the full cost of attendance, not just tuition, room, board, and books; and (2) allowing member schools to pay their athletes small amounts of deferred cash compensation (about $5,000 per year) for use of their NILs.

The Ninth Circuit, in an opinion by Judge Bybee, held that the cost of attendance was an acceptable alternative remedy. The court rejected cash payments, likening such payments to crossing the Rubicon, a slippery slope that would open the door to pay-for-play and undercut the student-athlete model.

Importantly, the court made the distinction here based on the concept of education. Covering the cost of attendance was another part of paying for the education of athletes. Providing NIL payments, by contrast, amounted to a form of pay-for-play. Interestingly, the amount athletes received for cost of attendance was roughly in the amount of the $5,000 payment that the court rejected.

Shawne Alston, a West Virginia University running back, and other athletes filed a class action antitrust case against the NCAA seeking to expand the holding in *O'Bannon*. The plaintiffs in *Alston* were current and former athletes in men's Division I FBS football and men's and women's Division I basketball. The defendants in the case included eleven Division I conferences as well as the NCAA. The plaintiffs challenged the current, interconnected set of NCAA rules that limit the compensation athletes may receive in exchange for their athletic services.

Following *O'Bannon*, the district court held that the NCAA rules violated antitrust law, and the consequence of this decision was that athletes could receive education-related benefits. These benefits included graduate school tuition, summer abroad programs, computers, and IPads. After the Ninth Circuit affirmed the district court's opinion, the NCAA appealed the case to the Supreme Court. *NCAA v. Alston*, 594 U.S. 69 (2021). Perhaps the NCAA hoped that the Supreme Court would expand upon its dicta in *Board of Regents* and create an antitrust exemption for the NCAA under the Sherman Act. It did not.

Instead, the Supreme Court affirmed the Ninth Circuit's decision. It agreed that the NCAA amateurism restrictions on athletes violated the Sherman Act as an anti-competitive restraint of trade. It found that the pro-competitive justification of amateurism would not result in a loss of consumer interest in college sports if athletes received education-related benefits. In other words, the Court found that allowing athletes to receive education-related benefits would not diminish fan interest in college football and basketball. The athletes did not raise the broader challenge of whether NCAA restrictions of non-education related benefits violated the Sherman Act on appeal.

Importantly, the Court rejected the NCAA's reliance on the dicta from the *Board of Regents* case. Perhaps the NCAA was hoping the Court would read that language as providing it with an antitrust exemption, but the Court made clear that all of the NCAA's rules are subject to antitrust scrutiny. The *Board of Regents* language—stating the NCAA should have ample latitude to maintain its tradition of amateurism—did not "suggest that courts must reflexively reject *all* challenges to the NCAA's compensation restrictions." *Alston*, 594 U.S. at 92.

In particular, the Court emphasized the changing economic dynamics in college sports. When it decided *Board of Regents*, college athletics was not a billion-dollar industry. The economic realities suggested to the Court that antitrust law should apply to the business of college athletics and the student-athlete amateurism model did not receive any sort of antitrust immunity.

Justice Brett Kavanaugh wrote separately to emphasize his view that the NCAA's restrictions on athlete compensation beyond education-related benefits also raised serious questions under the Sherman Act. His statement that "[t]he NCAA is not above the law" underscores this sentiment. Indeed, Kavanaugh suggested that the remainder of the NCAA's amateurism restrictions might violate the Sherman Act. It is important to note that none of the other eight justices joined in Kavanaugh's opinion. It is not clear whether they would agree with his views in a subsequent case.

So, the consequences of *O'Bannon* and *Alston* were that the NCAA cannot restrict athletes from receiving "education-related benefits." Such benefits include both the cost of attendance and *Alston* money, an annual stipend of $5,980, an amount related to academic scholarships.

An indirect consequence of *O'Bannon*, as explored in Chapter Four, was the decision of state legislatures to pass NIL laws. These laws prohibit the NCAA or its member institutions from interfering with the ability of athletes to receive compensation from third parties for use of their NILs.

The NCAA settled the most recent antitrust case, *House v. NCAA* in May 2024. Discussed in Chapter Six, this settlement provides for revenue sharing of television revenue with college athletes.

At the time of publication, the ensuing model remained unsettled, but reports indicated that the NCAA would allow schools to share up to twenty percent of their revenue with athletes.

4. THE COLLEGE BASKETBALL FBI INVESTIGATION

In 2017, the U.S. Attorney's Office for the Southern District of New York filed a number of indictments against basketball coaches, runners, and shoe company executives alleging mass corruption, bribery, and wire fraud. The criminal law theory was that by paying athletes to choose a particular university, these actors deprived the university of an amateur athlete, thereby defrauding the institution.

A jury convicted James Gatto, Merl Code, and Christian Dawkins of engaging in a scheme to defraud three universities Kansas University, the University of Louisville, or North Carolina State

University (N.C. State), all of which Adidas sponsored. The fraud scheme involved defendants paying tens of thousands of dollars to the families of high school basketball players to induce them to attend these universities, and covering up the payments so that the recruits could certify to the universities that they had complied with the NCAA's amateurism rules. *United States v. Gatto*, 986 F.3d 104 (2d Cir. 2021).

In response to the investigation, the NCAA acted swiftly, keen to preserve the image of college basketball. It announced the creation of the Independent Commission on College Basketball led by Condoleezza Rice. The Commission proposed a number of reforms subsequently adopted by the NCAA, including the creation of the IARP discussed above as well as allowing basketball players to hire agents and enter the NBA draft without losing their eligibility. Interestingly, the Commission also advocated for allowing basketball players to use their NILs. State laws enabled all athletes to use their NILs before the NCAA decided to implement this change as discussed below. Further, the NCAA imposed only minimal punishments against the universities involved in the investigation, despite having evidence from audio recordings and the testimony of subpoenaed witnesses.

5.   AGENTS AND DRAFTS

The Independent Commission on College Basketball's reforms have created a disparity between football and basketball players concerning the NCAA's no-draft and no-agent rules. Football players still lose their eligibility if they hire an agent or enter the NFL draft.

Note that receiving representation for NIL deals is not the same as hiring an agent under NCAA rules. 2023–24 NCAA Division I Manual, Bylaw 12.3. The NCAA rules distinguish between agent representation and legal representation. Having a lawyer present at a negotiation does not violate NCAA rules. Having an agent does unless it is an NCAA-certified basketball agent. Athletes also may have an agent prior to enrolling in college for purposes of baseball or men's hockey, both of which directly draft high school athletes.

Entering a professional draft also means that a college athlete loses their eligibility. 2023–24 NCAA Division I Manual, Bylaw 12.2.4. The exception is college basketball players, who can return to college after entering the draft without losing their eligibility.

One obstacle some athletes face are the age restrictions of professional sports leagues. The National Basketball Association (NBA) requires one year after completion of high school before it will allow an athlete to enter its draft. The National Football League (NFL) requires an athlete be three years out of high school in order to be eligible to enter its draft.

In 2004, former Ohio State star running back Maurice Clarett sued the NFL, arguing that its age requirement violated the Sherman Act. *Clarett v.*

NFL, 369 F.3d 124 (2d Cir. 2004). As a freshman, Clarett led Ohio State to the National Championship in football, winning the Fiesta Bowl in January 2003. Prior to the start of his sophomore year, the NCAA declared Clarett ineligible. Clarett had received impermissible benefits from an Ohio State booster. As a result, Clarett sought to enter the NFL draft in the spring of 2004.

Clarett was able to show that the draft constituted an unreasonable restraint of trade that ordinarily would violate antitrust law. All of the teams in the NFL had conspired to create a rule that would make him ineligible for the draft in the current year. The question in the case, however, was whether the non-statutory labor exemption applied to the case.

The purpose of the Sherman Act—preventing collective activity—is contrary to the purpose of the National Labor Relations Act (NLRA)—promoting collective bargaining. To reconcile this conflict between two federal statutes, the Supreme Court has created a non-statutory labor exemption from the Sherman Act. *United States v. Hutcheson*, 312 U.S. 219 (1941). This means that collective bargaining agreements are generally exempt from antitrust scrutiny.

In Clarett's case, the court found that eligibility rules were mandatory subjects of collective bargaining. As a result, the court held that the NFL's eligibility rule did not violate Clarett's rights under the Sherman Act because of the non-statutory labor exemption. The consequence of Clarett only having to wait a year before entering the draft likely played a role in the court's decision.

The Denver Broncos drafted Clarett the following year, but Clarett did not make the team. Sadly, Clarett committed armed robbery and weapons offenses in 2006 and spent almost eight years in prison.

CHAPTER FOUR
NAME, IMAGE, AND LIKENESS

Name, image, and likeness (NIL) refers to the ability of athletes to receive money from third parties for the use of their name, image, and likeness, typically to endorse a product. Historically, the NCAA retained control over athlete NIL and declared an athlete ineligible if they received money from third parties.

After the Ninth Circuit's decision in *O'Bannon*, which denied athletes licensing rights, the California legislature passed a bill in 2019 that gave California athletes the right to monetize their name, image, and likeness (NIL). The law specifically barred the NCAA as well as colleges and universities from interfering with this right. Set to go into effect in 2023, the California law spurred activity across the United States. Florida adopted a similar law, but set the effective date on July 1, 2021. Many other states adopted similar laws and amended their effective dates to match Florida's date.

Under state NIL laws, athletes can receive third party money in exchange for use of their NIL without losing their eligibility or suffering other discipline from the NCAA. As a result, behavior historically considered cheating is now permissible. As a private organization, the NCAA must follow state law. The first of the state NIL laws went into effect on July 1, 2021 and this change has clearly reshaped the landscape of college sports. Specifically, it has redefined amateurism in college athletics.

1.   EA SPORTS, VIDEO GAMES, AND O'BANNON

While the athlete's right to monetize their NIL began in 2021, one can trace the beginnings of the NIL era back to 1993. That was the year that EA Sports released its first video game involving NCAA teams, *Bill Walsh College Football*.

Former Apple employee Trip Hawkins founded Electronic Arts (EA) in 1982, as Apple was becoming a publicly traded company. EA struggled initially, but eventually found success with the launch of simulated sports games. It signed a contract with former Oakland Raiders coach, John Madden to develop a football video game. A Super Bowl-winning coach, Madden had become a well-known public figure as an NFL broadcaster. The popular Madden NFL series led to a similar game which had college teams instead of NFL teams. EA named its college game after former Stanford and current (at that time) San Francisco 49ers coach Bill Walsh.

The 1992 game (released in 1993) used 24 teams from the 1992 season and 24 historical teams. EA Sports did not have a license from the NCAA, so it used city or state names as well as university colors to identify the teams in the game. EA similarly programmed the different avatars, which reflected skin tones, hair styles, heights, weights, jersey numbers, equipment, home states, and physical abilities, to correspond to the skill levels of the individual players in identifiable ways. For instance, the Tallahassee quarterback had a rating of 100, which clearly represented 1992 Florida State

Heisman   Trophy-winning   quarterback   Charlie
Ward.

Similarly,   the   historical   teams   represented
national championship teams from prior years and
used the name of their cities. It was clear, for
instance, that Provo 84 was BYU's national
championship team and Atlanta 90 was Georgia
Tech's undefeated 1990 team. Other teams included
Pittsburgh 80, Clemson 81, Washington 91, Michigan
85, Texas 81, SC 79, Tallahassee 87, Columbus 79,
Miami 91, Nebraska 83, South Bend 88, State
College 86, Tennessee 85, Auburn 83, Alabama 87,
Georgia 80, and Baton Rouge 87. Perhaps previewing
modern developments, the game included a 16-team
playoff.

After issuing a second version of *Bill Walsh College
Football* in 1995, EA released a more elaborate
version in 1996, *College Football USA 96*. This was
the first version to feature all (108 at the time)
Division I-A collegiate football teams. It included
bowl games such as the Orange, Sugar, Fiesta and
Rose bowls. EA Sports' 1997 game, *College Football
USA 97*, was the first to involve the use of an NCAA
license to use player NIL. It featured University of
Nebraska quarterback, Tommie Frazier on the cover.
In 1998, EA renamed the series *NCAA Football 98*,
reflecting the use of the NCAA's license.

In 2005, EA signed a fifteen year exclusive deal
with ESPN giving EA exclusive first rights to all
ESPN content for sports simulation games. Later
that same year, EA struck a deal with the Collegiate

Licensing Company (CLC) for exclusive rights to college football content for the next six years.

The next iterations of the NCAA College football games included the NIL of well-known college football athletes on the cover of the game, even though the game itself did not include their names. The athletes on the cover included Reggie Bush, Charles Woodson, Carson Palmer, Shaun Alexander, Ricky Williams, Chris Weinke, Joey Harrington, Larry Fitzgerald, Desmond Howard as cover athletes.

The last NCAA College Football video game EA created was *NCAA Football 14*. EA ended the series at the time as a consequence of the *O'Bannon* litigation. With the advent of state NIL laws, EA will resume its series in the summer of 2024.

While not as prominent as its college football series, EA also released a college basketball series, *NCAA Basketball*, from 1998 through 2009. As with football, the basketball game identified players by uniform number, not name, even though the users could add player names. Like the football games, the series featured a star player on its cover each year, including Tim Duncan, Steve Francis, Carmelo Anthony, Kevin Durant, and Blake Griffin.

Over time, the technology in the EA games became more elaborate, with the player avatars increasingly reflecting the mannerisms and movements of the athletes. The licensing of game footage by the NCAA and ESPN enabled the games to make the avatars more and more realistic.

As discussed in Chapter Three, former UCLA star Ed O'Bannon noticed his avatar in the *NCAA Basketball* game. Along with a group of twenty current and former NCAA FBS football players and Division I basketball players, O'Bannon filed a lawsuit against the NCAA and CLC arguing that the NCAA's amateurism rules violated the Sherman Act because they prevented athletes from receiving NIL compensation. Around the same time, Arizona State quarterback Sam Keller sued EA, CLC, and the NCAA arguing that EA misappropriated athletes' NIL in its video games and that the NCAA and CLC had facilitated this tortious behavior.

A California federal district court consolidated the *Keller* and *O'Bannon* cases. Ultimately, the case evolved into a class action lawsuit involving all former athletes in the EA college sports games and all current NCAA FBS football and Division I basketball players. CLC and EA settled with the 24,000 former athlete plaintiffs for $60 million in 2016. The three named plaintiffs—Ed O'Bannon, Rutgers quarterback Ryan Hart, and Arizona State quarterback Sam Keller—received $15,000 each. The rest of the original twenty plaintiffs received $5,000, with the average player payout being $1,600.

The NCAA, however, chose not to settle. The case proceeded to trial as an antitrust case challenging the NCAA's rule against athletes receiving compensation for use of their NIL beyond the value of their grants-in-aid. As discussed in Chapter Three, the NCAA capped the grant-in-aid remuneration at tuition, room, board, and books. In particular, the plaintiffs sought an injunction against the NCAA enforcing its amateurism rule. Specifically, FBS football players and Division I men's basketball players sought the opportunity to receive compensation, beyond the value of their athletic scholarships, for the use of their NIL in video games, live game telecasts, re-broadcasts, and archival game footage.

With respect to NIL, the important part of the case relates to the two markets identified by the plaintiffs. The plaintiffs partially prevailed in the college education market. The plaintiffs advanced the idea that the amateurism rules restrained the athletes from competing for payments for their services as college athletes beyond the grant-in-aid amount. The Ninth Circuit held that the NCAA's justification of amateurism partially justified its restraint on compensation, but that athletes could receive the cost of attendance in addition to tuition, room, board, and books. 802 F.3d 1049 (9th Cir. 2015). The antitrust law required allowing increased competition for athlete services among universities, but a free market involving pay-for-play would compromise the product of amateur college sports in the entertainment market.

The second market, the group licensing market, did not create an antitrust issue, according to the court. Specifically, it found that the athletes would not be competing with each other for group licenses of their NIL for television or video games. To the contrary, the athletes would have an incentive to cooperate instead of compete because networks or companies like EA would want to purchase their NIL rights collectively, not individually.

2.   THE FAIR PAY TO PLAY ACT AND ALSTON

The direct consequence of the Ninth Circuit's decision in *O'Bannon* was the decision of the California legislature to explore a bill allowing athletes to receive remuneration for use of their NIL and placing a legislative limit on the reach of the NCAA. Economist Andy Schwarz, who had worked on the *O'Bannon* case, discussed the possibility of finding a new way to advance athlete rights with California Senator Nancy Skinner.

In May, 2019, Senator Skinner introduced the Fair Pay to Play Act, co-authored by Senators Scott Wilk and Steven Bradford. The California legislature passed the law on September 11, 2019. The Fair Pay to Play Act gave athletes enrolled in California's four-year public colleges and universities the right to monetize their NIL. Specifically, the act prohibited the revocation of a student's scholarship as a result of earning NIL compensation. It also prevented limits on an athlete's ability to use their NIL for a commercial purpose when not engaged in official team activities. Finally, the Fair Pay to Play Act also gave athletes the right to legal representation with individuals licensed by the state of California.

The initial effective date for the Fair Pay to Play Act was January 1, 2023. Subsequent adoption of similar laws by other states led to an acceleration of the effective date to July 1, 2021.

The first state to follow California in passing an NIL law was Florida. Florida's bill passed in June, 2020. It chose an effective date of July 1, 2021, two years earlier than California. Similar to California, Florida's NIL law proscribed institutions and the NCAA from punishing athletes for monetizing their NIL. In addition, Florida's NIL law prohibited athletes from signing endorsements or contracts that will conflict with endorsements that their schools already have in place. The Florida law also required college institutions to conduct financial literacy and life skills workshops for its athletes. In addition, it explicitly stated that scholarship grants awarded by a state university do not constitute compensation. Finally, the Florida NIL law provided that the duration of the athlete's contract may not extend beyond their enrollment at the university.

Many states rushed to pass bills of their own so the universities within their state would not be at a recruiting disadvantage. Joining Florida's effective date of July 1, 2021 were Illinois, Iowa, Kentucky, Louisiana, Maryland, Mississippi, New Mexico, Ohio, Oregon, South Carolina, and Tennessee.

The NCAA's initial response to the idea of allowing athletes to profit from their NIL was one of resistance and skepticism. Critics within the organization expressed concerns that relaxing the amateurism rules could lead to unintended consequences. The NCAA pointed to the possibility of an uneven playing field where schools with more significant financial resources could attract top talent by offering lucrative endorsement deals.

The NCAA's concerns extended to the potential loss of control over athlete endorsements and the risk of commercializing college sports excessively. It feared that allowing NIL compensation could lead to potential exploitation of athletes by third-party entities seeking to capitalize on the athletes' marketability.

An alternative strategy pursued by the NCAA has related to the NIL compensation that universities receive for the televising of its games. As discussed in Chapter Three, it appealed the *Alston v. NCAA* case to the United States Supreme Court in 2020. The practical consequence of *Alston* for the NCAA's member institutions is not that significant. *Alston* allows athletes to receive remuneration "related to" education. The court in *O'Bannon* developed this concept to differentiate cost of attendance payments from other pay-for-play remuneration.

[handwritten margin note: Diff. btwn Alston and O'Bannon]

Costs related to education include graduate school tuition, summer abroad programs, computers as well as *Alston* money, a payment of just under $6,000 per year that mirrors money available for academic scholarships.

One reason that the NCAA might have appealed *Alston* was to seek an antitrust exemption for college sports. An antitrust exemption would allow universities to keep all of the television money, instead of facing the continued antitrust threat and potential requirement of a competitive economic market for athlete services discussed in Chapter Six.

[handwritten note: Antitrust explanation]

Sherman Act = rule of "free competition"

The unanimous decision by the Supreme Court in *Alston* made clear that the NCAA did not receive any exemption under the Sherman Act. The Court rejected the dicta from *Board of Regents*, finding that it did not exempt the NCAA's restrictions on the market for college athletes.

Justice Kavanaugh's concurring opinion, which none of the other justices joined, went further. In explaining that the NCAA was not above the law, he opined that the NCAA's entire student-athlete model might violate antitrust law.

Interestingly, the timing and tone of Kavanaugh's opinion may be more important than its substance. Released June 21, 2021, just days before the effective date of state NIL laws, it symbolized the change to the student-athlete model that state NIL laws reflected.

Putting aside the actual antitrust question the Court decided in *Alston*, it was state law that took conduct previously barred by the NCAA—third party boosters providing benefits to athletes—and made it permissible. But the opinion from Kavanaugh signaled a rhetorical shift. The NCAA should no longer characterize payment of extra benefits as cheating because college sports were an economic endeavor, not just the amateur pursuit of education. And state NIL laws, not *Alston*, made this change a reality.

State law > Alston

Allowed athletes in state's w/o NIL laws to enjoy NIL benefits

3.   THE NCAA'S INTERIM NIL POLICY

On July 1st, 2021, the NCAA enacted an Interim NIL Policy that temporarily suspended the restrictions on the ability of athletes to profit from their NIL. The Interim NIL Policy defined name, image, and likeness (NIL) as the right of student-athletes to control and profit from the commercial use of their own names, images, likenesses, and other individual identifiers. This broad definition encompassed a wide range of commercial opportunities, including endorsement deals, social media sponsorships, appearances, and autograph signings. The policy still required that athletes adhere to the applicable state NIL laws. Further, this policy allowed athletes playing in states without an NIL law to enjoy NIL benefits.

Even with the ability of third parties to compensate athletes for use of their NIL, the NCAA Bylaws still barred member institutions from providing benefits to athletes beyond the scope of their grants-in-aid, which now included cost of attendance and other education-related costs.

The NCAA otherwise left the oversight of NIL to conferences, individual institutions, and state law. Under the interim NIL rule, the NCAA prohibited the following: (1) NIL compensation contingent on enrollment at a particular institution; (2) NIL compensation for athletic participation or achievement; (3) NIL compensation for work not performed.

Under the Interim NIL Policy, student-athletes can engage in various NIL activities without jeopardizing their eligibility or scholarships. These permissible activities include:

- Endorsement Deals: Athletes can enter into endorsement agreements with businesses and promote products or services using their NIL.

- Social Media Sponsorships: Athletes can monetize their social media presence by endorsing products or promoting brands on their personal accounts.

- Personal Appearances: Athletes can make paid appearances at events, autograph signings, and public gatherings.

- Online Content Creation: Athletes could generate revenue from online platforms by creating and monetizing content such as videos, podcasts, and merchandise.

While the Interim NIL Policy afforded athletes new financial opportunities, it also included certain regulatory restrictions to maintain fairness and protect the integrity of collegiate sports. Key restrictions included:

- No Pay-for-Play: The policy explicitly prohibited pay-for-play arrangements, ensuring that third parties do not tie compensation to athletic performance or recruitment inducements.

- No Use of Institution Marks without Approval: Athletes cannot use their institution's logos, trademarks, or other intellectual property in NIL-related activities without permission.

- Compliance with State Laws: Athletes and institutions must comply with applicable state laws related to NIL activities.

By adopting the interim NIL policy, the NCAA sought to comply with state law without sacrificing its student-athlete model. Its short term response sought to keep the athletes as amateurs, at least with respect to their universities, while working toward federal legislation. Specifically, the NCAA continued to pursue the antitrust exemption that the Supreme Court failed to give it in *Alston*.

4.   STATE COLLEGIATE NIL LAWS

Generally speaking, state collegiate NIL laws aim to strike a balance between allowing student-athletes to benefit from their personal brand and ensuring that these activities do not compromise the integrity of college sports. The specific provisions described below show how state laws work to achieve these dual objectives. To understand this relatively new landscape, a brief overview is instructive.

State collegiate NIL laws grant student-athletes the right to profit from their own NIL. This means athletes can earn money through endorsements, sponsorships, and other commercial activities without jeopardizing their eligibility to participate in college sports. Nonetheless, these laws often come with restrictions. Athletes generally cannot use university trademarks, logos, or copyrighted materials in their commercial activities without obtaining permission. This rule exists to prevent confusion and to maintain the distinction between the athlete's personal brand and the university's brand. For instance, a college football player from the University of South Carolina would not be able to use the Gamecock logo in an NIL advertisement or sponsorship without prior permission from the University.

Over time, however, some schools created licensing programs that allow athletes to use their school logos. The Brandr group, a sports marketing and licensing agency in Florida, sets up such programs. One program at the University of Texas allows group licensing programs involving three or more individuals from the same team or six or more individuals across university teams. Athletes at the University of North Carolina and the Ohio State University have participated in similar programs.

Many state NIL laws, as well as NCAA rules, require that any compensation received by student-athletes for their endorsements or commercial activities relate to the fair market value of the services provided. When the use of NIL became protected under state law, many imagined that athletes would engage in traditional endorsement deals like professional athletes had done for decades. On July 1, 2021, Fresno State basketball players Haley and Hannah Cavinder, aka the Cavinder twins, entered into such a deal with Boost Mobile with a billboard in Times Square. The idea of measuring whether the athlete provided value justifying the amount of compensation provided for the athletes NIL seemed easy to measure, as long as one examined other similar deals in the market for endorsements.

But the landscape shifted as boosters began to organize into collectives. The NIL deals became less about athletes marketing or endorsing products, although that continued for some. Instead, the deals with collectives became a way for boosters to engage in pay-for-play. To comply with state laws and NCAA rules, such deals place some requirements on athletes, but one wonders the degree to which such deals really reflect value provided by the athletes. Typical arrangements include public appearances, social media posts, and other interactions with members of the collectives at private events. It is also difficult to measure whether the value provided by the use of the athlete NIL relates to the amount of compensation provided. This is because the details of such contracts remain private and confidential both with respect to the amount paid and the amount of athlete participation required.

A second NCAA restriction that is part of some state laws relates to the inducement of athletes to attend a particular university through the promise of a particular NIL deal or set of NIL deals. Again, prior to the formation of collectives, this issue seemed easy to monitor. The idea of a particular booster waiting for their company to make an endorsement offer seemed easy to identify and regulate. But with collectives, the issue becomes more complicated, as the collective payment does not relate to promoting one particular company or product. Nonetheless, anecdotal evidence suggests that inducements are commonplace, with NIL simply being a form of pay-for-play. The question from each recruit to his prospective coach is simple: how much?

In early 2024, the NCAA was investigating University of Tennessee related to such inducements. The NCAA believed that Tennessee had major violations across several sports, including football for using NIL deals as inducements. The football case centered around the recruitment of star quarterback Nico Iamaleava, who signed a multi-million dollar contract with Spyre Sports Group, allegedly made contingent on his choosing to play football with Tennessee.

On January 31, 2024, however, the attorney generals of Virginia and Tennessee filed a lawsuit in federal court alleging that the inducement rule violated federal antitrust law. Federal district judge Clifton Corker issued a preliminary injunction barring the NCAA from enforcing all rules related to athletes and recruits negotiating compensation for NIL with collectives and boosters. *Tennessee & Virginia v. NCAA*, 2024 WL 755528 (E.D. Tenn. 2024). This injunction will remain in place until the court tries the case of *Tennessee & Virginia v. NCAA*, barring a successful appeal by the NCAA to the Sixth Circuit. Chapter Six explores potential consequences of this important case.

Without such an injunction, using an NIL deal to induce an athlete to attend a particular school not only violates NCAA rules, but also could constitute a federal crime. As discussed in Chapter Two, James Gatto, a former Adidas executive, has served a year and a half in federal prison for inducing a star basketball player to attend the University of Louisville by paying him and his family $100,000. *United States v. Gatto*, 986 F.3d 104 (2d Cir. 2021).

Beyond fair market value requirements and bars on inducements, some states require athletes to consult with legal counsel or university compliance officers before entering into NIL contracts. This helps protect the interests of the athletes and ensures that they understand the terms and implications of the agreements they're entering. Some states have required that the university provide a course on financial literacy to athletes, like Florida. It helps prevent the athlete from inadvertently violating any NCAA or state rules.

A contract review requirement provides further protection to college athletes from exploitative contracts and ensures that athletes make informed decisions. The legal professionals can provide more insight, identify any clauses that may be unfavorable, and educate the athlete on possible risks regarding eligibility.

The case of star quarterback recruit Jaden Rashada is one cautionary tale. Rashada initially verbally committed to play at the University of Miami. Rashada subsequently flipped, however, and signed a national letter of intent with the University of Florida. Rashada's decision related in large part to an alleged $13 million NIL contract he signed with the now defunct Gator Collective. Unfortunately for Rashada, the deal fell through, as the collective did not provide the money it allegedly promised. Florida released Rashada from his letter of intent and he enrolled at Arizona State.

The case of Gervon Dexter is another example of why athletes need NIL safeguards. Dexter, a former Florida Gators star defensive lineman who played in the NFL for the Chicago Bears, sued Big League Advance, a group with whom he signed an NIL deal. Dexter's agreement with Big League Advance paid him $436,485 while he was at Florida. But the agreement also provided that the NIL payments were in exchange for a 15% commission on Dexter's future earnings as a professional athlete.

Dexter, who clearly did not read the agreement carefully before signing it, executed the agreement within 24 hours of receiving it. His lawsuit claims that the agreement was predatory in violation of Florida's NIL and Athlete Agent laws. Big League Advance moved to have the case arbitrated, pursuant to the contract. *Dexter v. Big League Advance Fund II*, 2023 WL 6994189 (N.D. Fla. 2023).

Sometimes, athletes are the ones taking advantage of the lack of NIL regulations. Kadyn Proctor, a five-star, 6'7", 360-pound offensive lineman at the University of Alabama, decided to transfer to the University of Iowa, in his home state, at the end of his freshman season in 2023. Porter had started all fourteen games with the Crimson Tide, including its win over Georgia and loss to Michigan in the national semifinal game.

He transferred to Iowa after Coach Nick Saban's retirement and then abruptly decided to transfer back to Alabama two months later for the 2024–25 season. He received money from a contracting business, but apparently not from the collective that supports Iowa football. His sudden decision to transfer back created the appearance that he was playing Iowa—transferring for money and then never playing for the football team, but it appears that early reports may have overstated such allegations.

State law also might require athletes to disclose their NIL agreements to their universities or relevant state authorities. This reporting obligation ensures that the agreements follow the applicable laws and regulations. It helps prevent any undisclosed or unethical activities while allowing universities to monitor the activities of their athletes.

Reporting obligations provision improve transparency and accountability on every party involved. By requiring college athletes to report their NIL agreements, universities and state authorities can monitor potential conflicts of interest or violations of the established guidelines and laws.

a.   CALIFORNIA: SENATE BILL 206 (FAIR PAY TO PLAY ACT)

Gavin Newsom signed Bill 206, the original NIL bill, during a recording of LeBron James' show, *The Shop*. This Act had an original effective date of 2023, but the legislature amended it to match Florida's effective date of July 1, 2021.

Here are the key provisions, many of which other states emulated:

1. **Endorsement Rights**: The law prevents California colleges from penalizing student athletes for capitalizing on their NIL rights. This ensures that athletes can engage in endorsements and sponsorship opportunities without fear of punishment.

2. **Scholarship Protection**: Colleges cannot alter an athlete's scholarship based on earnings from their NIL rights. This protects athletes from losing financial support due to their entrepreneurial activities.

3. **NCAA Restrictions**: The NCAA cannot ban California colleges from participating in intercollegiate sports if student athletes decide to exercise their NIL rights. This prevents punitive measures against institutions that allow their athletes to benefit from these rights.

4. **Preservation of School Contracts**: The law acknowledges that colleges can still generate revenue for their athletic programs, and as such, student athletes cannot enter into agreements that undermine their school's existing endorsement contracts.

The Fair Pay to Play Act also addresses the financial hardships that many athletes face. Contrary to the misconception that all athletes receive full scholarships covering tuition, room, and board, the reality is that most do not. Athletes at Division II and III schools typically do not receive scholarships, and many of those schools lack generous financial aid packages.

Furthermore, research has shown that a significant number of college athletes live at or below the poverty line, spending extensive hours on their sports without sufficient time for part-time employment. To that end, the Act aims to encourage athletes to stay in school, complete their degrees, and resist the pressure to turn professional prematurely. It ensures that all college athletes, not just those at the elite level, can benefit from their NIL rights. These benefits could involve small local sponsorships, monetizing online content, offering lessons, or even coaching.

In essence, the Fair Pay to Play Act marked a significant step towards restoring equity and fairness for college athletes. By giving them the same rights as other students to profit from their own identities and talents, California helped pioneer a movement that has altered the landscape of college sports.

b.   FLORIDA: SB 646 (INTERCOLLEGIATE ATHLETE COMPENSATION AND RIGHTS)

Like the Fair Pay to Play Act, this law addresses the issue of allowing intercollegiate athletes at postsecondary educational institutions in Florida to earn compensation for the use of their NIL. The law aims to give these athletes the opportunity to benefit from their athletic success in a manner similar to how other individuals can profit from their personal brands.

Like California, many of the provisions of the Florida law are part of other states' NIL statutes. Key provisions of Florida's NIL law include:

1. **Definition of Intercollegiate Athlete**: The law defines an "intercollegiate athlete" as a student participating in an athletic program at a postsecondary educational institution. It does not define athletes as university employees.

2. **Right to Earn Compensation**: Under the law, intercollegiate athletes have the right to earn compensation for the use of their names, images, or likenesses.

3. **Postsecondary   Educational Institution Restrictions**: The Florida law prohibits postsecondary institutions from preventing athletes from earning NIL compensation. Additionally, institutions must   allow   athletes   to   secure representation by licensed agents or Florida-licensed attorneys to negotiate compensation for their NIL.

4. **Restrictions   on   Compensation**: Compensation earned by athletes for the use of their NIL must be "commensurate with the market value" of their name, image, or likeness. Compensation cannot relate to athletic performance or be contingent upon attendance at a specific

institution. Athletes can only receive compensation from third parties not affiliated with their educational institutions.

5. **Responsibilities of Athletes**: Athletes are responsible for ensuring that compensation for their NIL complies with the law and does not violate their university's contracts. Athletes must also disclose NIL contracts to their institutions.

6. **Responsibilities of Educational Institutions**: Institutions must not interfere with athletes' right to earn NIL compensation and must disclose to athletes any contract terms that conflict with their team contracts. Additionally, institutions must conduct financial literacy and life skills workshops for athletes to address financial management and other skills.

7. **Prospective Sponsor Responsibilities**: Sponsors offering compensation to athletes must ensure that the compensation is commensurate with the market value of the athlete's NIL. They also must negotiate terms that do not conflict with the athlete's team contract. Contracts with athletes under the age of eighteen must receive prior court approval.

8. **Duration of Contracts**: NIL contracts must cannot exceed the duration of the athlete's participation in intercollegiate

athletics. This means that contracts cannot exceed five years.

9. **Open Questions and Potential Litigation**: The law leaves certain terms and definitions open to interpretation, such as what constitutes "commensurate" compensation and who qualifies as a third party unaffiliated with the university.

10. **Implications for College Athletics**: Florida's NIL legislation has broader implications for college athletics, including potential impacts on recruiting, athlete parity, and the ongoing conversation about compensating student-athletes fairly.

Other notable NIL bills include the Georgia House Bill 617 (Name, Image, and Likeness) and Michigan Senate Bill 601 (Collegiate Athlete Fair Pay Act). Georgia's HB 617 allows athletes to receive compensation for their NIL, while prohibiting certain types of deals, such as those involving alcohol, tobacco, and gambling. Michigan's SB 601 grants athletes the right to profit from their NIL and prohibits universities from revoking scholarships because of NIL activity.

State collegiate NIL laws have reshaped the way athletes can benefit from their own name, image, and likeness. While these laws bring opportunities, they also introduce complexities related to fair compensation and potential conflicts of interest. Staying informed about evolving state laws and seeking appropriate legal guidance are essential for both athletes and universities as they navigate this new landscape.

State laws add other requirements including reporting contracts to the university, prohibiting NIL deals with certain kinds of companies—alcohol, tobacco, and gambling, and avoiding contracts in conflict with university contracts. States have modified their laws to keep a competitive advantage, including giving college coaches and university officials a more active role in NIL deals. Alabama repealed its NIL laws in light of the NCAA's permissive approach to NIL. The NCAA and conference leaders have advocated for a federal NIL law, but to date there has been no consensus on such a law.

5.   UNIVERSITY NIL POLICIES

While state NIL laws provide the parameters for the regulation of NIL deals, university policies also add a layer of complexity that athletes and third party boosters and collectives must consider. These include:

1. **Degree of University Involvement**: Universities can choose the extent to which they are involved in managing and promoting student-athlete NIL activities. Some universities may provide comprehensive support, while others may offer minimal assistance. Under current NCAA and state law rules, however, a university cannot be a party to an NIL contract.

2. **Fair Market Value**: Universities must determine how they will ensure that compensation for NIL activities aligns with the fair market value. This involves creating guidelines to avoid impermissible payments or preferential treatment.

3. **Use of University Logos and Marks**: Universities can decide whether athletes can use university logos, trademarks, and slogans in their NIL activities. This decision varies from one institution to another.

4. **Use of University Facilities**: Universities have the authority to establish policies concerning athlete use of university facilities for NIL activities. These policies may differ in terms of requirements, fees, and risk management.

5. **Conflicts with University Contracts**: Universities need to define the scope of "university contracts" where such contracts might conflict with NIL contracts. Each university must determine how to address conflicts between these contracts. The definition of what contracts constitute a conflict and the process concerning how to handle such conflicts can vary between institutions.

6. **Conflicts with University Institutional Values**: Universities have discretion to bar student-athletes from endorsing products

or services that conflict with their institutional values. Specific restrictions differ between universities.

7. **Timing of Student-Athlete Disclosures**: Universities can establish requirements for student-athletes to disclose potential NIL agreements in advance of signing. The timing and flexibility of these requirements may vary.

8. **Autographs and Memorabilia**: Universities can set rules regarding athlete involvement in autograph signings and memorabilia-related activities, including what items athletes can sign and sell.

9. **Agents and Other Professional Service Providers**: Universities have the discretion to outline procedures for athletes to disclose the use of agents, attorneys, or other professional service providers. These procedures may differ from one institution to another.

10. **Dispute Resolution**: Universities must decide on internal dispute resolution processes to address issues related to NIL. These processes can vary in terms of arbitration and mediation options.

One area of particular concern, either because of state law or university policy, relates to companies connected to the vices of alcohol, tobacco, cannabis, and/or gambling. Some states and schools have allowed athletes to enter NIL deals with companies previously considered taboo, such as alcohol companies and sports betting operators. These NIL deals with alcohol and gambling companies offer various benefits to all parties involved, providing financial support to athletes, promote local businesses, and generate national publicity. Even so, critics argue that college athletes should not associate with substances and industries considered risky or harmful, even if they are of legal drinking age. The debate revolves around responsible use and marketing strategies. Both alcohol and gambling companies attempt to address these concerns by emphasizing responsible consumption and lifestyle promotion,.

Two notable examples in this space are the NIL deal between Florida Atlantic University (FAU) quarterback N'Kosi Perry and the Islamorada Beer Company and deals between female athletes and MaximBet, a sports betting operator in Colorado.

Perry became the first college athlete to sign a deal with an alcohol-related company when he partnered with Islamorada Beer Company, a local brewery. Perry's unique partnership with Islamorada demonstrates the expanding horizons and diverse avenues available for athletes to leverage their NIL. Despite the optics, Perry's deal did not give rise to much public opposition.

MaximBet, on the other hand, garnered a more extensive public reaction. MaximBet offered NIL contracts to all female athletes in Colorado in all three divisions. These offers raised questions about the intersection of Colorado state law, institutional policies, and NIL deals.

Colorado's NIL laws and institutional policies surrounding student-athlete endorsements and partnerships differ from many other states. While many states and universities strictly prohibit deals with sports betting or gambling entities, Colorado's state law does not explicitly bar such partnerships. This unique legal framework is the key factor allowing MaximBet to extend its offer to female athletes in the state. The University of Colorado, for example, has not established category prohibitions in its policies, and this flexibility aligns with Colorado's NIL law. But a potential conflict arose because of the university's pre-existing deal with PointsBet, another sports betting company. The compliance office at the University of Colorado had to assess whether MaximBet's contracts with Colorado students conflicted with the university's agreement with PointsBet.

MaximBet, however, went out of business in December 2022. The crowded market for online sports betting and the fierce competition for gamblers with more established casino options has led a number of similar companies to fail. Put simply, the competitive market made MaximBet's business unsustainable.

The emergence of college athletes securing NIL deals with alcohol and gambling companies presents a new set of challenges and opportunities for the world of collegiate sports. While these partnerships offer financial benefits and promotional opportunities, they also raise ethical and regulatory questions for some.

6. COLLECTIVES

When state laws legalized athlete NIL deals in July, 2021, the initial deals involved individual athlete endorsements for companies. One of the most remarkable developments since 2021, however, has been the emergence and proliferation of NIL collectives across the United States. These collectives are private companies comprised of boosters and alumni of individual schools. Some of the most successful collectives include the 12 Man+ Fund (Texas A&M), Division Street (Oregon), the Grove Collective (Ole Miss), the Valiant/Champions Circle (Michigan), and the Classic City Collective (University of Georgia). These collectives have become pivotal players in facilitating NIL deals for athletes. Their emergence has sparked important discussions regarding their purpose, influence, and future trajectory.

NIL collectives are specialized programs devised to provide support and, in theory, safeguard the interests of athletes as they navigate the complex world of endorsement opportunities. Importantly, they are not exclusive to college athletes but are open to any athlete operating within the framework of NCAA bylaws. The recent landscape has seen the formation of over 120 known collectives, with almost all of the sixty-five Power conference schools either already having a collective or actively working towards establishing one. Typically, these organizations consist of a mix of prominent former athletes, alumni, local businesses, and donors who pool their resources to create valuable endorsement opportunities for athletes.

Despite their connection with universities, NIL collectives retain their independence as distinct entities. One of the primary objectives of NIL collectives is to provide athletes with endorsement opportunities. They streamline the complex process of securing these deals, thereby maximizing the earning potential of the athletes involved and saving time for the athlete.

Collectives go beyond merely brokering deals; they offer educational resources to equip athletes with the knowledge and skills required to monetize their personal brands effectively. In theory, this empowerment ensures that athletes can make informed decisions about the financial opportunities available to them.

Many NIL collectives engage in community-based initiatives that benefit not only athletes but also local businesses and fans. This fosters a sense of unity and mutual support within the university ecosystem.

While NIL collectives have attracted substantial attention and backing, they have not escaped controversy. A primary concern revolves around the potential for recruiting and transfer portal activities to adopt pay-for-play characteristics. Certain recruits have inked highly lucrative agreements with collectives, prompting valid queries about the fairness and competitiveness of the recruiting process. Consequently, the NCAA has endeavored to regulate collectives and curtail their participation in recruiting endeavors. Nonetheless, enforcing these regulations has presented formidable challenges, allowing collectives to persist.

Indeed, the common practice here looks much less like private endorsements and much more like legalized pay-for-play. On their face, collectives are just a group of boosters pooling their money to make paying players more efficient, in a streamlined way that can enhance recruiting.

And the transfer portal has heightened the importance of collectives. Schools no longer just have to recruit athletes to come to a university and join the football team. They now have to incentivize the athlete to stay for another year. As explored in Chapter Five, the dual windows of the transfer portal make recruiting a constant demand, with much of the recruiting related to convincing players to stay.

The utilization of million-dollar deals as enticements for recruiting prospects has become an especially pressing issue with respect to NIL collectives as the NCAA has started to try to regulate such deals. In the summer of 2022, Nick Saban of Alabama and Lane Kiffin of Ole Miss both chided then Texas A&M coach Jimbo Fisher for assembling the best roster money could buy. And yet, with state laws allowing for NIL, such deals do not violate NCAA rules unless they are inducements. Even then, as discussed in Chapter Six, attempts by the NCAA to limit such practices might violate antitrust law.

Even so, it is imperative to assess the actual impact of NIL collectives in the current landscape. Despite headlines depicting them as omnipotent entities, industry experts posit that their influence may be less pronounced than perceived. Opendorse CEO Blake Lawrence's data indicates a substantial disparity between collectives that have adeptly navigated the NIL landscape and those generating buzz through announcements but contributing minimally in practice. It seems like most players are receiving several hundred thousand dollars at most, with only the most sought after players receiving over a million dollars a season. In short, it is not clear the actual amount of payments football athletes are actually receiving for use of their NIL.

As NIL collectives continue to evolve, numerous pivotal factors will determine their trajectory. One key inquiry relates to the scope of their direct involvement in recruiting. Programs with more established coaches may have less of a worry here, but for some programs, the economic power of the collectives could lead to such individuals wanting a role in making recruiting decisions, as opposed to just funding them. Again, the NCAA is increasingly trying to restrict the involvement of collectives in recruiting by prohibiting boosters from engaging potential recruits in discussions about NIL agreements. Nevertheless, enforcing these regulations has proven to be a formidable task.

One of the first NIL infractions cases involved Florida State's football program. As discussed in Chapter Two, the NCAA sanctioned the university because an assistant football coach had arranged for a meeting between a transfer portal football recruit and a booster during which the booster offered an NIL deal. *Florida State University, Negotiated Resolution*, Case No. 020169, January 12, 2024. It is uncertain whether the NCAA will ultimately be able to enforce its anti-NIL inducement rule in light of federal antitrust law. *Tennessee & Virginia v. NCAA*, 2024 WL 755528 (E.D. Tenn. 2024).

Perhaps the growing reputation of collectives may make meeting with recruits unnecessary. Coaches might reference historical deals negotiated by collectives to substantiate their legitimacy. Ultimately, the success of collectives may hinge on continued appetite of donors to fund them. For most donors, a return on investment is important. Usually this is less about financial return and more about the success of the team. If a donor extends a substantial deal to an athlete who fails to perform well, this might influence their inclination to participate in future NIL arrangements. Over time, market forces could prompt donors to become more selective with their investments. In the short term, though, the desire to spend money to invest in one's college program of choice seems to be growing.

As a general matter, NIL collectives provide a legitimate avenue for boosters to financially support athletes—a practice that the NCAA has historically prohibited. Despite the contentious debates and challenges collectives have produced, it is becoming increasingly evident that educational institutions must grapple with this emerging reality. As the NIL landscape undergoes further transformation, the role of collectives in college sports remains a subject of fervent debate, with their implications for recruiting, athlete remuneration, and the overarching NCAA framework still uncertain.

It is worth noting that NIL collectives offer unique advantages to college athletes that traditional endorsement deals often do not. A key factor is ownership and profit-sharing. Athletes or their representatives often have ownership stakes in collectives, allowing them to retain a more substantial portion of their earnings as compared to deals with external companies that take a significant cut. By directly selling merchandise through their platforms, collectives can retain up to 100% of the profits, creating a sustainable revenue stream.

Additionally, collectives can empower athletes to shape their careers, gain valuable experience in business negotiations, and make a positive impact on their communities. This level of autonomy and financial support provides college athletes with unprecedented opportunities to secure their financial futures.

Another significant development in this area is the rise of The Collective Association (TCA), a newly formed trade association that serves to link collectives and advocate for their common interests. TCA's objectives extend beyond advocacy; it also serves as a repository for best practices and offers a unified voice shaping the development of the NIL market. In July 2023, seven NIL collectives, all affiliated with prominent football-playing schools, established TCA: Happy Valley United (Penn State), Classic City Collective (Georgia), Spyre Sports Group (Tennessee), The Grove Collective (Ole Miss), The Battle's End (Florida State), House of Victory (USC), and Champions Circle (Michigan). This group continued to grow, adding over a dozen other collectives for Power conference schools within a few months.

TCA's ambitious agenda includes navigating the conflicts between NCAA NIL regulations and state NIL laws as well as registering and verifying agents working with athletes. TCA wants to manage NIL contracts in a way that furthers the status quo and does not transform student-athletes into university employees. Further, TCA seeks to promote collaborative efforts between collectives and college athletes to make a positive impact on local communities.

Among the institutions leading the charge in this ever-evolving NIL landscape is Texas A&M, which has garnered praise for its innovative approach. The 12th Man+ Fund collective associated with Texas A&M has attracted recognition from industry leaders. The 12th Man+ Fund, however, has not been without controversy, particularly because of the ongoing tension between NCAA regulations and state-level NIL legislation discussed below. For instance, Texas has enacted laws that allow donors to receive priority points for contributing to a collective, a practice seemingly at odds with NCAA rules. Essentially these priority points reward donors by giving them priority access to special seats, and game tickets.

In October 2023, the University of Utah's NIL Collective, The Crimson Collective, gifted the entire Utah football roster new, 2024 Ram 1500 Big Horn trucks as part of a deal with an NIL-focused video platform FTW360. Each football player on scholarship received a new truck, with the insurance and lease costs paid for by the collective. The deal requires the athletes to participate in a community service project within a year. With the trucks retailing for $61,000, the deal is worth over $1 million. The leases renew every six months and extend for the duration of the athlete's enrollment at the university. Covered in the Crimson Collective and FTW360 logos, the trucks also promote the launch of the collective's new streaming app Utah360°.

Other schools and their collectives could potentially follow suit. Offering a high school football player, a brand-new truck seems like an enticing recruiting pitch, at least in the current NIL market. While the concept of providing college athletes with new cars is not new in the world of NIL, offering the cars to the entire roster at the school is. It is possible car dealerships will provide cars to prominent student athletes in exchange for promotional and marketing services and with the condition that the car bears the dealership's logo.

Collectives capitalize on alumni and supporters used to hearing about donation campaigns, capital drives, scholarship funds, ticket sales, merchandise sales, and events organized by their alma mater. In this context, NIL collectives are an addition to these well-established communication channels. What remains unknown is how these collective efforts impact athletes in a growing and largely unregulated market.

Overall, NIL collectives have emerged as powerful catalysts in the ever-evolving landscape of college sports and athlete endorsement opportunities. These specialized programs have not only facilitated lucrative deals for student-athletes but have also empowered them with knowledge and autonomy. While controversies and challenges persist, the influence of these collectives is undeniable, and their role in shaping the future of the NIL landscape remains essential. With the establishment of trade associations like The Collective Association (TCA) and the innovative approaches of institutions like Texas A&M, the future of student-athletes leveraging their name, image, and likeness for endorsements and community impact appears economically promising. As the debate surrounding NIL legislation continues, collectives provide a valuable avenue for student-athletes to navigate this evolving terrain while retaining control over their identities and financial opportunities.

7.   BOOSTERS

In the world of college sports, a distinctive blend of tradition and passion has always prevailed, drawing in enthusiastic fans and devoted financial backers known as "boosters." These boosters have long had considerable influence. Much of the NCAA's amateurism rhetoric focused on protecting athletes from boosters with the idea that their money would corrupt the athletes, or at least cost them their eligibility.

NIL laws, however, have reversed that orientation. Instead of being wary of boosters, athletics departments have invited boosters in, given them unprecedented access, and encouraged their much needed participation in collectives.

Many boosters are individuals who wholeheartedly commit themselves to their university's athletic programs, going to great lengths to lend their support. Their contributions come in various forms, such as monetary donations, volunteering their time, and even facilitating employment opportunities for athletes. The NCAA defines boosters as representatives of the institution's athletic interests, encompassing alumni, fans, or anyone with a vested interest in their university's sports teams. These boosters are instrumental in furnishing the resources essential for student-athletes to thrive in both their athletic and academic pursuits.

One of the primary responsibilities of boosters is to bolster their university's athletic department through financial donations. These financial contributions are pivotal in funding scholarships, state-of-the-art facilities, and coaching staff—all integral components for the success of collegiate athletic programs. In essence, boosters serve as the lifeblood of these programs, ensuring that student-athletes have the necessary resources and opportunities to excel in their chosen sports.

Further, boosters can lend their time and expertise to various facets of the athletic program, including the delicate realm of recruiting. While NCAA rules impose stringent limits on booster involvement in recruiting activities, they can still tip off university coaching staff about promising prospects in their regions. This underscores the passion and dedication that boosters harbor for their alma mater's sports programs and their desire to contribute to the team's successes.

Boosters undeniably wield significant influence over the fortunes of athletic departments nationwide, providing the critical financial support required to sustain and elevate college sports programs. Prominent figures like Phil Knight at Oregon and Jimmy Rane at Auburn have poured substantial resources into their alma mater's athletic endeavors, enabling the construction of cutting-edge facilities and the attraction of top-tier coaching talent. In essence, boosters play an indispensable role in recruiting prospective athletes, indirectly influencing their decisions by enhancing the appeal of these programs.

NIL, however, has shifted the focus from supporting the athletic department generally and investing in facilities to paying for athlete NIL. Boosters increasingly are pooling their donations into collectives, not athletic departments. And general university giving is decreasing with funds once donated to academics now becoming collective donations.

While the NCAA has grappled with regulating booster involvement for over a century, recent changes in NIL regulations have introduced novel challenges. Boosters can now enter into NIL agreements with athletes, provided they operate independently of the university and its athletic department. They technically cannot utilize contracts to entice athletes to enroll, but they can still offer lucrative NIL opportunities.

Some boosters have found innovative ways to navigate the NIL rules to benefit university athletes. In response, the NCAA has issued new guidelines to clarify the role of boosters in recruiting and NIL deals. These guidelines explicitly prohibit boosters from directly recruiting athletes and emphasize that NIL deals should not serve as a means to directly pay players to enroll or compete for a particular school. The NCAA is attempting striking a balance between allowing athletes to profit from their NIL and what it perceives as the integrity of the recruiting process, where the amount of NIL money available is not the central driving force in college choice.

Additionally, the guidelines expand the definition of boosters to encompass third-party entities that promote athletics programs, assist with recruiting, or provide benefits to recruits and enrolled student-athletes. This broader definition aims to ensure that collective groups and organizations receive to the same recruiting restrictions as individual boosters.

8.   COMPLIANCE AFTER NIL

For a generation, athletic department compliance offices had the difficult task of keeping athletes away from third-party boosters. Under NCAA rules, the university was responsible for any benefit paid by any third party to any athlete. The focus, then, related to making sure athletes did not receive any benefits that would threaten their athletics eligibility.

In a post-NIL world, third-party benefits for athletes no longer violate NCAA rules because of the new state laws that became effective on July 1, 2021. Payments that would have constituted cheating are now not only permissible but also highly coveted.

A central role of the compliance office, then, has become to track such contracts and payments. Some state laws require tracking of such contracts and payments; other universities require such tracking. One can imagine that these roles will continue to evolve.

The compliance office also has its traditional role of monitoring the provision of illegal benefits to athletes from the university and university officials. But such benefits are less of a concern and likely are de minimis as compared to the NIL compensation available to some athletes.

While moving slowly in light of the seemingly common practice of using NIL deals as inducements, the NCAA enforcement committee has begun to monitor activity. Its first case of major infractions related to NIL involved the University of Miami. The investigation revolved around a meeting set up between two key recruits of Miami's women's basketball team, Haley and Hanna Cavinder, the aforementioned Cavinder twins, and John Ruiz, a well-known University of Miami booster. The Miami head basketball coach, Katie Meier, arranged this meeting.

Following this meeting, the Cavinder twins transferred from Fresno State to the University of Miami. Ruiz, already recognized as one of the nation's leading NIL boosters, continued to make waves. His trio of ventures, LifeWallet, MSP Recovery, and Cigarette Racing, have all brokered endorsement deals with numerous college athletes. The NCAA flagged this engagement because it deemed the meeting as impermissible since the players had not officially committed to Miami.

In February 2023, after thorough investigation, the NCAA entered into a negotiated resolution with Miami. *University of Miami (Florida), Negotiated Resolution*, Case No. 020161, February 24, 2023. The NCAA imposed a one-year probation on Miami, attributing it to an impermissible contact violation. The negotiated resolution also included a fine of $5,000, a 1% cut from the women's basketball budget, and a slight modification in its recruiting practices. But the University could maintain its association with booster John Ruiz. This event highlighted the challenges associated with the new NIL guidelines and the inherent risks of NIL recruiting inducements under NCAA rules.

Similarly, the University of Florida found itself facing national scrutiny for the actions of its now-defunct Gator Collective. The collective allegedly offered a significant amount of NIL money to Jaden Rashada, a star quarterback recruit. Unconfirmed reports indicated that the Gator Collective offered a $13 million endorsement deal, spread across 3–4 years, to entice Rashada to enroll at Florida. Crucially, this deal hinged on his enrolment at Florida, in violation of the NCAA's guidelines. Rashada subsequently decommitted from Miami, where he allegedly had signed an NIL deal, and committed to Florida. Following Rashada's commitment to Florida, the Gator Collective reportedly reneged on the promised sum, prompting Rashada to ask the University to release him from his letter of intent.

This series of events led to unique lawsuit filed in May 2024. Rashada sued the University of Florida's head football coach Billy Napier, its former director of player engagement Marcus Castro-Walker, and Florida booster Hugh Hathcock. This is the first known time a college athlete has sued his coach or a booster over an NIL dispute.

Rashada alleges the University of Florida outbid Miami's NIL offer, offering $13.85 million to Miami's $9.5 million. After Florida released him from his letter of intent, Rashada enrolled at Arizona State University, where his father played collegiate football. Rashada went on to play quarterback for the Sun Devils in the 2023 season, and appeared in three games, prior transferring to the University of Georgia in the spring of 2024.

NCAA regulations prohibit boosters from interacting with recruits or using the allure of NIL money to convince players to choose a specific school. Receiving NIL compensation cannot be contingent on enrolling at a school. The complaint mentions a "zip code clause" in Rashada's contract, requiring him to reside in Gainesville, Florida. Zip code clauses seek to tie athletes to the Universities they sign endorsement contracts with, without expressly making the agreement contingent on enrollment. Even though the NCAA has specifically prohibited NIL deals from being contingent on enrollment, these zip code clauses are an attempted work around.

The contract was reportedly terminable at will by both parties, likely the reason why Rashada is not suing for breach of contract. The seven count complaint alleges fraudulent misrepresentation and fraudulent inducement, aiding and abetting fraud, civil conspiracy to commit fraud, negligent misrepresentation, tortious interference with a business relationship, aiding and abetting tortious interference, fraud in the inducement, and vicarious liability against Velocity Automotive Solutions LLC, the company owned by UF donor, Hugh Hathcock. The underlying claim of his tortious interference claim is that the Florida representatives defrauded Rashada out of his $9 million Miami NIL contract and that they fraudulently induced Rashada to abandon his agreement with Miami.

As damages, the complaint requests punitive damages and lost profits. Rashada also claims Florida coach Billy Napier promised him a "partial payment" of $1 million upon signing his National Letter of Intent to attend Florida, that his commitment to Florida was contingent on a four year $13.85 million NIL deal brokered through Florida's now defunct NIL Collective, the Gator Collective, now rebranded as Florida Victorious.

Shortly following Rashada's tumultuous recruitment and release from his letter of intent, the NCAA opened an investigation into Florida in the summer of 2023. Fortunately for Florida, as a result of the injunction issued in *Tennessee & Virginia v. NCAA*, 2024 WL 755528 (E.D. Tenn. 2024), the NCAA sent a letter to its schools in February 2024 explaining it was pausing all open enforcement cases involving third party participation in NIL-related activities. This injunction, however, will not stop discovery from proceeding in the Rashada case or limit potential ramifications for Coach Napier at Florida.

The Rashada situation raised questions about the use of NIL deals in the recruitment process and whether they constituted a form of pay-for-play, which would be a violation of NCAA rules. The NCAA remains unwavering in its view that NIL is distinct from pay-for-play. It believes that NIL should relate only to compensation for actual NIL use. It should solely empower collegiate athletes to monetize their name, image, and likeness. Yet, university-based NIL collectives often tread the blurry line of pay-for-play. Indeed, the practical reality of NIL deals seems much more like a pure pay-for-play system used to recruit star players, not an amateur system that permits athlete endorsements.

A testament to this ambiguity was the NCAA's revised bylaw introduced on January 1, 2023. It empowered NCAA investigators and enforcement personnel to rely on circumstantial evidence when probing NCAA rule infringements, contrasting with the earlier mandate of definitive on-record sourcing.

The guidelines initially promulgated by the NCAA expressly prohibit pay-for-play. Yet, given the lack of clarity on defining an athlete's fair market value, and the absence of a cap on compensation, determining what constitutes pay-for-play as opposed to mere endorsement remains vague. As of the writing of this text, the NCAA has not announced sanctions for the University of Florida in the alleged pay-for-play deal involving Jaden Rashada. This incident highlighted the need for institutions and student-athletes to navigate the complexities of NIL regulations while respecting contractual obligations.

As discussed in Chapter Two, Florida State became the first football program to receive sanctions for NIL inducement violations. And the current investigation of Tennessee has led to a preliminary injunction barring enforcement of the NCAA's NIL rules. Chapter Six explores the future of this litigation.

9. THE QUESTION OF UNIVERSITY INVOLVEMENT

The initial response to the passage of NIL laws included many athletes signing endorsement deals with companies. But within the first year, athletics boosters began to organize, forming collectives. These collectives combine resources and then enter into deals with athletes or groups of athletes to provide compensation to larger groups of players, not just star athletes.

In October 2022, the NCAA offered additional guidance on the permitted role of the university with respect to the NIL contracts between athletes and third party boosters and collectives. First, the NCAA made clear that schools may not compensate athletes beyond tuition, room, board, books, cost of attendance, and education-related costs. So, universities still cannot compensate their athletes for use of their NIL under NCAA amateurism rules. 2023–24 NCAA Division I Manual, Bylaw 12.5.1.1(f). Also, university employees, including coaching and athletics department staff cannot provide benefits to athletes not available to non-athlete students. 2023–24 NCAA Division I Manual, Bylaw 16.02.3. Institutions can, however, finance and assist athletes with personal development services. 2023–24 NCAA Division I Manual, Bylaw 16.3.

The guidance indicated, however, that the university can play a significant role in helping connect athletes to third party collectives and boosters. Specifically, NCAA rules allow universities to engage NIL entities to inform athletes of NIL opportunities; engage NIL entities to administer a marketplace that matches athletes with NIL opportunities (without university involvement in the deal); provide information to athletes about NIL opportunities, including providing information and directory information about the NIL entities; provide stock video/graphics to NIL entities; promote the athlete's NIL activity provided there is no value or cost to the institution; provide donor information or facilitate meetings between a donor and an NIL entity.

NCAA rules do prohibit communication with an NIL entity about a specific athlete request or demand for compensation; proactively assisting in the development of the athlete's NIL activity; providing services to support the NIL activity; providing access to equipment to support the athlete's NIL activity; allowing the athlete to promote their NIL activity during required activities for athletics including practices and games; and providing assets to a donor as an incentive for providing funds to an NIL entity.

In short, the university and its employees (including coaches) can help facilitate the NIL deals. Under NCAA rules, they cannot be a party to those deals or use those deals to entice athletes to attend their university by negotiating NIL deals.

Nebraska's Harper Murray was one of the top volleyball players in the country. In August 2023, she signed a deal with Avoli, a new volleyball shoe brand. The parties, however, terminated the contract because it violated Nebraska's contract with Adidas. Adidas pays Nebraska $4.85 million annually and provided over $6 million in equipment to Nebraska in 2023. Nebraska and Adidas are in the seventh year in an eleven-year contract with a total value of $128 million. The contract gives Adidas exclusive rights to market and sell Official Nebraska volleyball merchandise, including shoes. Nebraska does not allow Murray to wear Avoli shoes in competition, as this would violate the school's contract with Adidas. In addition, Murray may not promote Avoli shoes on her social media channels while wearing her Nebraska uniform.

This case highlights the potential for conflicts between NIL deals and school contracts. As NIL becomes more widespread, it is likely that more cases like this will arise. This case shows the limitations of NIL endorsement deals. While athletes are free to enter into agreements with whomever they choose, their school's existing brand deals place limits on the scope of the NIL contracts.

Some have argued that this brand conflict creates a health and safety issue as the athlete is not free to select the shoe, or equipment, that best fits them. In professional sports, players can choose what they wear for their health and safety benefit. It is important for student-athletes and their legal teams to carefully review all contracts before signing them, to ensure that they are not in violation of any school rules or regulations.

The rise of collectives, explored in earlier in this chapter, has alleviated some of the NCAA's concerns and exacerbated others. To that end, the NCAA has indicated that it may allow universities to take a more active role in the NIL process. Further rule changes may be forthcoming. A new state law in Texas, passed in the summer of 2023, has accelerated possible changes.

What some universities would like to do is to merge collectives with their athletic foundations. This would give athletic departments more control over the NIL money paid to their athletes. The first step is for fundraising groups that are legally separate yet closely partnered with universities to start paying athletes for NIL endorsements. In Texas, for example, the new law allows fundraising groups such as the Longhorn Foundation or the 12th Man Foundation—which support the athletic departments at Texas and Texas A&M, respectively—to raise money for NIL deals. Arkansas and Oklahoma have passed similar laws. These new laws forbid the NCAA and its conference from punishing any school that incentivizes fans who donate to NIL collectives.

In October, 2023, the NCAA discussed a series of proposed changes that would allow schools to:

- Proactively assist in the development/creation of NIL activity.

- Provide services such as tax preparation and contract review.

- Provide access to equipment (such as cameras, podcast studios, etc.) for NIL activity.

- Communicate with school sponsors about NIL opportunities for their athletes, including securing specific opportunities.

While the future is unsure, the NIL market and the NCAA's attempts to regulate it are likely to continue to evolve.

10. THE CHARLIE BAKER ERA

On December 15, 2022, the NCAA welcomed its sixth President, Charlie Baker. Baker replaced Mark Emmert, who had served as president since 2010. Before this role, Baker had a distinguished career as a businessman and politician. He was the 72nd governor of Massachusetts, the "executive in residence" at General Catalyst Partners, and the CEO of Harvard Pilgrim Health Care. Notably, he also played collegiate men's basketball for Harvard during the 1977–78 season. Baker formally began his tenure as the NCAA President on March 1, 2023.

Baker's vision for the NCAA is clear and ambitious. In his open letter, "The Path Forward," he shared his aspirations, the challenges ahead, and a commitment to transparency. One of his priorities is gender equity. Baker's letter noted, "After an exhaustive third-party gender equity assessment in 2021, the NCAA has been making strides to ensure women's sports receive equivalent backing and that their experiences are as enriching as those in men's sports." On the topic of inclusion in sports, especially concerning the participation of transgender athletes, Baker emphasized the importance of balancing inclusion with competitive fairness. He suggested that sports-specific criteria, based on scientific evidence, may be necessary. The achievements of transgender swimmer Lia Thomas, who won an NCAA Division I title in 2022, have led to some calling for reform of NCAA regulations with respect to transgender athletes.

Additionally, Baker announced the establishment of an NCAA Health Insurance Fund, designed to support Division I, II, & III athletes who sustain sports-related injuries that require continued care post their college sports careers.

Tackling the topic of NIL, Baker expressed support for athletes monetizing their NIL. Even so, he emphasized the necessity for a standardized system to maintain transparency and fairness for both universities and athletes. He envisions a system with a "deal registry, agent certification, and a standardized contract for deals." Multiple legislative proposals aim to implement such a system, including "The College Athletes Protection & Compensation Act," "The Amateur Athletes Protection and Compensation Act," and "The College Athlete Economic Freedom Act." While these proposals are still in the discussion phase, the NCAA has voiced its desire for a federal law.

Departing from previous NCAA stances, Baker seems receptive to the organization engaging in the facilitation of sports betting. Despite the NCAA's earlier attempts to limit sports betting to Nevada, Baker recognized the potential benefits, especially since thirty-eight states have legalized it after the Supreme Court's decision in *Murphy v. NCAA,* discussed in Chapter Ten. *Murphy v. NCAA*, 584 U.S. 453 (2018). Even so, he's wary, noting that many athletes are within the prime betting demographic (ages 18 to 22), and a careful approach is paramount.

In March 2023, a congressional hearing took place on name, image, and likeness regulations and how they have drastically changed college sports. Since 2021, the NCAA has continuously attempted to seek an antitrust exemption from Congress that would supersede the myriad state NIL laws.

In December, 2023, President Baker proposed that presidents and chancellors consider legalizing a pay-for-play model, with a subdivision allowing for athletes to share in NIL revenue generated by television broadcasts. His proffered approach contemplates schools investing $30,000 per year into an enhanced educational trust fund for at least half of the institution's eligible student-athletes. It remains to be seen how this proposal will be adjusted by the settlement in the *House* case, discussed in Chapter Six.

In May 2024, the NCAA Board of Governors and Power conferences voted to tentatively approve the *House* settlement. NCAA President Charlie Baker and the commissioners released a joint statement. "This settlement is [a] road map for college sports leaders and Congress to ensure this uniquely American institution can continue to provide unmatched opportunity for millions of students. . . We look forward to working with our various student-athlete leadership groups to write the next chapter of college sports." For better or worse, this decision and its consequences will define Baker's legacy. To be sure, the settlement signals a seismic shift in college sports.

11. NON-SCHOLARSHIP IVY LEAGUE ATHLETES

The Ivy League remains the only Division I athletic conference that forbids its member schools from awarding athletic scholarships. This policy, instituted in 1954, reflects the belief that student-athletes should gain college admission based on academic merit rather than athletic prowess. While some critics say the policy financially handicaps student-athletes, the Ivy League defends its stance. The League argues that its policy guarantees equal access to quality education for all students, irrespective of their athletic capabilities or financial standing.

But the availability of NIL endorsements has tested the league's stance on athletic scholarships. Detractors believe the Ivy League's policy discriminates against its athletes, preventing them from monetizing their NIL in contrast to athletes from other institutions. The future of the Ivy League's scholarship policy is uncertain, but the emergence of NIL payments has undoubtedly drawn attention to it.

In March 2023, two basketball players from Brown University, Grace Kirk and Tamenang Choh, initiated a class action lawsuit against the Ivy League and its eight member institutions challenging the prohibition on athletic scholarships.

Choh & Kirk v. Brown University, No. 3:23-cv-00305-AWT (D. Conn. 2023). Specifically, the lawsuit contends that the League's policy effectively constitutes a price-fixing arrangement, violating federal antitrust law. Further, the suit alleges that the Ivy League inadequately provides financial aid to its student-athletes and fails to justly reward them for their on-field performance. In defense, an executive director from the Ivy League emphasized that their student-athletes reap benefits beyond academic scholarships, including "a path for lifelong success."

During the 2023–24 season, men's basketball players from Dartmouth College formed a union. Rather than using antitrust law, then, these athletes used labor law as a tool to receive compensation from the university, as explored in more detail in Chapter Six. The historic vote took place on March 5, 2024, with the players voting 13–2 to unionize. The vote came just weeks after a regional office of the National Labor Relations Board held that the athletes were university employees for purposes of the National Labor Relations Act. *Decision and Direction of Election, Trustees of Dartmouth College*, 01-RC-325633 (NLRB Feb. 5, 2024).

As such the athletes are university employees, at least for the purposes of organizing. The next step would be to enter into a collective bargaining agreement with Dartmouth. Further, the athletes can claim employee status with respect to other federal statutes, entitling them to other benefits, such as minimum wage under the Fair Labor

Standards Act (FLSA) or access to health care under the Affordable Care Act. This might not happen soon, however, as Dartmouth plans to appeal the regional director's decision. Dartmouth has also indicated that it has no intention of entering into a collective bargaining agreement with the basketball players' union.

12. HEALTH BENEFITS AND INSURANCE

Student-athletes face a heightened risk of injury, compelling access to quality health care. Historically, the NCAA did not mandate its member schools to offer health insurance to these athletes. As a result, many student-athletes bear the financial weight of their own health care, with some even forgoing essential medical treatments. As mentioned earlier, by unionizing, NCAA student-athletes could collectively seek health benefits and insurance.

The NCAA has recently taken steps to address the issue of health care for student-athletes. In 2018, the NCAA adopted a new policy that requires member schools to provide health insurance to all student-athletes. But the new policy does not require member schools to cover all costs associated with health care. Recognizing that student-athletes still needed access to quality health care, the NCAA Division I Board of Directors voted unanimously to expand health care coverage for college athletes to take effect in August 2024. The NCAA's Transformation Committee recommended this initiative, called holistic student-athlete benefits model, in January 2023.

Furthermore, under the new rules, the NCAA
mandates each member institution to confirm their
provision of academic support, career counseling for
current and past athletes, life skills development,
and covering out-of-pocket medical expenses. Each
member institution must also attest to offering
mental health services and adherence to concussion
management protocols, and supply funds for degree
completion up to ten years following a college
athlete's eligibility if they had a full scholarship or
received financial aid in a head count sport.

13. EA V. BRANDR

Brandr Group is a full-service agency that prides
itself on being "experts in taming the 'wild west' of
NIL marketing." Brandr has deals to negotiate
licensing contracts for 54 Division I schools
represented in the upcoming EA Sports college
football game. Brandr is suing EA Sports claiming
that EA is trying to circumvent its agreements to
negotiate for athletes to participate in the football
game. The Brandr Group either has "exclusive" or
"preferred" group licensing rights, which the
company defines as three or more athletes on a
school's team, or six or more across multiple sports,
while using school imagery.

EA and Brandr had been in contact multiple times
from 2021 through 2022 about EA's plans for the
game in offering NIL money to athletes featured in
the game. Ultimately, EA chose to work with
OneTeam Partners over Brandr to help facilitate the
group licensing deals with athletes. EA is offering

deals with the help of OneTeam that athletes can "opt into" directly without any involvement from Brandr.

In Brandr's complaint, Brandr alleged that the current deal as of July 2023 is $500 per athlete with no royalties. Brandr and the College Football Players Association claim this is below fair market value. Brandr's main point is that it must be able to negotiate on behalf of the athletes at schools for which it has contracts and that EA's decision to ask athletes to directly opt-in without the involvement of Brandr amounts to tortious interference. Brandr believes that student athletes are not receiving fair market value for their NIL rights and the contractual rights asked for may limit other NIL gaming opportunities. The court had denied Brandr's temporary restraining order (TRO), then went on to outline the likelihood of success on the merits in its lawsuit.

As of July 2023, both parties agreed to a joint stipulation, extending the deadline for EA to respond Brandr's complaint. In December, 2023, Brandr agreed to drop the lawsuit, paving the way for the release of the EA Sports college football video game in the summer of 2024.

14. HIGH SCHOOL NIL LAWS

While NIL laws primarily pertain to college athletes, their influence has also trickled down to the high school level. High school students aspiring to play college sports are becoming more aware of their personal branding and social media presence, as these factors can impact their future opportunities under NIL regulations. The growing trend of NIL opportunities for high school athletes and the implications for their eligibility and participation in high school sports have prompted discussions on various aspects of this matter.

Nationally, the NCAA interim policy and subsequent state NIL laws have universally authorized student-athletes in utilizing their name, image, and likeness for monetary gain. But this universal authorization is not the same for high school college students. A major reason is that unlike colleges or universities, public or private, there is no central, national regulatory body like the NCAA for high schools.

Currently around thirty states have adopted NIL rules for high school athletes, but concerns arise from the lack of uniformity across states. The disparate regulations can lead to inequalities and complexities in recruitment, endorsement deals, and eligibility, depending on a student's location. The lack of standardized guidelines can also lead to confusion among young athletes and their families about their rights and responsibilities in navigating NIL opportunities.

As of July 1, 2023, only thirty of the fifty states allow high school students to monetize their NIL. These states include Alaska, California, Colorado, Connecticut, District of Columbia (D.C.), Idaho, Illinois, Iowa, Kansas, Louisiana, Maine, Maryland, Massachusetts, Minnesota, Nebraska, Nevada (limited, see below), New Hampshire, New Jersey,

New Mexico, New York, North Carolina, North Dakota, Oklahoma, Oregon, Pennsylvania, Rhode Island, Tennessee, Utah, Virginia, and Washington.

Here is a sampling of some of the different state approaches:

i.   **Alaska**: In Alaska, the ASAA (Alaska School Activities Association) permits high school athletes to capitalize on their Name, Image, and Likeness (NIL) rights, but with a specific condition. Athletes may engage in commercial endorsements, as long as these endorsements do not involve any affiliation with their school team, the school itself, or any ASAA entity. This rule appears to strike a balance between allowing athletes to benefit from their NIL while maintaining a clear distinction between their personal endorsements and their school affiliations.

ii. **Arkansas**: Arkansas has seen recent amendments in its approach to NIL rights for high school athletes. Under House Bill 1649 signed by Governor Sarah Huckabee Sanders, athletes admitted to an institution within the state or have signed a National Letter of Intent (NLI) can pursue NIL deals. This supersedes the previous AAA's (Arkansas Activities Association) rule on amateurism, which prohibited athletes from receiving compensation for the use of their name, image, or likeness. The focus here is on athletes who have secured college commitments, allowing them to explore

NIL opportunities without violating the AAA's amateurism policy.

iii. **California**: As one of the first states to allow high school athletes to participate in NIL agreements, California enables athletes to enter into commercial endorsements without a restriction on NIL activities, provided that their school or team has no association with the endorsement. This approach aims to provide athletes with the freedom to benefit from their personal brand while avoiding conflicts with their educational institutions.

iv. **Illinois**: The Illinois High School Association (IHSA) follows the trend of other states by permitting student-athletes to engage in NIL activities while retaining their eligibility. In line with this, athletes must ensure a clear separation between their NIL activities and their participation in interscholastic sports. The emphasis here is on maintaining the distinction between an athlete's personal brand ventures and their involvement in school sports.

v. **Louisiana**: The LHSAA (Louisiana High School Athletic Association) allows high school athletes to monetize their NIL rights, and an association with Eccker Sports provides educational resources for athletes pursuing NIL opportunities. This highlights the importance of educating student-athletes about the implications and opportunities associated with NIL, while also giving them the freedom to engage in such activities.

vi. **Maryland**: Maryland's policy on NIL aligns with many other states, allowing student-athletes to participate in NIL activities. Maryland, however, stands out by prohibiting the use of NIL to promote video games. Moreover, the state association takes a strict stance on the formation of collectives supporting schools through NIL activities, preventing employees, contractors, and vendors of member schools from participating. This approach aims to ensure the integrity of student-athlete endorsements.

vii. **Missouri**: In Missouri, the Missouri State High School Activities Association's (MSHSAA) updated handbook states that "qualified" high school student-athletes can earn compensation from NIL activities. Notably, these athletes cannot receive deals that specifically represent the sport they are involved in, preserving their amateurism status. This approach reflects the intention to prevent direct promotion of athletic prowess that might compromise the amateur nature of high school sports.

viii. **Oklahoma**: Oklahoma's approach allows student-athletes to earn profits from NIL activities without jeopardizing their amateur status. But there are limitations. Athletes cannot use school marks or apparel in such deals, and cannot tie compensation to athletic achievements. This approach ensures that student-athletes can benefit from their NIL while maintaining a clear distinction between their academic and athletic pursuits.

ix. **Pennsylvania**: Pennsylvania allows student-athletes to engage in NIL activities without losing their high school eligibility. Even so, a unique aspect is that individuals affiliated with the high school or employed by it cannot arrange NIL deals or paying players. This approach emphasizes the separation between the school and NIL deals, preventing undue influence or conflicts of interest.

x. **Rhode Island**: In Rhode Island, student-athletes can monetize their NIL, provided there is no connection to their team, school, or the Rhode Island Interscholastic League. This aligns with the overarching approach of allowing athletes to benefit from their personal brands while ensuring that they do not exploit school for personal gain.

Overall, the various NIL high school laws generally permit athletes to benefit from their NIL rights, but differ in terms of eligibility criteria, restrictions on endorsements, and affiliations with educational institutions. These differences reflect the evolving landscape of NIL rights and the unique considerations of each state.

Unlike colleges, most high schools lack the resources and infrastructure to provide comprehensive oversight and support for athletes engaging in NIL activities. Colleges have compliance officers who ensure athletes adhere to regulations, but many high schools may struggle to offer the same level of guidance. This disparity in support could expose young athletes to the risk of entering unfavorable contracts, potentially undermining their future eligibility and overall well-being. Insufficient advisory programs could leave high school athletes vulnerable to exploitation, especially given their relative inexperience in negotiating complex financial and contractual arrangements.

One of the primary concerns centers around the capacity of adolescents to make sound financial decisions. The impetus behind NIL policies was to address the financial challenges faced by college athletes. Similarly, high school athletes can benefit from NIL deals, but they might not possess the necessary life experience to make informed choices about endorsement contracts, financial planning, and long-term career implications. Without proper guidance and education, high school athletes might be at risk of making decisions that hinder their future prospects or lead to unnecessary financial burdens.

Highly visible high school athletes with significant potential, like Bronny James, Mikey Williams, or Arch Manning, can attract lucrative NIL deals. While these deals may seem attractive on the surface, there is a potential for third parties to exploit or undervalue these athletes. Corporations might be eager to secure young talent at a lower cost, banking on their future success. Cases of corruption and unethical behavior have surfaced in the past, indicating that some entities are willing to go to great lengths to secure promising athletes. The lack of oversight and proper guidance could exacerbate these vulnerabilities.

Engaging in NIL activities can introduce high school athletes to complex tax and legal considerations. Without proper understanding, these athletes might inadvertently violate tax regulations or face legal complications. The burden of going through these complexities might be overwhelming for young athletes, potentially leading to unforeseen consequences and unintended legal consequences. Navigating the intricate tax implications of monetizing NIL for high school athletes presents a multifaceted challenge. Parents and administrators need to help high school athletes understand that NIL agreements are more than swift profit opportunities. Rather, these agreements demand careful execution, meticulous tracking, and precise reporting for tax considerations.

For high school student-athletes, many of whom are dependents on their parents' tax returns, comprehending their dependency status holds paramount importance. Earnings derived from NIL arrangements could potentially impact their dependency classification, shifting tax filing responsibilities. This becomes especially critical in relation to educational credits linked to tax submissions. The transition to college introduces further nuances, as NIL earnings have the potential to influence Expected Family Contribution (EFC) calculations for financial aid, potentially altering the amount of Pell Grant awards. Seeking guidance from financial professionals becomes imperative to evade unforeseen consequences related to signing NIL contracts.

The designation of athletes (or their parents) as independent contractors is common in NIL agreements. In this capacity, athletes assume responsibility for remitting income taxes, as well as social security and Medicare taxes, which some NIL contracts do not withhold. Even if athletes receive payments in cash or through platforms like Venmo, they must record them as taxable income. Precise record-keeping of all received payments, coupled with receipts, invoices, and contracts, becomes pivotal to avert future tax-related mistakes.

As with other forms of income, NIL earnings are subject to federal and state taxes. State-level taxation hinges on residency, with the athlete's home state claiming state taxes on income. States where athletes conduct NIL deals or where the athlete attends college, even if non-resident, may also impose taxes. Navigating the intricate tax regulations of different states is critical to avoid dual taxation and ensure adherence.

Athletes must disclose all earnings stemming from NIL activities, including endorsements, sponsorships, and merchandise sales. Even compensation in non-monetary forms can be taxable income. In the case of products received as compensation, athletes must report their fair market value. Grasping the tax implications of agent fees also is important. Payments made to licensed agents might be deductible as business expenses, whereas fees from non-licensed agents are not.

Because the tax issues can be quite complicated, athletes and their families need to seek professional guidance in many situations. Educational institutions can also help by integrating NIL-related financial education into their curricula. Collaborating with CPAs, tax experts, and professionals to discuss the tax and business facets of NIL can equip athletes with crucial life skills and ensure compliance with tax statutes.

One instructive approach to high school athlete NIL contracts is that of Pennsylvania, where the implementation has been cautious and restrictive. The Pennsylvania Interscholastic Athletic Association (PIAA) approved NIL bylaws, but only for a select group of nationally recognized athletes. This approach aims to limit the influence of NIL deals to only a few high-profile individuals, reducing the potential impact on the broader high school athletic community.

The Pennsylvania Interscholastic Athletic Association (PIAA), the governing body for high school athletics in the state, introduced a new rule that allows high school athletes in Pennsylvania to monetize their NIL rights. Like the rules for college athletes, the PIAA's NIL rule sets specific guidelines to maintain a separation between athletes and their schools or governing bodies. Specifically, state rules bar athletes from using their school's logos, names, and nicknames in any promotions or endorsements to safeguard intellectual property and privacy rights. In addition, both high school and college rules in Pennsylvania prohibit athletes from entering NIL deals related to adult entertainment, gambling, alcohol, tobacco, vaping, prescription drugs, controlled substances, and weapons.

Further, there are distinctions between high school and college NIL rules. Notably, the PIAA's rule explicitly forbids boosters, collectives, and alumni from assisting high school athletes in obtaining NIL deals. This contrasts with the collegiate landscape where boosters and alumni have played a significant role in facilitating NIL deals for college athletes. A recent amendment to Pennsylvania's collegiate NIL law removed the provision that prevented schools from arranging NIL deals for their athletes. High school athletes, however, do not have access to these types of NIL support networks until they transition to the college level.

Enforcement and reporting mechanisms also differ between the two rules. The PIAA's rule places enforcement responsibility on individual school districts throughout the state, allowing for variations in implementation from district to district. By contrast, universities generally enforce the collegiate rule. Additionally, the high school rule mandates that athletes report any NIL deals to their school's athletic department within seventy-two hours of receiving the deal. In the college rule, an amendment has removed the requirement for athletes to report deals to their school within a week.

The implementation of the PIAA's NIL rule represents a significant development in the evolving landscape of NIL rights for athletes. Whether at the high school or college level, navigating the complexities of the NIL space can be challenging. While the potential for high school athletes to secure NIL benefits now exists, concerns remain about the unknowns associated with these opportunities. PIAA Executive Director Bob Lombardi expressed the belief that only a select few high school athletes in Pennsylvania are likely to secure NIL deals because of the state's limits.

While NIL policies have the potential to provide financial opportunities for high school athletes, they also raise serious concerns about exploitation, decision-making capacity, and the lack of support and oversight. It remains important for educational institutions, state legislatures, and athletic associations to strike a balance between empowering athletes and protecting their interests. Implementing robust advisory programs, standardized guidelines, and educational resources can help young athletes navigate the complexities of NIL while safeguarding their future successes and well-being.

15. HIGH SCHOOL NIL AND
NCAA ELIGIBILITY

Recall the *Lasege* case from Chapter One. *NCAA v. Lasege*, 53 S.W.3d 77 (Ky. 2001). When an athlete receives remuneration for playing a sport prior to enrolling in college, that athlete loses eligibility in that sport. 2023–24 NCAA Division I Manual, Bylaw 12.2.5. It is different, as recounted in the Prologue, if the college sport is not the same sport as the prior pro sport, like professional skier Jeremy Bloom being eligible to play college football at Colorado. *Bloom v. NCAA*, 93 P. 3d 621 (Colo. Ct. App. 2004).

With state laws entitling high school athletes to receive NIL money, such remuneration in theory does not impair the athlete's college eligibility. But the line between salary and NIL can blur, creating eligibility issues.

Matthew and Ryan Bewley are brothers who played basketball at Overtime Elite Academy, an "elite basketball academy" high school in Georgia. While students at Overtime Elite, the Bewleys both signed an agreement with the school that included academic scholarships and remuneration in exchange for the sale and transfer of their NIL rights. Effective on July 1, 2021, the agreement warned that accepting its "negotiated market value compensation package" risked the loss of NCAA eligibility.

The Bewley brothers subsequently accepted athletic scholarships to play basketball at Chicago State University. In July 2023, the Bewleys applied for NCAA eligibility. On October 31, 2023, the NCAA denied their application, finding them ineligible to compete one week prior to their first game for Chicago State.

Two other former Overtime Elite players, Rob Dillingham and Kanaan Carlyle received a different response from the NCAA, which found them eligible to play. In 2022, Overtime Elite had changed its agreement by offering athletes a "scholarship option" instead of a "salary."

The Bewleys filed a lawsuit against the NCAA and sought a temporary restraining order and ultimately, a preliminary injunction that would keep the NCAA from enforcing its eligibility decision. *Bewley v. NCAA*, 2024 WL 113971 (N.D. Ill. 2024). They argued that not only was the NCAA's decision inconsistent, but it also violated the Illinois NIL law. Denying the Bewleys' motion, the court held that they were unlikely to succeed on the merits because the contract in question was clearly an employment contract. While the contract included NIL rights, it reflected a much more extensive employment relationship, according to the court.

The Bewleys also raised an antitrust claim, but the court was unwilling to grant an injunction based on it in light of the lack of undeveloped nature of the record. It is possible the case will continue with discovery. But the Bewleys will not be able to receive the remedy they wanted—immediate eligibility.

While there was a clear difference, at least from the court's perspective, between an NIL deal and an employment contract, one can imagine similar situations arising. This is particularly true as high school athlete NIL contracts become more common. Athletes will need to be careful to make sure such contracts do not interfere with their eligibility to play intercollegiate sports.

16. EVALUATING THE VALUE OF NIL

For some athletes, the passage of state NIL laws has proved invaluable with respect to the way in which it has altered college athletics. These advantages include financial empowerment, gender equity, academic incentives, and an enhanced sense of competitive balance.

NIL money represents a monumental departure from the traditional limitations placed on college athletes by the NCAA. It is a new opportunity to be able to generate income while concurrently pursuing an education and an athletic career. With the advent of NIL rights, athletes are now able to engage in various commercial activities, including endorsements, appearances, and social media promotions, all while staying within NCAA regulations.

Student-athletes can accrue NIL money through diverse avenues, including: (1) direct payments for promotional activities; (2) receipt of free or sponsored products or services in exchange for promotion; (3) affiliate marketing on social media platforms; (4) brand ambassadorships; and (5) appearances in commercials, advertisements, and digital content.

To truly appreciate the value of NIL, it is instructive to draw parallels with professional sports licensing. Professional sports unions, such as the NFL and MLB Players Associations, derive substantial revenue from licensing agreements with video game publishers and trading card manufacturers. College athletes now can reap similar benefits from licensing deals. For example, Electronic Arts agreed to disburse roughly $60 million to more than 24,000 former college athletes for the use of their likenesses in video games. Licensing fees can range from 10% to 15% of a game's revenue, potentially yielding thousands of dollars per athlete.

Apparel licensing agreements offer additional revenue, with notable college athletes potentially earning thousands of dollars annually. Nike's licensing deal with the NBA, valued at $1 billion over eight years, translates to approximately $275,000 per player annually. Comparing NIL to professional sports demonstrates that earning capability for top collegiate athletes.

The income of social media influencers whether on Instagram, Tik Tok, or Twitch, provides further benchmarks for estimating college athlete earnings. Social media has created an additional level of earning capability for student-athletes.

Early estimates the average income from NIL deals for all Division I athletes falls within the range of $1,000 to $10,000. In 2022–23, boosters spent approximately $1.7 billion on NIL, with half or more of that revenue going to Power conference football athletes. Such athletes are more likely to receive between $10,000 and $50,000 annually with around five players receiving in excess of $100,000 per year. As college football consolidates and the transfer portal becomes more competitive, these amounts are likely to increase. By contrast, the average deal across all sports at non-Power conference schools was $1440 in the 2022–23 year.

On average, collectives have about $3 million to spend annually, with some spending between $7 and $10 million per year. Again, these numbers are likely to increase, particularly as the market becomes more transparent.

Noteworthy exceptions exist on the higher end of the spectrum, where athletes with substantial social media followings or extraordinary athletic potential have earned significantly more. Athletes can earn income through sponsored Instagram posts, with rates typically predicated on follower count. For instance, high school basketball sensation Bronny James, son of NBA legend LeBron James, boasts an estimated NIL valuation of $7.5 million. LSU's gymnast Olivia Dunne, with over 11.3 million social media followers, commands an estimated NIL value of $3.4 million. Athletes like UCLA's Madison Kocian and UNC's Cole Anthony have generated approximately $4,000 per Instagram post. These examples underscore the potential for substantial earnings via NIL contracts. Even those with smaller followings, colloquially known as nano-influencers, can leverage their social media reach to generate NIL profit.

Indeed, social media furnishes a novel and accessible source of revenue for college athletes. Popular live streaming platforms such as Twitch offer another tool to gain additional income. For example, athletes can host a live stream where they are playing a video game and gain followers to grow their platform on other social media sites like Instagram. College athlete streamers with sizable followings can amass substantial monthly incomes based on their viewership, thereby diversifying financial opportunities.

Some of the positive impacts of NIL on college sports include:

1. **Earning Opportunities for a Wide Range of Athletes**: One of the most notable benefits of NIL is the wide range of athletes who can now earn income. This encompasses stars in high-revenue sports, walk-ons, and those participating in non-revenue sports. This diversity counters initial predictions that only a select few would benefit significantly under NIL laws.

2. **Empowering Female Athletes**: NIL has not disadvantaged female athletes; instead, it has arguably empowered them. Female athletes have thrived in the NIL space, earning money, and gaining a platform to promote gender equity in sports. This change has bolstered women's sports and elevated its charismatic athletes.

3. **Transparency and Fairness**: NIL has eradicated questions and suspicions surrounding athlete financial situations. Previously, inquiries about athlete finances were common, often with racial undertones. Now, these concerns have largely dissipated, fostering a more transparent and equitable environment.

4. **Education and Staying in School**: NIL enables athletes to continue their education while earning money. This option benefits those who prioritize education and provides additional opportunities for schools to retain athletes for longer durations. The money some athletes receive can disincentivize them from leaving college early for the pros.

5. **Talent Distribution**: NIL has the potential to disperse talent across a wider range of schools, augmenting competitive balance. Athlete decisions can now factor in financial considerations, contributing to a more equitable distribution of talent.

6. **Financial Literacy**: NIL promotes financial literacy among athletes, equipping them with the knowledge to make informed decisions about contracts, taxes, savings, and investments. It furnishes valuable real-world business experience.

NIL has also offered important benefits to female athletes. Decades of exclusion, inequality, and limited opportunities have marred the history of women's involvement in college sports. Despite the presence of Title IX, male athletes enjoyed superior financial backing, media exposure, and personal branding opportunities, while their female counterparts have endured systemic disparities. While Title IX has increased involvement and scholarship opportunities for women, NIL rights have the potential to serve as a further catalyst to increased economic opportunities for female athletes.

With NIL, every NCAA female athlete now possesses a platform to share her narrative, affording her a voice and platform previously unavailable. This change carries far-reaching consequences for the future of women's college sports. NIL's impact on women in college sports becomes evident through the endorsement deals and sponsorships secured by female athletes. In the most recent March Madness basketball season, four out of the top five NIL earners were women. As of May 2022, female basketball players ranked third in NIL earnings across all NCAA sports, trailing only football and men's basketball players. Additionally, other women's non-revenue sports like volleyball, softball, swimming, and diving outpaced several men's non-revenue sports in terms of NIL earnings.

These statistics stand in stark contrast to the historical disparities faced by women athletes in college sports. Despite Title IX regulations, numerous athletic departments still fall short in providing equitable financial support, facilities, and opportunities for female athletes. This unequal treatment extends to media coverage, where women's sports have historically received inadequate representation, with just 5.1% of overall sports coverage on platforms like SportsCenter devoted to women's sports in 2019.

NIL legislation is bridging this gap by creating fresh opportunities for female athletes to earn income, gain recognition, and advocate for important causes. Female athletes are now securing endorsement deals and sponsorships that were previously elusive. This increased visibility not only benefits the athletes themselves but also challenges traditional gender biases and stereotypes in sports.

NIL allows women to bypass traditional barriers to exposure and its accompanying benefits. This applies not only to high-profile college athletes with substantial social media followings but also to lesser-known athletes who can leverage their unique skills and content to secure NIL agreements. Athletes like Emily Cole of Duke track and field, Audrey and Nicole Nourse of USC beach volleyball, Jaiden Fields of UGA softball, and many others have harnessed NIL to create opportunities and amplify their influence.

The future of women's athletics holds promise, with NIL empowering female athletes to receive the recognition and financial benefits they rightfully deserve. As more and more female athletes utilize NIL to break down barriers and enact change both on and off the field, one can anticipate a future that is more equitable and prosperous for women in college sports. NIL is not merely reshaping how the perception and support of women in college sports, but also equipping them with the tools to shape their own futures and inspire the next generation of female athletes.

Beyond its impact on gender equality, NIL is opening unique opportunities for star athletes. One example is Caleb Williams, the Heisman Trophy-winning quarterback for the University of Southern California. A generational talent and the first pick in the 2024 NFL draft, Williams possesses unusual leverage due in part to NIL. His father has suggested that he could have opted to return to college for his senior year and not enter the draft if he did not want to play for the team that has the first pick. Historically, star players would never make such a decision, but in the NIL era, Williams can receive sufficient endorsement money to support a decision to delay entry into the NFL if he chose to make that decision.

Indeed, Williams enjoys NIL deals with prominent companies such as Fanatics, AT&T, Beats by Dre, and United Airlines among others. Pete Nakos of the sports news outlet, On3, valued Williams' NIL revenue at $2.8 million, fifth overall in college athletics. For reference, the first pick in the 2022 NFL Draft, Travon Walker, received a $3.5 million salary after a bonus. Williams has also reportedly wanted to explore receiving a share of ownership of whichever NFL decides to draft him. One can imagine a future in which star college athletes

leverage college NIL money against NFL money
when deciding when to enter the NFL draft.

Another example of the increased opportunities
NIL offers is Shedeur Sanders, the quarterback for
the University of Colorado. The son of NFL Hall of
Famer and Colorado head coach Deion Sanders,
Sanders is one of the most marketable college football
players in the country. The younger Sanders has an
extensive portfolio of endorsement deals, including
with Adidas, Gatorade, Beats by Dre, and Mercedes-
Benz. Sanders has also launched his own
merchandise line, which includes apparel,
accessories, and collectibles. According to On3
Sports, his NIL deals are worth $4.8 million
annually, making him one of the highest-paid
athletes in college football.

Beyond the remuneration, Sanders' NIL deals
have also helped him to build his brand and to
increase his exposure and have made him one of the
most recognizable college football players in the
country. Further, Sanders has used his NIL deals to
promote social justice and to support Historically
Black Colleges and Universities (HBCUs). A former
HBCU player himself at Jackson State, Shedeur
Sanders has served as a role model for other college
athletes, and worked to enhance opportunities for
other athletes.

Likewise, other college athletes are using their
NIL opportunities to make a difference in the world.
They are donating their NIL earnings to charities,
starting their own nonprofits, and raising awareness
for important causes. USC quarterback Caleb

Williams offered his offensive line an NIL deal, a paying it forward sentiment that is becoming more common in NIL arrangements.

Some other examples include:

- Nick Evers, University of Oklahoma quarterback: Evers is donating a portion of his NIL earnings to the Make-A-Wish Foundation.

- Tyler Linderbaum, Iowa offensive lineman: Linderbaum donated $30,000 to the University of Iowa Children's Hospital.

- Dillan Gibbons, Florida State offensive lineman: Gibbons started a GoFundMe fundraiser to help his friend Timothy, who has autism, attend his first college football game. The fundraiser raised over $55,000.

- Blake Corum, former University of Michigan running back: Corum started the Blake Corum Foundation to provide uniforms and other sports equipment to underprivileged youth.

- Harry Miller, Ohio State center: Miller is donating all of his NIL earnings to humanitarian efforts in Nicaragua.

- Jack Bech, LSU tight end: Bech is donating a portion of his NIL earnings to the Dreams Come True Foundation, which grants wishes to sick children.

- Stetson Bennett IV, former University of Georgia quarterback: Bennett and four of his teammates started the DGD Fund, which donates to a variety of charities, including the ALS Association and Hilinski's Hope, a foundation that supports mental health awareness in college football.

NIL in college sports represents a transformative change that offers numerous positive outcomes. It empowers athletes from various sports, enhances gender equity, eliminates financial questions, promotes education, spreads talent, and fosters financial literacy. This new era in college athletics holds promise for athletes to capitalize on their hard work, talent, and marketability while simultaneously benefiting universities and brands.

CHAPTER FIVE
THE TRANSFER PORTAL

For decades, the NCAA rules had the practical effect of limiting transfers by athletes from one institution to another. In the past few years, however, rule changes and litigation have opened the door to widespread transfers by athletes. The current environment is a free agency of sorts, without contracts that limit future movement. Recruiting has become a constant and never-ending pursuit, with coaches having to recruit new athletes as well as recruit their current athletes to stay.

This chapter details these changes and this new landscape of the transfer portal.

1. THE EVOLUTION OF NCAA TRANSFER RULES

Historically, the NCAA imposed a "residency rule." The residency rule allowed transfers to participate in the practices and workouts of the team, but prohibited participation in athletic competitions for one year (two semesters or three quarters) after the transfer. 2017–18 NCAA Division I Manual, Bylaw 14.5.5.1. For undergraduate students at four-year universities, the residency rule applied to all transfers, unless the NCAA granted a hardship exception.

For graduate students, a separate graduate transfer rule applied. 2017–18 NCAA Division I Manual, Bylaw 14.5. It required transfers in bowl subdivision football, basketball, baseball, and men's ice hockey to follow the residency rule and sit out for a year.

An additional requirement under the old transfer rule required that the athletic director release the athlete to transfer before the athlete could receive any eligibility. Over time, the NCAA began increasingly granting transfer waivers.

In 2017, the NCAA changed the transfer rule to allow graduate students to be immediately eligible to play. In October 2018, it launched the transfer portal, where athletes could officially renounce their current scholarship and provide notice of their desire to transfer.

In 2021, the NCAA broadened its rule again, granting the ability of athletes to transfer one time without any restriction on athletic participation. 2023–24 NCAA Division I Manual, Bylaw 14.5.

This change has dramatically affected college sports. Many coaches do not sign a full complement of high school seniors, choosing instead to fill their roster with transfers. In 2023–24, over three thousand players entered the transfer portal. This kind of free agency means that the star player on a less successful team could find himself helping a stronger team to a championship the following season.

As of the fall of 2023, the NCAA rules did not allow a second transfer without the imposition of the residency requirement. 2023–24 NCAA Division I Manual, Bylaw 14.5. It began to decrease its former practice of granting waivers readily for athletes trying to transfer a second time.

This new practice of limiting the second transfer led to a lawsuit filed in December 2023 challenging the practice. In December, 2023, Ohio Attorney General Dave Yost led a seven-state lawsuit alleging that the limit on transfers violated the Sherman Act. The states involved as plaintiffs are Ohio, Colorado, Illinois, New York, North Carolina, Tennessee, and West Virginia. The West Virginia federal district court granted a preliminary injunction against the NCAA. *Ohio v. NCAA*, 2023 WL 9103711 (N.D. W.Va. 2023). Specifically, it temporarily barred enforcement of NCAA Bylaws 14.5 and 12.11.4.2, the latter of which provides for restitution by the university that allows an ineligible player to participate. 2023–24 NCAA Division I Manual, Bylaw 12.11.4.2. The injunction will remain in place at least until the end of the Spring 2024 semester. Chapter Six explores possible future consequences of *Ohio v. NCAA*.

In April 2024, the NCAA proposed a rule change to remove restrictions on additional transfers beyond the first one. The same requirements for transfers otherwise apply—the student must be in good academic standing at their current institution and meeting progress-toward-degree requirements.

2. THE APPLICATION OF TRANSFER PORTAL RULES

In light of the shifting NCAA transfer rules, it is instructive to explain their application to individual athletes.

1. Timing and the NCAA Transfer Portal:

- Athletes should start the transfer process only when certain about their decision.

- An athlete's current scholarship remains intact once while initiating the transfer process. Even so, the guarantee of a future scholarship for the following academic term disappears. If an athlete decides to stay at their current school after starting the transfer process, the university can rescind their scholarship.

2. Accessing the NCAA Transfer Portal:

- To access the NCAA Transfer Portal, an athlete must provide written notice to their university's designated administrator.

- Without written notice, NCAA coaches at other institutions cannot contact or otherwise recruit athletes.

3. Transfer Window by Sport:

- Depending on the sport, there are specific transfer windows during which athletes can enter the NCAA Transfer Portal. These windows are related to championship selections for each sport (e.g., bowl game announcements for fall sports).

4. Walk-Ons:

- If an athlete was a walk-on at your previous college, an athlete can be a walk-on at your new college, regardless of whether their previous college recruited them or offered scholarships in their sport.

5. Redshirting:

- As of April 2021, D1 athletes transferring schools for the first time no longer have to redshirt for a year before competing.

- Subsequent transfers may require sitting out a season unless you obtain a waiver from the NCAA.

- Redshirting can still be beneficial for adjusting to a new school and coach.

6. Eligibility Clock:

- Athletes are eligible to compete in games for four years, with a five-year clock to complete those four years.

- The clock starts when an athlete become a full-time student and typically pauses when an athlete is not a full-time student.

7. Transferring Between Divisions:

- Transferring from D3 to D2 or D1 requires registration with the NCAA Eligibility Center.

- Transferring to another D3 school only requires filling out the NCAA Self-Release form.

- NAIA students transferring to an NCAA school may need approval from the NCAA Eligibility Center, a permission-to-contact letter, and a release from their current NAIA school.

8. **Multiple Transfers:**

- NCAA colleges allow multiple transfers. Some transfers used to come with penalties, especially if one transfers to a four-year college for the second time, but the proposed rule would eliminate any penalties.

- The nature of the penalty varies depending on specific circumstances, but can include sitting out for a season prior to receiving eligibility. Again, this is not likely to exist under the rule change.

9. **Minimum GPA:**

- Most colleges require a GPA of 2.0 to play a sport. Even so, four-year schools might have higher GPA requirements for transfer students from two-year colleges.

10. **Junior College Transfer Rules:**

- Transferring between two-year colleges generally does not require a release for other junior college coaches to contact you.

- Transferring from a junior college to a four-year school involves meeting NCAA eligibility requirements and GPA requirements specific to the school.

11. NCAA Graduate Transfer Rules:

- An athlete can participate in sports as a graduate student, but must meet certain requirements, such as graduating from their current college, having remaining eligibility on their five-year clock, and enrolling in a graduate school that offers their sport.

12. Assistance:

- NCAA transfer rules can be complex and sport-specific. Athletes should seek assistance from experts or resources like NCSA to navigate the transfer process and gain a better understanding of the rules applicable to their situation.

These rules are essential for student-athletes considering transferring between colleges within the NCAA system. They provide guidance on eligibility, scholarship considerations, and the transfer process.

3.   IMPACT OF THE TRANSFER PORTAL

Created on October 15, 2018, the NCAA Transfer Portal has become a polarizing topic of discussion in the world of college athletics. The NCAA originally intended transfer portal to be a compliance system to develop an efficient transfer process for athletes who are looking to switch to a different school and play for said school's team. As it functions, the portal is an online database platform available to coaches, players, and schools. The Transfer Portal provides a way for athletes to express their interest in playing for other programs.

The growth of the transfer portal since its inception has been exponential. In 2018–19, 4.076 football players entered the transfer portal. By 2021–22, that number had doubled to 8,242. It increased to 8,699 in 2022–23, with 3,284 of those players being FBS schools. The University of Colorado and Ole Miss were particularly active in the portal prior to the 2023 football season. With the arrival of new coach Deion Sanders, Colorado sent seventy-one players into the portal and acquired eighty-six new players through the portal. Ole Miss coach Lane Kiffin, using his Twitter mantra of "Come to the Sip" sent forty-eight players into the portal and brought in fifty-six new players.

With the introduction of the Transfer Portal, the intrigue surrounding NCAA transfer approvals has heightened. Part of this heightened interest relates to the novelty of a digital tool managing the process, and part relates to the portal itself being inaccessible to the media and the general public.

The Transfer Portal serves as an organized system for handling a complex process. Among those who benefit most from its creation are compliance administrators. The time-saving capabilities of the portal are significant, though the exact amount of time saved can vary depending on the unique challenges of each transfer case. Prior to the portal, certain aspects took immense amount of time to perform, but now the portal allows for completion within minutes.

Dede Allen, the associate director for compliance and academics at Alaska Anchorage, praised the transfer portal as one of the most remarkable uses of technology in recent times. Allen recognized that the portal ensures that everyone who needs access to the information can obtain it promptly. The portal effectively streamlines players' transfer goals without unnecessary obstacles.

Even so, the use of the portal in Division II is optional for some schools, which can lead to occasional frustration. Still, it represents a significant step in the evolution of this system, especially considering that it's only been in operation for a short time.

Sean McAndrews, associate athletics director for compliance and game administration at West Virginia State, has noted that the portal saves valuable time for compliance tasks, allowing administrators in Division II, who often have multiple roles, to be more efficient.

The NCAA transfer portal's best attribute remains its dynamic and up-to-the-minute functionality. This feature empowers compliance administrators to swiftly compile reports encompassing a diverse array of data metrics. These reports can encompass statistics on the volume of athletes actively seeking transfers, categorized by sport, institution, or conference.

The portal plays a pivotal role in assisting the NCAA's research team by serving as a centralized repository for transfer-related data. It also eradicates the necessity of relying on individual educational institutions or conferences for information pertaining to the movement of athletes. This aggregated data proves to be an invaluable asset for NCAA members as they engage in in-depth analyses and strive to enhance the overall transfer process. It not only streamlines administrative tasks but also fosters a more informed and data-driven approach to transfer policies and regulations within the NCAA.

The Transfer Portal connects to Division I's new notification-of-transfer model, introduced for the 2018–19 academic year. This model empowers student-athletes by allowing them to request entry into the portal without needing permission from their current school. Once a student-athlete expresses this desire, the school has two business days to submit the information.

It is important to note that individual schools are responsible for establishing policies regarding portal requests. Even so, there is a downside for student-athletes. Their current school can reduce or terminate athletic aid at the end of the term in which the athlete makes the transfer request.

Therefore, before entering the portal, athletes should have discussions with their families about how they will finance their college education if another scholarship opportunity does not materialize. If an athlete decides to withdraw from the portal, the original school can reinstate them on the roster and restore their athletic aid.

This new system provides accountability for athletes and protects the investments made by schools in the recruiting process. Previously, in Division I, athletes had to seek permission from their coach to contact other schools for transfer opportunities. If denied, they could appeal to the athletic director. Those athletes who transferred without permission were ineligible for athletic aid at their new school. The current transfer portal represents a significant improvement over the old, labor-intensive process, streamlining administrative tasks and providing a centralized platform for managing transfers.

There is a prevalent misconception surrounding the NCAA Transfer Portal, relating to transfer waivers. Many individuals mistakenly believe that the transfer portal directly influences the decisions the NCAA makes regarding transfer waivers. Such waivers allow for transfers when the rules do not allow them. But the transfer portal serves a different purpose even while indirectly drawing attention to the NCAA's waiver process.

In Division I of the NCAA, athletes can typically transfer once to another four-year NCAA school without losing the eligibility to compete immediately. The athlete receives this privilege as long as they meet specific academic eligibility requirements.

The transfer rules can create challenges for NCAA athletes. One example involved Tez Walker, a wide receiver for the University of North Carolina Tar Heels. He was a two-time transfer, having previously played at North Carolina Central and Kent State. The NCAA deemed Walker ineligible by the NCAA prior to the start of the 2023 season because he had transferred twice.

Walker appealed to the NCAA for a waiver to restore his eligibility for the 2023 season. He cited his desire to be close to his sick grandmother and the COVID-19 pandemic as reasons for his transfers. The NCAA, however, denied his request, making Walker ineligible for the 2023 season.

Walker's case drew significant public attention to the NCAA's transfer rules, which some argued were too restrictive. Walker's supporters pointed out that he did not play his freshman season at North Carolina Central because of the pandemic, and that he transferred to Kent State in search of a better opportunity. They also argued that the NCAA should consider Walker's mental health challenges. The NCAA initially defended its decision, arguing that its rules are in place to protect athletes from academic and athletic exploitation. Additionally, the NCAA claimed that its rules help to maintain competitive balance among schools and that the University of North Carolina did not include key information in its appeal. Walker's case demonstrates the challenges that athletes face in the current college sports landscape. It is also a reminder of the power that the NCAA still can have over the lives of athletes.

On October 5, 2023, the NCAA reversed its decision and granted Tez Walker eligibility to play in the 2023 season. The NCAA said that it had received new information from the University North Carolina not previously disclosed. Prior to the recent rule change, two-time transfers typically had to sit out for a season after a second transfer. But the NCAA's transfer rules allow for a waiver and a grant of immediate eligibility if the athlete has a "bona fide reason" for transferring. In Walker's case, the NCAA found that his sick grandmother provided the bona fide reason to transfer from Kent State in Ohio back to his home in North Carolina.

It is important to understand that the transfer portal itself does not determine the outcomes of these waiver requests. Instead, the responsibility for evaluating and deciding on waiver requests lies with NCAA staff members who process them. The NCAA assesses such requests on a case-by-case basis. The approval of waiver requests hinges on whether they align with the eleven waiver standards established by Division I rules. To gain approval, the request must demonstrate extenuating and extraordinary mitigating circumstances that were beyond the athlete's control. In cases where the NCAA denies waivers, athletes may appeal to the Division I Committee for Legislative Relief.

Most waiver requests typically fall into several categories, such as the absence of participation opportunities at the previous school, egregious behavior, athlete injury or illness, or family member injury or illness. Even so, some requests do not fit neatly into these predefined categories and their evaluation depends upon the overall circumstances surrounding the transfer.

It is important to acknowledge that many of the waiver requests that receive significant attention come from the revenue sports of men's and women's basketball and football. These sports naturally draw more scrutiny, and when there is disagreement with waiver decisions, the NCAA often faces criticism. Even so, the NCAA assesses each waiver case independently, based on its unique case. The transfer portal's role is primarily to facilitate the transfer process and streamline administrative tasks, making it distinct from the waiver decision-making process.

Under the proposed rule, fewer cases will face restrictions related to transfers. Those that do will most often relate to athletes who are not in good standing academically.

The NCAA Transfer Portal represents a significant advancement in managing student-athlete transfers, enhancing efficiency and transparency in the process. While it has garnered substantial interest and some opposition, its central function is not directly related to making waiver decisions. Instead, it serves as a valuable tool for simplifying administrative procedures and simplifying transfer-related tasks, marking a positive step forward in the realm of college athletics.

While the new rule marks an additional step for athlete flexibility and freedom, it raises additional questions about the need to rethink the overall model. An environment where coaches constantly recruit athletes can provide opportunity for some, but undermine the traditional model of player development.

Former Kentucky and current Arkansas basketball coach John Calipari has suggested as much, noting he is considering having only eight or nine scholarship athletes on his basketball team. If players have the ability and are even likely to move schools on an annual basis, the incentive for coaches to develop the athletes diminishes.

The free agency type arrangement also diminishes loyalty on both sides of the athlete-coach relationship, with each incentivized to pursue short-term gain. A better model, at least for the revenue sports, might be one that created two-year contracts in which athletes agreed to stay for a two-year term as part of a revenue sharing agreement.

While the future is uncertain, the Transfer Portal is likely to remain central to the success and failure of college sports teams, at least in the next five years.

CHAPTER SIX

THE CHANGE AGENTS
OF ANTITRUST AND
EMPLOYMENT LAW

1. THE CHANGE AGENT
OF ANTITRUST LAW

Three change agents exist to the NCAA's student-athlete model: antitrust law, employment law, and conference realignment. This chapter and the next consider the ways in which these agents have effectuated change and might have future impacts as well.

Antitrust law is a problem for the NCAA because its organization constitutes, by its very nature, a horizontal restraint of trade. All of the participants in the market for college athletics have united under the umbrella of the NCAA. This means that economic competition between schools for athletic recruits is non-existent.

Historically, the NCAA challenged this conception of its organization on the basis that its member institutions offer education, with sports being a part of that education. In other words, intercollegiate sports is non-economic in nature. Student-athletes participate not as part of an economic market, but as part of an avocation while pursuing a degree.

Much in the same way that the Supreme Court's decision in *Federal Baseball Club v. National League*, 259 U.S. 200 (1922) decided baseball did not constitute interstate commerce because exhibitions took place in one location and were non-economic in nature, a decision that college sports is non-economic seems dubious. The Court in *Board of Regents* in 1984 noted as much, and since then, college sports has become a multi-billion dollar industry annually. *NCAA v. Board of Regents of University of Oklahoma*, 468 U.S. 85 (1984).

Under the rule of reason, though, the NCAA's rules can exist if they promote economic competition in an alternative market. The amateurism defense in this context suggests that the success of the product in the market—college sports viewership and attendance in the entertainment market—depends upon the student-athlete model. In other words, without the NCAA's limits on athlete compensation and requirements that athletes pursue a degree, college sports would lose its distinctiveness in the market and become economically damaged in a way that would hamper its ability to compete economically. The argument is that these horizontal restraints are essential to the character of the product in the market, with the restrictions in the market for athlete services enabling universities to compete in the market for entertainment.

The NCAA had long argued that the dicta in *Board of Regents* established as much and provided an antitrust defense to its limits on athlete compensation. In *Alston*, the Supreme Court finally rejected this reading of *Board of Regents*, holding definitively that the NCAA is subject to antitrust laws. It explained that amateurism, on its face, does

not justify the NCAA's economic restraints, at least
with respect to limits on compensation "related to"
education. *NCAA v. Alston*, 594 U.S. 69 (2021).

Justice Kavanaugh's concurrence suggested that
the NCAA's other rules might also violate antitrust
law because they were not essential to preserving the
product in the market. If anything, his opinion has
emboldened plaintiffs to challenge NCAA rules under
the Sherman Act.

Indeed, the amount of money paid to college
athletes seems to have little or no effect upon the
desire of fans to attend and watch the games. The
implementation of NIL payments has shown as
much. This echoes the same NCAA argument that
the Court rejected in *Board of Regents*: televising the
games has not decreased attendance at games. If the
NCAA rule in question does not protect the product
of college sports in a way that its absence would lead
to diminished interest, then the rule lacks
justification under the Sherman Act.

As explored below, one wonders how far the
antitrust law really goes. If fans and alumni literally
just cheer for the laundry, then the NCAA's entire
scheme violates federal law. In other words, if Duke
fans will attend the Duke basketball games and
cheer for the team as long as they wear Duke jerseys,
then all amateurism rules, including academic ones,
fail as a defense under the Sherman Act.

Academic rules, however, seem to have more of a
justification, to the extent that the reason people
spend money to support college sports in the market

relates to the participants in sport being actual students. Many college sports fans are not fans of professional sports, or at least, not to the degree that they are fans of college sports.

Economic limits, such as the current bar on pay-for-play, seem less promising under the Sherman Act. With NIL payments doing little to deter fan interest, payments from universities to athletes also seem unlikely to negatively impact the market for college sports. The shift would simply be expanding the class of acceptable payors, from third party boosters to universities. If anything, the amount of remuneration may be more likely to have an impact on the market for college sports. But leaving the question up to the free market would be exactly the remedy that antitrust law would promote.

One can see why the NCAA and its members institutions have continued to lobby Congress for an antitrust exemption after the Court declined to accord on in *Alston*. But after months of advocacy and a series of hearings, a federal NIL law exempting the NCAA and its member institutions from antitrust law seems unlikely. One recent report indicated that the NCAA and the Power conferences had collectively spent over $15 million in this lobbying effort.

The other ominous part to the equation for the NCAA and its member institutions relates to the calculation of economic damages under the antitrust law. For violations of the Sherman Act, parties must pay treble damages—tripling the amount of economic damage calculated by the jury. And the Sherman Act also provides for attorneys' fees, with the losing party responsible for paying the winner's lawyers. This provision encourages plaintiffs' lawyers to bring antitrust cases, even where their clients cannot afford to pay their fees.

Over time, one can imagine these costs becoming unsustainable. The *House* case, discussed in the next subsection, has an estimated damages amount in excess of $4 billion. Compliance with antitrust law by removing economic limits on pay-for-play could be even worse. Without restrictions, the market for athlete services becomes an open one, with star players going to the highest bidder coming out of high school.

Athletic departments may argue that this market will be shallow. After all, most athletic departments lose money. Even for the twenty or so schools that turn a profit, the amount of money does not seem to allow for many multi-million dollar contracts.

But in an open market, all bets are off, with the historical win-at-all-costs mantra likely to emerge. The current expansion of NIL and increasing annual contributions to collectives reflects this reality.

This means in practice that the massive redistribution from revenue to non-revenue sports will diminish if not disappear. Fans will certainly pressure athletic departments to spend more revenue on a star offensive tackle than on facilities and uniforms for the wrestling team or the lacrosse team. Non-revenue sports will quickly become club sports, perhaps with the exception of the few elite programs in the country like Stanford and Texas that regularly produce Olympic athletes.

The proposition becomes even more controversial when faculty realize that the university is spending tens of millions of dollars annually on athletes instead of academics. The current model largely silos athletics money from the academic budget, but one wonders if entrepreneurial presidents might see the largesse of college football revenue as a tool by which to boost academic departments.

Title IX, explored more thoroughly in Chapter Nine, will serve as a bulwark of sorts, but may only have limited applicability. It requires gender equity in the sense that the breakdown by gender of athletic scholarships offered must be proportional to the gender breakdown of the entire student body. This could mean that a few women's sports survive at a varsity, scholarship level, but only enough to achieve proportionality with football and men's basketball.

Athletics departments could circumvent these requirements in several ways. First, if athletes were employees of a private organization, whether a university foundation or collective, Title IX's limits presumably would not apply. This argument would be stronger with collectives given the nature to which some universities control their foundations. Second, athletes could be employees of the conference for purposes of pay-for-play. And with the NCAA not subject to Title IX (*NCAA v. Smith*, 525 U.S. 459 (1999)), conferences would similarly be unlikely to invoke Title IX scrutiny as institutions not funded by federal government.

Another option to avoid antitrust scrutiny relates to labor law. The National Labor Relations Act (NLRA) and the Sherman Act are both federal statutes, but they have opposite goals. The NLRA promotes collective activity in the market through collective bargaining. The Sherman Act bars collective activity by employers as a restraint of trade.

The Supreme Court has held that a non-statutory labor exemption exists. That means that collective bargaining agreements between multiple employer units (potentially like the NCAA and its member institutions) with labor unions are exempt from antitrust law. *Brown v. Pro Football, Inc.*, 518 U.S. 231 (1996).

Creating a management-union relationship with the NCAA and college athletes would serve to bar antitrust claims against NCAA rules, as long as such rules were the product of a collective bargaining agreement with college athletes. The reason that the NCAA rules would be exempt from the Sherman Act is because the rules would be the product of collective bargaining.

In particular, a collective bargaining agreement would have the advantage of regulating player movement, creating a salary structure for players, and even imposing a salary cap. Athletes should consider the degree to which a free market model is preferable, for their interests, to the collectively bargained model adopted by almost all professional sports leagues.

There are, however, a number of obstacles to such a union framework. First, athletes would have to be university employees, a distinction that universities and the NCAA may not want to concede (see discussion later in this chapter). Further, many athletes would be employees of public institutions in states that are "right to work" states that ban public employee unions. Those states would need to amend their labor statutes to allow college athletes to form a public union.

As in the Title IX context, having the conferences serve as employers might be one way around the "right to work" state public union problem. Another way would be to have athletes be employees of collectives. Foundations might be another possibility, but as with Title IX, the close connection some have with the university might infringe upon right to work laws. The current move in Texas and other states to merge collectives with university foundations would give rise to the same set of problems.

Other complications could include whether all of the athletes can be in the same union. The economic position and demands of revenue sport athletes might be very different from non-revenue sport athletes. Nonetheless, with the recent formation of a union by Dartmouth basketball players, a union-based approach seems more possible than before.

Having described the antitrust threat, the next question is how the current antitrust challenges to NCAA rules and policies might fare going forward. There are a growing number of cases challenging NCAA rules under antitrust law.

2. HOUSE V. NAT'L COLLEGIATE ATHLETIC ASS'N

In 2020, named plaintiffs Grant House, an Arizona State University swimmer, Tymir Oliver, a former defensive lineman for Illinois, and Sedona Prince, a former TCU basketball player brought a class action antitrust claim against the NCAA. *House v. NCAA*, 545 F. Supp.3d 804 (N.D. Cal. 2021). The plaintiffs challenged the subset of NCAA rules that "prohibit student-athletes from receiving anything of value in exchange for the commercial use" of their NILs. Specifically, these bylaws prohibit student-athletes from endorsing any commercial product or service during their academic tenure, regardless of whether they receive compensation, as stated in Division I Bylaw 12.5.2.1. They also deny student-athletes any compensation for their NIL from external employment, as outlined in Division I Bylaws 12.4.1, 12.4.1.1, and 12.4.2.3. Further, student-athletes cannot use their NIL to promote personal business ventures or engage in self-employment, according to Division I Bylaw 12.4.4.

The state laws passed in 2021 do make some of these bylaws now unenforceable, at least with respect to remuneration from collectives, boosters, and other third parties. But the challenged rules also allegedly prohibit NCAA member conferences and schools from sharing the revenue they make from their broadcasting contracts with networks, marketing contracts with companies that make sports apparel, social medial sponsorships, and other commercial activities that involve the use of athlete NILs.

Specifically, the Plaintiffs argue that the NCAA violated the Sherman Act in two main ways: (1) by preventing student-athletes from receiving compensation for the use, sale, and licensing of their NILs, and (2) by banning student-athletes from entering the market that involves the utilization, licensing, and sale of their NILs.

The court has certified three classes of plaintiffs in the case. First, there is the "Declaratory and Injunctive Relief Class," which includes all current and former student-athletes who have competed in an NCAA Division I athletic team anytime from four years before the filing of the Complaint (2016) until the judgment date. This class seeks an injunction to prevent the NCAA from capping the NIL revenue this class can earn.

Next is the "Social Media Damages Sub-Class" which includes athletes at Power conference schools who competed from 2016 to the present. These plaintiffs aim to recover NIL revenue, including potential social media earnings, that NCAA rules blocked them from pursuing.

Last is the "Group Licensing Damages Sub-Class," which includes athletes from NCAA Division I basketball or FBS football teams at Power conference schools from 2016 to the present. These plaintiffs seek a share of the revenue generated from the group licensing of game broadcasts.

According to the plaintiffs, the market in question for all of these antitrust claims is the nationwide market for the labor of NCAA Division I college athletes. Using the antitrust analysis from *O'Bannon* and *Alston*, the plaintiffs claim that consumer demand for college sports either cannot justify any of the restrictions on athlete compensation and revenue sharing, or alternatively, are unnecessary to achieve the desired pro-competitive effect in the market for college sports.

As in the earlier antitrust cases, the question becomes the degree to which the product of college sports (and its uniqueness) relates to the degree to which athletes receive compensation for the use of their NILs. If compensation for NILs reduces consumer demand in the market for college sports, then the restraint on NIL in the market for the services of college athletes will have some justification. If, on the other hand, NIL compensation does not affect the market demand for college sports, then the NIL restrictions violate antitrust law, with the court trebling any damages incurred.

To be clear, two distinct sets of NIL revenue were at issue in the case. First, the plaintiffs seek hypothetical NIL revenue that athletes could have earned from third parties between 2016–21 prior to the passage of state NIL laws on July 1, 2021. Second, the plaintiffs seek a share of the actual revenue earned by universities from their use of athlete NILs from 2016 to the present. This revenue includes compensation from the telecasts of college football and basketball games using group licenses.

Evidence from the fan response to the legalization of third party NIL payments—an absence of any negative effect on the market for college sports whatsoever—suggests that, at least with respect to third party payments, the NCAA rules violated antitrust law. And it likewise seems difficult for the NCAA to prove that sharing television revenue with college football and basketball players will do anything to decrease the economic demand for such sports.

Restyling the case as *In re College Athlete NIL Litigation*, the court has set it for trial in January 2025. Experts have estimated damages exceeding $4 billion.

Two other similar antitrust cases also followed *House. Carter v. NCAA* alleges that rules prohibiting schools from paying athletes violate antitrust laws, and *Hubbard v. NCAA* relates to retroactive *Alston* payments to athletes.

In May, 2024, the parties agreed to a proposed settlement of this case. The settlement, reported at $2.7 billion, also reportedly included a revenue sharing model going forward. This model would provide athletes with around 20% of the revenues per year as part of a ten year agreement. Part of the agreement also would include a reduction in the number of sports, and a move to make all sports head count sports, eliminating partial scholarships. Reports estimated the cost of this settlement at $300 million over ten years, or $30 million per year. Even if this settlement moves forward, it is not clear how it might bar future antitrust lawsuits challenging the fixing of the revenue at 20%.

The *Carter* case and the *Hubbard* case also are reportedly part of the settlement, with the plaintiffs in those cases dropping them.

Other changes might relate to the dropping of some non-revenue sports and the tightening of athletic department budgets. The NCAA also has to sort out how the new model complies with Title IX (see Chapter Nine).

3.   CHOH & KIRK V. BROWN UNIVERSITY

In March, 2023, former Brown men's basketball player Tamenang Choh and current women's basketball player Grace Kirk filed a class action lawsuit against the eight Ivy League institutions—Brown University, Columbia University, Cornell University, Dartmouth College, Harvard University, the University of Pennsylvania, Princeton University, Yale University—and the Ivy League Council of Presidents. *Choh & Kirk v. Brown University*, No. 3:23-cv-00305-AWT (D. Conn. 2023). Their lawsuit alleged that the Ivy League Agreement violates § 1 of the Sherman Act. The Ivy League Agreement is the agreement between the Ivy League schools not to provide scholarships for participation in intercollegiate athletics.

The lawsuit claims that the Ivy League universities are horizontal competitors in two distinct, but related, markets. First, they compete in the market for educational services for athletically and academically high-achieving ("AAHA") students. Second, they compete in the market for the athletic services of the AAHA students seeking to play for Ivy League teams.

While the plaintiffs allege that this restraint of trade is a per se violation of the antitrust law as a horizontal agreement, it is more likely that the court will assess the antitrust challenge under the rule of reason, as it typically does in cases involving college and professional sports. This may take the form of the shortened "quick look" rule of reason, but will nonetheless require balancing of a pro-competitive justification in an alternative market with the restraint in question.

In addition, the plaintiffs' complaint separately alleges that the Ivy League holds both monopoly and monopsony market power as the dominant providers of AAHA student education and purchasers of AAHA student athletic services. The anti-competitive effect, according to the Plaintiffs, is the suppression of competition between Ivy League schools where there exist no adequate substitutes (with apologies to Duke, Notre Dame, Georgetown, Stanford, and Rice).

Beyond the horizontal restraints that plaintiffs claim, they also allege that the Ivy League and its institutions have no pro-competitive justification for the restraints. Specifically, the plaintiffs argue that the Ivy League Agreement is unnecessary to (1) permit University Defendants to field teams in large numbers of intercollegiate sports; (2) assure competitive balance in athletics among University Defendants; (3) maintain or enhance academic excellence of University Defendants; and (4) allow University Defendants to provide financial aid, need based or merit, to non-AAHA students (given their sufficient resources from their individual billion dollar endowments). The plaintiffs conclude that even if a pro-competitive justification existed, a less restrictive alternative exists if the defendants "simultaneously maintain or enhance their academic excellence through agreement on minimum or average academic admissions standards, or both."

Unlike in *House*, the defendants here do have a number of possible pro-competitive justifications for maintaining their policy of not offering athletic scholarships. These include: (1) Ivy League student athletes are not a market that antitrust law ought to protect; (2) athletes are free to attend other colleges that offer solid athletic programs and impressive academics; (3) Ivy League schools do not have enough resources to pay for athletic scholarships and the money should go elsewhere; and the need to preserve the prestigious academic environments offered by these institutions.

The defendants have moved to dismiss the case, with a hearing set for May, 2024.

4.   OHIO V. NCAA

In December, 2023, the Attorney General of Ohio filed an antitrust suit against the NCAA on behalf of Ohio and six other states: Colorado, Illinois, New York, North Carolina, Tennessee, and West Virginia. *Ohio v. NCAA*, 2023 WL 9103711 (N.D. W.Va. 2023).

The plaintiffs sought a temporary restraining order blocking the NCAA from enforcing its transfer rule.

This meant convincing the court to bar enforcement of NCAA Bylaw 14.5, the transfer eligibility rule. 2023–24 NCAA Division I Manual, Bylaw 14.5. This bylaw allows athletes one transfer without restriction or consequence. But a second transfer requires that the athlete sit out for a season without eligibility to play in games, unless the NCAA grants a hardship waiver. The motion also requested that the court prohibit enforcement of NCAA Bylaw 12.11.4.2. 2023–24 NCAA Division I Manual, Bylaw 12.11.4.2. This bylaw allows the NCAA to punish universities for allowing two-time NCAA transfers to participate in games without receiving a waiver from the NCAA.

The plaintiffs' theory of the case related to its argument that the transfer rule violated the Sherman Act. As in *Alston*, *O'Bannon*, and *House*, the plaintiffs in *Ohio* claimed that the rule in question— the transfer rule—constituted an impermissible horizontal restraint of trade. By denying an athlete the ability to transfer a second time, the NCAA denies universities to compete for the athlete's services in the market for college athletics.

The district court granted the plaintiffs' motion for a temporary restraining order and subsequently entered a preliminary injunction against the NCAA enforcing its transfer rule. The injunction will remain in place at least until the end of the Spring 2024 semester.

To grant the restraining order, the court had to find a likelihood of success on the merits. In other words, it found that the plaintiffs had a reasonable chance of succeeding if the case goes to trial. First, the court explained that the horizontal restraint was the same kind that the Court disapproved of in *Alston*—a limit on the competition for athlete services. It pointed out that while the restraint in *Alston* related to paying the athletes "education related costs," the restraint in question in this case was more direct. The transfer rule places a direct consequence on competing in the market for a two-time transfer. This consequence is a one-year delay in eligibility to play.

The court found that the relevant market was the United States, and highlighted two broad categories of "sport-specific" labor markets—(1) the revenue sports market for the services of college football athletes and men's and women's basketball athletes; and (2) all other men's and women's Division I athletes. According to the court, the transfer rule harms athletes in three ways: (1) when making the decision whether to transfer; (2) when athletes decide to transfer and seek a new institution; and (3) when the NCAA denies two-time college athletes the ability to compete immediately at a new institution. The court also found that this rule harms consumers of college athletics by weakening their teams when transfers cannot play for a year.

The court also concluded that the NCAA's procompetitive justifications under the rule of reason were unlikely to survive antitrust scrutiny and were pretextual in nature. Specifically, the court rejected the idea that the transfer rule promoted "amateurism." Finding that the term amateurism did not have an ascertainable meaning, the court cast serious doubt on the idea that the transfer rule served to distinguish college sports from professional sports in the market. The court similarly rejected the idea that roster stability was a pro-competitive justification. It found no meaningful distinction between first-time transfers and second-time (or even subsequent) transfers. Indeed, the transfer rule really has nothing to do with athletes maintaining amateur status.

And even if the NCAA could establish a pro-competitive justification for the transfer rule, the court found that there were a number of less restrictive alternatives available and preferable to a one-year gap in eligibility. The academic rules already in place achieve the stated goals of the transfer rule. To the extent that the goal of the rule is to promote academics, the current progress toward degree requirements and minimum eligibility requirements already accomplish as much. Athletes cannot transfer unless they are in good standing and meet minimum grade-point average requirements.

Finally, the court found that athletes would suffer irreparable harm under the transfer rule if not allowed to compete. The court scheduled a trial for the summer of 2024. For the time being, college athletes can transfer multiple times without compromising their eligibility, even for a season.

As discussed in Chapter Five, the NCAA has recently proposed a new transfer rule that eliminates the restriction on the number of transfers an athlete can make. If the NCAA membership adopts the rule, the *Ohio* lawsuit will become moot.

5.   TENNESSEE AND VIRGINIA V. NCAA

When the NCAA issued its interim guidance on NIL in July, 2021, it articulated two basic limits on NIL. First, athletes could only receive NIL payments as just compensation for services rendered. In other words, boosters and collectives cannot offer payments to athletes without requiring something in return, whether appearances, advertisements, social media posts, or other promotional activities.

Second, universities, boosters, and collectives cannot use NIL deals as inducements for recruits to choose to play at their school. Further, this rule is not just an NCAA rule. Some state NIL laws also proscribe the same kinds of inducements.

The rationale behind these rules relates to an amateurism-type distinction that the NCAA is trying to make. Allowing athletes to enter into third-party endorsement deals does not compromise the athlete's relationship to the university. Even with NIL deals, then college athletes can maintain an amateur status much in the same way that Olympic athletes are amateurs. They receive third-party NIL payments for endorsements but do not receive pay-for-play, compensation for participating in athletic competitions.

Both payments independent of services rendered and inducement payments look like dressed up versions of pay-for-play. Paying an athlete "NIL money" but not requiring the athlete to render any services seems as if the payment is really for their participation in intercollegiate athletics. Similarly, using an NIL deal to induce an athlete to enroll in a university, whether after high school or as a transfer, also seems like a version of pay-for-play. As an inducement, the NIL payments serve to compensate the athlete for choosing to attend that particular school, even if the athlete ultimately renders services in exchange for the NIL money.

This amateurism distinction, however, may be one without real consequence now that state laws have legalized NIL payments. When athletes receive tens or hundreds of thousands of dollars, it does not seem to mean something different based on the identity of the payor. The origins of such payments do not seem to create a meaningful difference with respect to whether athlete participation is amateur or professional, despite the NCAA's rhetoric to the contrary. The NIL deals exist for athletes because of their status as athletes, even if not technically pay-for-play. If anything, remuneration from one's university (which has long existed in the form of tuition, room, board, and books) seems more closely connected to the historical student-athlete ideal than third-party booster payments do.

A coda to the anti-NIL inducement rule relates to its connection to federal criminal law. Interestingly, the NCAA amateurism rules give rise to mail fraud and wire fraud claims. If payments to athletes violate NCAA rules such that they deprive a university of an amateur athlete, that payment is a federal crime. And the use of NIL inducements seems similar to the federal bribes for which James Gatto and others have served time in prison. *United States v. Gatto*, 986 F.3d 104 (2d Cir. 2021).

In late 2023, the NCAA enforcement committee began increasingly investigating cases of NIL inducement—the use of NIL deals to recruit star athletes. In Chapters Two and Four, the Florida State and Miami cases offer early examples of attempts to sanction such inducements. In both cases, the universities entered into negotiated resolutions with the NCAA. *Florida State University, Negotiated Resolution*, Case No. 020169, January 12, 2024; *University of Miami (Florida), Negotiated Resolution*, Case No. 020161, February 24, 2023.

In early 2024, the NCAA was investigating University of Tennessee related to such inducements. The NCAA believed that Tennessee had major violations across several sports, including football for using NIL deals as inducements. The football case centered around the recruitment of star quarterback Nico Iamaleava, who signed a multi-million dollar contract with Spyre Sports Group allegedly made contingent on his choosing to play football with Tennessee.

On January 31, 2024, however, the attorney generals of Virginia and Tennessee filed a lawsuit in federal court alleging that the inducement rule violated federal antitrust law. Federal district judge

Clifton Corker issued a preliminary injunction barring the NCAA from enforcing all rules related to athletes and recruits negotiating compensation for NIL with collectives and boosters. *Tennessee & Virginia v. NCAA*, 2024 WL 755528 (E.D. Tenn. 2024).

As in *Ohio v. NCAA*, the question in the case with respect to the issuing of a preliminary injunction related to the court's view that the plaintiffs had a likelihood of success on the merits and that failing to issue an injunction would cause irreparable harm. Like in *O'Bannon* and *Alston*, the court found that the NIL inducement rule likely constituted a horizontal restraint of trade. Specifically, barring inducements prohibits the discussion of price in the market when an athlete weighs one scholarship offer against another. Such an agreement to not discuss price until after one commits to a school suppresses price competition by limiting negotiating leverage and, as a result, knowledge of value.

The court similarly found that the NCAA would be unlikely to show adequate pro-competitive justifications for the NIL rule, and further, the absence of other less restrictive alternatives. While the NCAA contended that allowing collectives to offer NIL deals as a recruiting inducement "would eviscerate the distinction between the collegiate structure and professional sports and undermine the unique balance of academics and athletics that the NCAA structure provides," the court did not agree. Specifically, the court found that the timing of when athletes entered NIL deals was immaterial to their status as amateurs. In short, the court rejected the NCAA's thin distinction between NIL payments as legitimate amateurism payments and NIL inducements as illegitimate professional pay-for-play payments.

The court also found that the NCAA's current eligibility rules and academic requirements were far more successful, and less restrictive, means of promoting amateurism. To the extent that college athletes has an amateurism component after the advent of NIL payments, it relates to the educational requirements imposed by the NCAA. Finally, the court also rejected the NCAA's argument that the NIL-inducement rule protects competitive balance or athlete welfare as pro-competitive defenses justifying the economic restraint.

As with the transfer rule case, the injunction against the NCAA sanctioning NIL-inducements will stay in place for months, at least until the case goes to trial. That does not, however, seem imminent.

On March 1, 2024, NCAA President Charlie Baker indicated that the enforcement committee would cease investigating and prosecuting NIL-inducement violations. His memo announcing this change in approach indicated his belief that the NCAA should shape NIL policy in the boardroom, not the courtroom. And yet, barring intervention by Congress, the NCAA will face the same decision— change its amateurism rules or face another antitrust case.

6.   EMPLOYEE ATHLETES?

The historical answer to this question has been no. But it is possible that this may change soon. Before exploring the answer of courts to this question, it is worth highlighting some of the many consequences of determining that athletes are university employees.

A determination that college athletes are university employees would have significant and far-reaching consequences. Athletes would have to pay taxes on their remuneration, and their university employers would have to accord all of the human resource benefits it accords other employees. This would likely include health insurance. In addition, a series of federal and state employment laws, not just the NLRA, would apply to athletes. These include workers' compensation, unemployment compensation, anti-discrimination, health and safety, and disability laws. Finally, as explored in several cases below, the Fair Labor Standards Act (FLSA) and parallel state laws would apply, requiring colleges and universities to pay athletes minimum wage and overtime.

In 1977, Texas Christian University (TCU) running back Kent Waldrep sued for workers' compensation benefits after sustaining a broken neck during a game against the University of Alabama. Waldrep's injury resulted in permanent paralysis from the neck down.

Waldrep's lawsuit turned on whether he was an employee of the university. The Texas Court of Appeals affirmed the jury's 10–2 finding that

Waldrep was not an employee of TCU. *Waldrep v. Texas Employers Insurance Association*, 21 S.W.3d 692 (Texas Ct. App. 2000). Specifically, the court noted that Waldrep did not have a contract of hire and TCU did not direct his "work." Waldrep could not receive to workers' compensation benefits.

More recent challenges by athletes to their classification as employees have come under the Fair Labor Standards Act (FLSA). The FLSA requires employers to provide their workers with the federal minimum wage. College athletes have argued that they are employees for purposes of the FLSA which entitles them to minimum wage.

The language of the FLSA provides that "employers" must pay their "employees" a minimum wage and overtime pay for hours worked in excess of the statutory workweek. 29 U.S.C. §§ 206(a), 207(a)(1). The statute defines an "employee" as "any individual employed by an employer." 29 U.S.C. § 203(e)(1). To "employ" means "to suffer or permit to work." 29 U.S.C. § 203(g). This circular language does little to provide an answer as to whether college athletes are university employees.

In 2016, University of Pennsylvania women's track and field athletes Gillian Berger and Taylor Hennig sued the NCAA alleging that the NCAA's limits on compensation violated the FLSA. They claimed that their athletic participation demonstrated they were employees. Because they were employees, Penn owed them minimum wage for the time they spent on their sport. The district court granted the NCAA's motion to dismiss the case. And the Seventh Circuit Court of

Appeals affirmed. *Berger v. NCAA*, 843 F.3d 285 (7th Cir. 2016).

Both courts rejected the idea that college athletes are university employees. The Seventh Circuit highlighted the "revered tradition of amateurism in college sports," which is an essential part of the "economic reality" of the relationship between the athletes and Penn. Because "generations of Penn students have vied for the opportunity to be part of that revered tradition with no thought of any compensation," the court concluded that Penn students participate in sports as part of their educational experience because it is beneficial to them. This rhetoric echoes the NCAA's conception of student-athlete. Sports are a part of education and athletes participate for the love of the game, not for compensation.

A similar case brought by University of Southern California football player Lamar Dawson and a class of similarly situated athletes reached the same result. Dawson sued for minimum wage under the FLSA for the time he spent playing football. Interestingly, though, Dawson claimed to be an employee of the NCAA and the Pac-12 conference, as opposed to his university. He argued that the NCAA and the Pac-12 acted as an employer of the class members by "prescribing the terms and conditions under which student-athletes perform services." Dawson thus sought recovery of the wages, including overtime pay that the joint employers, the NCAA and Pac-12, failed to pay as required under the FLSA.

The district court dismissed the case for failure to state a claim and the Ninth Circuit affirmed. *Dawson v. NCAA*, 932 F.3d 905 (9th Cir. 2019). The Ninth Circuit found that the FLSA did not apply to Dawson and other plaintiffs as they were neither employees of the NCAA nor the Pac-12. The court explained that the plaintiffs had no expectation of compensation, that the NCAA and the Pac-12 did not have the power to hire and fire, and were not conducting their business to evade the requirements of the FLSA.

In 2021, college athletes Ralph "Trey" Johnson, Stephanie Kerkeles, Nicholas Labella, Claudia Ruiz, Jacob Willebeek-Lemair, and Alexa Cooke, and a class of plaintiffs brought an FLSA claim against Division I universities and the NCAA. The athletes sought payment for their "work" as athletes on behalf of the university, including minimum wage and payment for overtime.

As in *Berger* and *Dawson*, the defendants sought to dismiss the case for failure to state a claim. Unlike the courts in those cases, the district court in *Johnson* held that the plaintiffs had alleged a colorable claim under the FLSA, allowing their lawsuit to move forward. *Johnson v. NCAA*, 556 F. Supp. 3d 491 (E.D. Penn. 2021).

The court began by rejecting the arguments of the defendants as circular. It explained that the defendants were arguing that the NCAA and its member schools do not have to pay the plaintiffs a minimum wage under the FLSA because the plaintiffs are amateurs, and that plaintiffs are amateurs because the NCAA and its member schools have a long history of not paying athletes like the plaintiffs.

The court also emphasized the multi-billion dollar nature of college sports, noting that this revenue was possible only because of the athletes. It cited the plaintiff's claim that the NCAA and its members do not conduct sports primarily for the benefit of the student athletes who participate in them, but rather for the monetary benefit of the NCAA and the universities that those athletes attend. The court also noted the plaintiffs' claim that college athletics are not part of the educational opportunities provided to athletes. Rather, athletics interferes with the academic opportunities available to athletes. The court also commented on the FLSA's definition of employer, noting that it is a very broad definition.

Finally, the court applied the seven factor test from *Glatt v. Fox Searchlight Pictures, Inc.*, 811 F.3d 528 (2d Cir. 2016) to assess whether the plaintiffs could make a showing that they are university employees. *Glatt* assessed whether interns are employees. The seven factors are the extent to which: (1) the intern and the employer clearly understand that there is no expectation of compensation; (2) the internship provides training that would be similar to that which would be given in an educational environment; (3) the internship is tied to the intern's formal education program by integrated coursework or the receipt of academic credit; (4) the internship accommodates the intern's academic commitments by corresponding to the academic calendar; (5) the internship's duration is limited to the period in which the internship provides the intern with beneficial learning; (6) the intern's work complements, rather than displaces, the work of paid employees while providing significant educational benefits to the intern; (7) the intern and the employer understand that the internship is conducted without entitlement to a paid job at the conclusion of the internship. The court found that factors 3, 4, and 6 favored the plaintiffs, which was enough to overcome the motion to dismiss. Factors 1 and 7 were unfavorable to the plaintiffs, and 2 and 5 were neutral.

The defendants appealed the district court's decision and the Third Circuit is considering the case. No matter the Third Circuit decision, athletes will probably continue to litigate this question of whether they are university employees, perhaps until the Supreme Court weighs in on the question.

7.   COLLEGE ATHLETE UNIONS?

Yes, college athletes can, in theory, form unions but only if they are employees for purposes of the National Labor Relations Act. The National Labor Relations Act unhelpfully defines employees as follows: "The term 'employee' shall include any employee, and shall not be limited to the employees of a particular employer ..." National Labor Relations Act § 7, 29 U.S.C. § 152(3) (2012).

Athletes in "right to work" states face an additional obstacle. Right to work states bar the formation of public unions. As such, athletes who are employees of public universities in right to work states cannot form unions. Right to work states, for the most part, are in the Southeast, although some other states, most notably Wisconsin, also bar public unions.

If football players at SEC schools want to unionize, they would either need to be employees of some non-public entity or states would have to amend their right to work laws. Depending on the economic arrangement, it is possible, for instance, that athletes could be employees of university foundations, athletic conferences, or even the NCAA. For an exploration of a model centered around college athletes being employees of a conference, *see* William W. Berry III, *Amending Amateurism*, 68 ALA. L. REV. 551 (2016).

Athletes at Northwestern University had initial success making a similar claim that they were university employees. Led by quarterback Kain Colter, the Northwestern football players filed a lawsuit to gain employee status in order to unionize.

In March 2014, the NLRB's regional director in Chicago Peter Ohr ruled that the scholarship recipient members of the Northwestern football team were employees of the university. *Northwestern University*, 2014–2015 NLRB Dec. (CCH) ¶ 15,781 (Mar. 26, 2014). The athletes thus were eligible to hold a representation election to determine if a majority of the employees wanted to be represented for purposes of collective bargaining by a union (College Athletes Players Association) that would serve as their exclusive bargaining representative.

The essence of the decision was that the scholarship football players met the criteria for being classified as employees in light of the following: (1) they provide a valuable service to the university (as demonstrated by the substantial revenue and public relations benefits the university receives), (2) universities compensate them (with scholarships that include tuition, fees, books, room and board), (3) universities require athletes to perform services for the university as a condition of receiving that compensation, and (4) supervisors employed by the university (their coaches) control their "work."

The regional director also stressed: (a) the players spend huge amounts of time on their football duties, sometimes as much as 40 to 50 hours a week, which is far more than they spend on their studies; (b) the work for which the players are compensated, playing football, has no relationship to their degree-seeking academic work and they receive no academic credit for it; (c) the university employees who supervise the players are not faculty, but rather non-academic coaches; and (d) the compensation the players receive is not financial aid for academic purposes.

Two years later, the NLRB vacated the regional director's decision and the election, deciding that whether or not the athletes were university employees, a bargaining unit including only them and not players for the other universities in the Big Ten would not be appropriate. *Northwestern University*, 362 N.L.R.B. No. 167 (Aug. 17, 2015). The Board noted these other universities are all public institutions over which the Board has no jurisdiction. The Board offered no opinion on whether athletes were employees for purposes of the NLRA.

Interestingly, the NLRB has also assessed whether graduate assistants are university employees. In a 2004 case involving Brown graduate students, the Board found that graduate assistants were not "employees" after considering four factors: (1) the status of graduate assistants as students; (2) the role of the graduate student assistantships in graduate education; (3) the graduate student assistants' relationship with the faculty; and (4) the financial support they receive to attend Brown University. *Brown University*, 342 N.L.R.B. 483 (2004). Specifically, the Board found that the relationship between the graduate assistants and Brown was primarily an educational one, not an economic one.

In 2016, the NLRB reversed its decision in *Brown* in holding that graduate assistants at Columbia were university employees and had the right to unionize. *The Trustees of Columbia University in the City of New York*, 364 N.L.R.B. No. 90 (Aug. 23, 2016). The Board explained that the fundamental error of the *Brown* decision was to frame the issue not in terms of the existence of an employment relationship, but rather on whether some other relationship between the employee and the employer is the primary one. In other words, just because the graduate assistants are students in graduate programs does not preclude them also from being employees in their role as teaching assistants and instructors.

The same analysis may also apply to college athletes. Whether courts consider them to be employees could turn on whether their time at the university is more educational or more economic. But courts could also find that their athletic pursuits and concurrent compensation means that they are employees even if they are also students.

In 2021, NLRB General Counsel Jennifer Abruzzo opined that college athletes are employees for purposes of the NLRA. She further indicated a willingness to bring actions against institutions classifying college athletes as "student-athletes" to the extent that such classifications chill athletes' chapter 7 activity under NLRA or otherwise violate athletes' right to organize pursuant to section 8(a)(1).

Subsequently, in May, 2023, the NLRB regional office in Los Angeles filed a lawsuit against the NCAA, the Pac-12, and the University of Southern California. The suit alleged that the three institutions have acted as joint employers and violated federal labor laws by failing to treat their athletes as employees. Specifically, the NLRB claims that these employers have deliberately misclassified men's and women's basketball players and men's football players as "student-athletes" in order to deprive the players of their rights under the NLRA, including the right to unionize. The NLRB seeks an order requiring the university, the conference, and the NCAA to cease classifying the athletes as "student-athletes" and instead reclassify them as employees.

In 2023, Northwestern faced an unfair labor practice complaint lodged with the NLRB by Michael Hsu, leader of the College Basketball Players Association (CBPA). This complaint was a reaction to Northwestern labeling its players as "student-athletes" during an internal investigation into hazing allegations against their head football coach, Pat Fitzgerald. Hsu commented, "The intent is to deter players from realizing and accepting their legitimate rights, not as student-athletes but as employees." He further added, "This complaint is an avenue for the NLRB to take appropriate action. I hope it isn't simply dismissed."

In the fall of 2023, men's basketball players at Dartmouth College filed a petition with the NLRB to form a union. The Dartmouth case is a bit different than the Northwestern, as Dartmouth is an Ivy league school that does not offer athletic scholarships. Both cases signal a desire on the part of some to move from the status quo of student-athlete to a model of employee-athlete.

In February, 2024, NLRB Regional Director Laura Sacks issued a decision finding that the athletes on the men's basketball team at Dartmouth were employees of the college, at least for purposes of the National Labor Relations Act (NLRA). *Decision and Direction of Election, Trustees of Dartmouth College,* 01-RC-325633 (NLRB Feb. 5, 2024). The regional director reached her conclusion based on two key facts. First, Dartmouth has the right to control the work performed by the athletes. It schedules practices, workouts, film sessions, and games, all of which it requires athletes to participate in as part of the team.

Second, the Dartmouth athletes perform this work in exchange for compensation. Although the athletes do not receive grant-in-aid scholarships, the regional director highlighted a number of economic benefits. She explained:

> As members of the basketball team representing Dartmouth, the players on the team receive valuable apparel and equipment. Each year, each player receives six pairs of basketball shoes (valued at $1,200); lifting shoes; travel shoes; a backpack; a duffel bag; unlimited socks; three hoodies; a zip sweatshirt; a quarter-zip shirt; two pairs of athletic pants; compression undergarments; a long-sleeved shirt; approximately ten short sleeved shirts; a windbreaker; three pairs of shorts; and showering shoes. Every other year, the players also receive a Nike parka with Dartmouth's logo; a Nike hat with Dartmouth's logo; Nike Dartmouth polos; practice gear; and a large travel bag. The players estimate that in 2023, the equipment was valued at $44,242 or approximately $2,950 per player. Each player also receives two tickets for each away game and four tickets for each home game. These tickets have an estimated value of $1,200 over the course of a 30-game season; however, the players may not sell the tickets. Dartmouth pays for all travel, lodging, and meals required for away games at a substantial cost per player per season. Further, Dartmouth provides room and board for each player during the six-week "Winterim" break at a significant cost per player. Players may also receive valuable Winterim parking passes.

Dartmouth Peak Performance, a program for varsity athletes, provides academic support, career development, sports and counseling psychology, sports nutrition, leadership and mental performance, strength and conditioning, sports medicine, integrative health and wellness, and sports science and innovative tech. As discussed in more detail below, many of these supports are available to other Dartmouth students through other programs, but Dartmouth Peak Performance is a comprehensive program designed exclusively for varsity athletes who wish to create a "championship culture."

So even for a largely non-revenue sport that loses money annually, the costs can be significant even without scholarships. And that is before the athletes get compensation under the FLSA for minimum wage.

After the regional director's decision, Dartmouth men's basketball players had clearance to form a union. On Tuesday, March 5, the players voted 13–2 to form a union. This historic decision established the first ever college athlete union.

The consequences, however, remain uncertain. Dartmouth appealed the decision of the regional director to the NLRB asking for extraordinary relief. The Board denied the request but did not opine on the merits. Dartmouth will presumably file a standard appeal to the Board, and if the athletes prevail, to the federal appellate court. It seems possible, if not likely, that such litigation would continue beyond the graduation date of the current team members.

Once the certification becomes final with no further appeals, there will still be the matter of collective bargaining. Dartmouth has indicated that it has no intention of entering into a collective bargaining agreement with its basketball players' union.

Ultimately, Dartmouth will have to bargain in good faith pursuant to the NLRA, but will not have to reach a collective bargaining agreement unless it finds favorable terms. The question of good faith bargaining also opens an additional avenue for litigation that could delay any agreement for years. Another obstacle relates to NCAA rules against pay-for-play. Although the current antitrust litigation suggests that the current amateurism model's may disappear, in the meantime direct salary payments by Dartmouth to its basketball players would render athletes ineligible and prevent the team from playing in the NCAA basketball tournament. Needless to say, both the short-term and long-term consequences of this historic college athlete unionization are not certain, but likely contested both by Dartmouth and the NCAA.

CHAPTER SEVEN

THE CHANGE AGENT OF CONFERENCE REALIGNMENT

In addition to the potential changes resulting from antitrust and employment litigation, the movement of schools from one conference to another has reshaped the current landscape and potential future of college athletics. This chapter recounts the recent changes, including the dramatic moves from the Pac-12 in 2023.

1. CONFERENCE REALIGNMENT

The first modern wave of conference realignment occurred in 1991, with Arkansas and South Carolina moving to the Southeastern Conference (SEC), expanding it to 12 teams and allowing for a lucrative conference championship game in football. Soon after, Florida State joined the Atlantic Coast Conference (ACC) and Penn State joined the Big Ten. In 1996, the Big 8 Conference and the Southwest Conference joined to form the Big 12.

In 2003–04, Boston College, Miami, and Virginia Tech all left the Big East to join the ACC. The ACC paid $5 million to settle a lawsuit filed by the Big East over the defections. Conferences began to restructure their contracts with member institutions, imposing economic penalties for leaving and instituting waiting periods.

As television money increased, however, further shifts became inevitable. The rise of the Big Ten

Network, and the University of Texas's own network opened the door to more lucrative arrangements that depended access to major media markets. The SEC, ACC, and Pac-12 have all followed suit, establishing their own television networks.

The next major shift of schools between conferences came during this growth, beginning in 2011, with the SEC expanding to add Missouri and Texas A&M; the Big Ten expanding to include Rutgers, Nebraska, and Maryland; the ACC again raiding the Big East in welcoming Louisville, Pittsburgh, Syracuse, and Notre Dame (in basketball only).

Most recently, the SEC expanded again to add Texas and Oklahoma, arguably the two strongest football programs in the Big 12, in the fall of 2021, with the membership scheduled to commence in 2024–25. This addition makes the SEC a super-conference of 16 teams. This move threatened the landscape of major college football so significantly that three of the other four Power conferences—the Big Ten, the ACC, and the Pac-12 subsequently announced an "alliance," presumably to defend against the SEC in the market.

This alliance was short-lived, however, as the USC and UCLA announced in the summer of 2022 that they were leaving the Pac-12 to join the Big Ten in 2024–25. The current map remains uncertain, other than that the SEC and the Big Ten will thrive with long-term lucrative television deals. The SEC reported revenue of $777.8 million for the 2020–21 fiscal year; the Big Ten signed a $1.2 billion annual television deal in 2022 (for 2023 through 2030).

The summer of 2023 brought another series of changes, leading to the demise of the Pac-12 conference. At the root of the collapse was the inability of the commissioner to secure a new television deal on par with the other Power conferences.

In late July, Colorado announced that it was returning to the Big-12. Oregon and Washington subsequently agreed to become part of the Big Ten. Arizona, Arizona State, and Utah then followed Colorado to the Big-12. Finally, Stanford and California-Berkeley moved to the ACC, along with SMU. Those moves left Oregon State and Washington State as the only remaining members of the Pac-12.

As of the Fall 2024, college sports will have four mega-conferences with 16 or more members—the SEC (16), the Big-12 (16), the Big Ten (18), and the ACC (18, with 17 in football without Notre Dame). With a college football playoff expanding from four to twelve teams in 2024–25 (and perhaps fourteen soon after), the college football model continues to creep in the direction of mirroring the National Football League.

What is clear is that football television revenue is driving the conference realignment and threatens the status quo of college sports. For this reason, the Knight Commission has called for separating out college football from the NCAA and the rest of intercollegiate athletics. The CFP, which oversees the college football playoff, discussed this option of college football leaving the NCAA in August 2022. It subsequently voted to expand the college football playoff from four to twelve teams.

While separating out football has some appeal, it might not be without cost. Having football separated from the rest of college athletics would prevent the pressure of increased commercialization and athlete compensation from spreading to other sports, except perhaps college basketball. It would make privatization easier, open the door to unionization and collective bargaining, and isolate a virtually professional sport from the other non-revenue sports seemingly more suited to an amateur student-athlete model. The cost might be, though, a diminution in the revenue distribution currently occurring in many athletic departments, particularly in the Power conferences. One solution, particularly if football programs become entities separate from the university, would be to have the football program pay licensing fees to use the logos, trademarks, emblems and colors of the team.

Such a model, though, might diminish the market for college football, as at least some segment of the fans seem to want the athletes to be students, not just professionals. It would beg the question of whether there is some substantive connection to the student-athlete model that makes boosters, alumni, and fans care about the games. Alternatively, it could demonstrate that these individuals are really just rooting for the laundry.

In addition, one wonders whether an evolving model will cut many institutions out of the big paydays likely to come. The lack of diversity of teams participating in the college football playoff over its history underscores this point, with the move toward a super-league or two super-leagues seeming imminent. It is also not clear that schools currently in the Big Ten or SEC are safe. One could imagine a new league that takes the most marketable programs and leaves out other, less successful programs. The SEC, for instance, might replace Mississippi State with Clemson; the Big Ten might replace Minnesota with North Carolina.

Notre Dame, which as of 2024 remained independent in football, remains the university arguably with the most power to affect the landscape in the near future in the way that Oklahoma, Texas, UCLA, and USC recently have. Its tradition and multi-million dollar single team television contract suggests that its brand will be part of any future professionalization of college football, even as its administration rests on its academic strength and historical embrace of amateurism.

During the wave of realignment over the past two decades, conferences have sought to impose safeguards to discourage schools from leaving. These safeguards have led to litigation.

In 2013, when Maryland decided to leave the ACC to join the Big Ten, the ACC sued Maryland to require it pay the exit fee contained in the conference constitution. The ACC changed withdrawal fee in

2012 to three times the conference's annual operating budget. This meant that Maryland owed $52 million.

Maryland argued that it possessed sovereign immunity and thus did not have to pay the exit fee. A North Carolina court rejected Maryland's argument and found for the ACC. *ACC v. University of Maryland*, 751 S.E.2d 612 (N.C. Ct. App. 2013). Specifically, the court held that as a matter of public policy, sovereign immunity could not be a defense for a cause of action based on a contract. After the court's decision, Maryland and the ACC settled for $31.3 million.

Two years earlier, West Virginia sued the Big East conference in an attempt to avoid paying an exit fee. West Virginia argued that the fee violated antitrust law, even though it had signed the contract. In order to receive an immediate release, West Virginia settled for $31 million, with the Big 12 schools paying $20 million of the exit fee.

Rutgers similarly faced litigation with the Big East when it left for the Big Ten. The issue for Rutgers was the 27 month required waiting period. It settled its lawsuit for $11.5 million paying more than the initial $10 million in order for an agreement to allow it to leave early.

Texas and Oklahoma faced a similar waiting period when leaving the Big-12 to come to the SEC. The schools chose to wait an additional two years rather than violate their contract with the Big-12. Part of the rationale was the current media rights contract, which required the schools to forfeit their rights to remuneration if they left early.

The ACC schools currently face a similar issue with a long-term media contract. Both Clemson and Florida State have expressed a desire to leave the conference because its television deal has fallen significantly behind the Big Ten and the SEC. The current media rights deal with ESPN extends through 2036. Under the deal and the ACC constitution, the ACC would retain the rights to televise the games of the school, even if they left the ACC. The ACC's new exit fee is $120 million.

2.   THE ACC LITIGATION

After the decision of the College Football Playoff (CFP) to include two one-loss teams, Alabama and Texas, over undefeated Florida State, FSU amped up its rhetoric against the ACC and made noises about filing a lawsuit enabling it to leave the conference.

On December 21, 2023, the day before the FSU Trustees voted on whether to sue the ACC, the conference filed its own lawsuit in North Carolina. The suit sought a declaratory judgment concerning the economic consequences of FSU leaving the ACC. The next day, Florida State filed its own a lawsuit in the Florida courts seeking a declaratory judgment freeing it from the ACC constitution without consequence.

After recounting the many ways which it believes that the ACC has failed its members, particularly in reference to its media contracts, Florida State specifically argued that the penalties under the league constitution for leaving are unenforceable. Florida State claims that these penalties violate Florida antitrust law.

Likewise, FSU asserts that the penalties are unenforceable because they are penalties and not damages. Victims of breached contracts are entitled to the benefit of the economic bargain, but cannot punish the other party as a consequence for the breach.

FSU also argues that the ACC materially breached its contract with FSU, breached its fiduciary duties to FSU under that contract, and frustrated the purpose of the contract, particularly by entering into a sub-market media deal of lengthy duration. FSU also argues that the media grant of rights contract is unenforceable because it materially contradicts the ACC constitution and bylaws. Finally, FSU argues that the ACC punishments are unconscionable and against Florida public policy.

The gap between what the parties believe FSU might owe the ACC remains significant. The conference exit fee is $140 million, but including estimates of the overall cost of the media rights that the ACC would lose, some have estimated the damages to be as much as $572 million. Presumably, FSU and the ACC will settle at some number between those estimates, but regardless of the final outcome, it will be a messy divorce. If and when the split occurs, the ACC will lose one of its two strong football brands. And FSU will pay hundreds of millions of dollars for the privilege of leaving the conference.

In March, 2024, Clemson followed Florida State and filed its own lawsuit against the ACC in South Carolina state court. The suit challenged the enforceability of the ACC's contract with Clemson, specifically its $140 million exit fee and its grant of media rights to the ACC through 2036. The ACC countersued the following day in North Carolina asking for declaratory relief on the same two issues.

While Clemson's claims seem speculative at best, this case and the Florida State case make their exits from the ACC increasingly possible. The question will be the price tag, and whether the universities can negotiate an amicable settlement with the ACC.

What remains unclear, however, is whether the SEC or the Big Ten would be interested in adding Clemson and/or Florida State. Geographically, the SEC would make more sense, but it is not clear that the SEC wants to expand further, at least at the current moment.

Further complicating the picture, Florida Attorney General Ashley Moody has sued the ACC after it failed to provide the details of the Grant of Rights agreement between the ACC and ESPN. Moody claims the agreement is a public record under Florida law. The ACC and Mecklenburg County Judge Louis A. Bledsoe, who is presiding over the ACC-FSU litigation, disagree.

Bledsoe found that FSU waived its "sovereign immunity" by being a member of the ACC. As a result, the secrecy of the agreement between the ACC and ESPN is legitimate and protected. Moody argues that contracts involving a Florida state entity (here, FSU) are public record, regardless of whether they occur out of state.

3.   THE END OF THE PAC-12

In recent years, the Pac-12 conference has encountered notable financial hurdles, with revenue generation being a core issue. While other Power conferences like the SEC and Big Ten have secured lucrative television and media rights deals, the Pac-12 has struggled to keep pace. This revenue gap has hindered the conference's ability to invest in new facilities, recruit outstanding coaching staffs, and attract elite talent. A significant factor contributing to the Pac-12's financial predicament is its geographic spread. In contrast to conferences with more centralized locations, Pac-12 schools ranged from Arizona to Washington and California to Colorado. This dispersed membership has made it logistically challenging to create regional rivalries and generate the same level of fan interest and television viewership seen in other conferences.

As the conference's television contracts neared their end, the potential revenue from new deals remained uncertain. Negotiations for a television deal with ESPN stalled when the Pac-12 sought $50 million per school, far above ESPN's offer of $30 million. Additionally, the Pac-12's hesitancy regarding NIL further hampered its ability to draw top talent and generate revenue.

The first significant blow to the conference was the decision of UCLA and USC to leave and join the Big Ten in 2022. With these moves scheduled to take effect in 2024–25, Colorado announced that it was returning to the Big 12 in July 2023. The University of Arizona, Arizona State University, and the University of Utah followed Colorado in August, 2023. Finally, the University of California and Stanford announced a future move to the Atlantic Coast Conference in August 2023, leaving Oregon State and Washington State as the only remaining members. The conference had one final year, 2023–24, before its unfortunate implosion.

UCLA paid a particularly steep cost for leaving California Berkeley and the Pac-12. UCLA has to pay $30 million over three years to Cal, a form of "Calimony." UCLA anticipates an increase of $60 million in annual revenue from the Big Ten, while Cal expects an additional $11 million from the ACC.

As the ten schools departed, a dispute arose concerning the incoming revenue from the 2023–24 media rights deal. The two remaining conference members, Oregon State and Washington State, sued the other ten schools. They obtained a preliminary injunction to enable them to control the conference, including making decisions about potential new members. This was important because the ten leaving members had insisted that they were still members of the conference until they officially left in the summer of 2024.

The schools ultimately settled, with the leaving schools taking an unspecified amount of television revenue from the 2023–24 season while also paying a portion back to the two remaining members. The departing schools paid Oregon State and Washington State $65 million for departing, which along with the 2024–25 media rights contract, leaves the two schools with $255 million.

Oregon State and Washington State will join the West Coast Conference as affiliate members and play league games—with the exception of football and baseball—against WCC schools for the 2024–25 and 2025–26 seasons.

The most important sport in this agreement is basketball, as the Beavers and Cougars will be in the same basketball conference as Gonzaga and Saint Mary's for two seasons. This will give the WCC eleven basketball members for two years.

Earlier in December 2023, Oregon State and Washington State reached a football scheduling agreement with the Mountain West Conference. All twelve Mountain West teams will play seven traditional conference football games in addition to one contest against either Washington State or Oregon State for a total of eight league games.

While conference realignment remains unpredictable and perhaps geographically comical, it seems likely that the shuffling will continue, particularly if television networks believe that consolidation of brands will produce increased national interest.

CHAPTER EIGHT

COACHES

The rise in college football coach salaries over the past two decades has been exponential. In 2023, the top head coaches in the country made in excess of $10 million per year. And assistant coaches make in excess of $1 million a year with the top assistant coaches approaching $3 million per year. Seven-time national champion Nick Saban received the highest salary, $11.4 million for the 2023 season.

College basketball coaches are not far behind. In 2023, Bill Self was the first to top $10 million with other top coaches making in excess of $5 million per year.

These revenue sport coaches have benefitted significantly from the economic model that limits the compensation received by college athletes. The result has been a robust free market in which college coaches have seen significant salary increases. To be sure, some of this increase has also resulted from the public roles coaches take in their universities and communities, as well as the connection between athletic success and enrollment at some universities.

Coaches have succeeded by perpetuating the image that they, more so than the players, bear responsibility for the success or failure of the team. When presidents, athletic directors, and fans view the coach as indispensable in the success of the program, it alters the bargaining power in a way that most employees do not enjoy. Interestingly, the real value in such coaches might not lie in the preparation of the team and the coaching of the game, but rather in the ability to recruit better players than one's opponent. Regardless of the reality, the perception remains that coaches enable the success of a program which results in their ability to command exorbitant salaries.

Indeed, the unusual success of Nick Saban provides the impetus for placing importance on the person serving as head coach. During his recently ended tenure at Alabama, Saban's teams won a remarkable twelve division titles, nine conference championships, and six national championships in seventeen years. The myth that a university's next coach can be the next Saban enables coaches to receive lucrative contracts which allow them to collect millions of dollars even after they have failed to achieve championship-level success.

1.   ANTITRUST LIMITS ON CAPPING COACH SALARIES

Reformers have called for the NCAA to place caps on coach compensation. But antitrust law prevents caps on coach salaries.

In *Law v. NCAA*, 134 F.3d 1010 (10th Cir. 1998), a group of basketball coaches successfully challenged such a cap. In the 1990s, the NCAA promulgated a rule limiting annual compensation of certain Division I entry-level coaches to $16,000. Basketball coaches affected by the rule filed a class action challenging the restriction under Section 1 of the Sherman Antitrust Act.

The court found that in the market for college basketball coaches, the restriction constituted an unreasonable restraint of trade. The imposition of this salary cap amounted to price-fixing. The NCAA did not have any pro-competitive justification for the rule. As a result, the court enjoined the NCAA from enforcing its rule.

In addition to the inability of the NCAA to place a cap on coach salaries, the unusual shift in bargaining power has led to universities entering into disadvantageous contracts with coaches. The perhaps mistaken perception that quality college football coaches are somehow scarce in the market has led to universities agreeing to contracts with large buyout provisions.

Typically, term employment contracts cover a specific time period with the management having the option to terminate the employee. If there is cause for termination, the employee does not receive any additional money. If there is not cause for termination, the employee receives the remainder of the amount due under the contract if the employee had completed the term.

Coach contracts usually define cause with reference to moral turpitude, but do not include job performance. For instance, the University of Mississippi fired its football coach Hugh Freeze for cause in 2017 after finding he used a university cell phone to call an escort service on multiple occasions.

In other industries, poor job performance can be grounds for termination for cause. But for college coaches, losing every game still does not provide cause for termination. With impatient alumni wanting championships, universities continue to pay record amounts in coach buyouts. In the 2022 fiscal year, Power conference schools paid former head coaches over $90 million. In November 2023, Texas A&M fired head football coach Jimbo Fisher, triggering a buyout of over $77.6 million.

2. THE DINARDO CASE

This gap in bargaining power has not always been the case, however, as evidenced by Vanderbilt University's contract with its former football coach Gerry DiNardo in the 1990s. Under the contract with DiNardo, DiNardo was responsible of paying the remaining amount owed to him back to the university if he left early.

When DiNardo left Vanderbilt to accept the head coaching job at Louisiana State University (LSU), Vanderbilt sued to collect the $281,886.43 due under the contract. *Vanderbilt University v. DiNardo*, 174 F.3d 751 (6th Cir. 1999). DiNardo argued that the damages amounted liquidated damages that were punitive and did not reflect the amount of damage suffered by Vanderbilt.

Unlike tort cases in which the plaintiff can recover damages for pain and suffering as well as punitive damages, damages in contracts cases can only be for the amount due under the contract. The court found for Vanderbilt, determining that the amount reflected the cost to the university of DiNardo's leaving. A quick examination of the lack of success of the Vanderbilt team both before and after DiNardo's tenure coaching the team demonstrates this cost. DiNardo was able to win five games in three out of his four seasons at Vanderbilt. Between his predecessor and his two successors, Vanderbilt only enjoyed one other five win season.

The decision in DiNardo's lawsuit coincided with his only bowl victory at LSU. LSU boosters paid the money he owed to Vanderbilt. Two seasons later, LSU fired DiNardo, paving the way for Nick Saban to become LSU's coach and subsequently win a national championship.

3. PEPPER RODGERS, JIM O'BRIEN, MIKE LEACH, AND TODD MCNAIR

DiNardo is not the only coach at a major program to be involved in employment litigation. In the early 1980s, Georgia Institute of Technology (Georgia Tech) head football Franklin C. "Pepper" Rodgers brought a breach of contract lawsuit against the Georgia Tech Athletic Association. Georgia Tech had fired Rodgers in 1979, and the parties dispute which of the perquisites of his job as a head coach continued for the two years remaining on his contract. *Rodgers v. Ga. Tech. Athletic Assn.*, 303 S.E.2d 467 (1983).

When Georgia Tech fired Rodgers, it agreed that as an employee of the Association, he would still receive "various insurance and pension benefits and perquisites" as he became eligible for, but the parties could not agree to what constituted perquisites. In the litigation, Rodgers composed a list of twenty-nine items, including car insurance and expenses, general expense money, meals at the Georgia Tech training table, eight season tickets to home football games, tickets to Georgia Tech basketball games, Atlanta Falcons home football games, pocket money for the football games, parking, services of a secretary and an administrative assistant, travel to coaching conventions, country club fees, profits from his television show, a life insurance policy, and other benefits.

The court found that the contract was ambiguous as to the meaning of perquisites and whether that consisted of benefits available to all association employees or also included benefits given to the head football coach. The court adopted Rodgers' reading of the contract—that he should receive benefits beyond that of a general Association employee. But the court drew a line limiting his recovery to items not related to Rodgers actually performing the job of head football coach, since he no longer had that job. So, Rodgers received the perquisites of being a coach, such as tickets, meals, expenses, and country club memberships, but not those related to performing the job—the use of a secretary and administrative assistant, as well as the travel to coaching conventions.

Ohio State basketball coach Jim O'Brien sued his university after termination. Prior to his firing, O'Brien had been successful on the court, leading the Buckeyes to the Final Four in the 1998–99 season. In 2004, however, an ongoing lawsuit forced O'Brien to disclose that he made a payment of $6,000 to recruit Aleksandar Radojević in 1997. O'Brien claimed that the loan of his own money did not violate NCAA rules because Radojević had already lost his amateur status.

At the time, the NCAA had declared Radojević, a 7'3" center, ineligible because he had received money from his team in Montenegro. The Toronto Raptors drafted Radojević in the first round of the 1999 NBA draft, but he had a short-lived career in the NBA and in Europe as a result of a series of injuries.

Ohio State Athletic Director Andy Geiger fired O'Brien upon learning about the payment, and O'Brien sued for wrongful termination. *O'Brien v. Ohio State University*, 859 N.E.2d 607 (Ohio Ct. of Claims, 2006). While the NCAA infractions committee found that O'Brien's payment was a major infraction, the Ohio court nonetheless found that Ohio State improperly fired O'Brien.

Of particular importance was the language of O'Brien's contract. His contract required him to follow NCAA rules and report any potential violations to Geiger. But it also prohibited Ohio State from firing O'Brien for cause unless he "materially breached" his contract.

The court found that O'Brien's payment and NCAA rule violation breached the contract, but was not a material breach. It relied on the common law definition of material breach. A material breach occurs when a party fails to do something that is so fundamental to a contract that the failure to perform that obligation defeats the essential purpose of the contract or makes it impossible for the other party to perform under the contract.

With no verdict or sanction from the NCAA at the time of the termination, it remained possible for O'Brien to continue to coach, performing his obligation under the contract. As a result, the court found that Ohio State improperly terminated O'Brien. This is because the court concluded that his breach was not material.

Ohio State complained that it should not have to wait for the NCAA to render a decision before firing O'Brien. But the court emphasized that Ohio State had structured O'Brien's contract to require it to wait if it wanted to fire him with cause.

The consequence of firing a coach without cause in most contracts is that the university pay the coach the remainder of the salary due under the contract. Because O'Brien had not materially breached the contract, Ohio State had fired O'Brien without cause. The Ohio court decision, affirmed by the Ohio Court of Appeals, awarded O'Brien $2.4 million in damages.

Coach Mike Leach's case against Texas Tech University was less successful than the cases of Rodgers and O'Brien. Leach was the architect of the potent Air Raid offense and one of the most colorful and jovial of college football coaches. His problems arose from a conflict with a player who alleged mistreatment after receiving a concussion. The player, Adam James, was the son of ESPN football analyst Craig James, which gave the incident public notoriety.

Texas Tech suspended Leach and subsequently terminated him for cause on the grounds that he had failed to adhere to the terms of the suspension and fully cooperate with the school's investigation. Leach then sued Texas Tech for wrongful termination to recover the $2.5 million he claimed the university owed him under his contract. *Leach v. Texas Tech University*, 335 S.W.3d 386 (2011). The Texas Court of Appeals dismissed Leach's suit on sovereign immunity grounds. In other words, the State of Texas, as a sovereign, is immune from liability and suit.

Leach argued that (1) the state had waived that immunity by entering into a contract with him, (2) he was bringing a whistleblower claim, meaning sovereign immunity did not apply, and (3) a dismissal of his breach of contract claim constituted an unconstitutional taking and denial of due process under the federal Constitution and the Texas Constitution. But the Court found none of these claims had merit against the shield of sovereign immunity.

Professionally, Leach recovered and enjoyed continued success as the head coach of Washington State and then Mississippi State, where he coached until he died unexpectedly in December, 2022. But he continued to fight the reputational damage of his firing at Texas Tech, hiring an investigator and filing open records requests that continued beyond the end of his life.

Perhaps the most complicated of recent college coach lawsuits involved University of Southern

California (USC) assistant football coach Todd McNair, whose litigation against the NCAA lasted a decade. The case emerged out of the NCAA's investigation of USC star running back Reggie Bush, the 2005 Heisman Trophy winner and member of the 2004 National Championship team. As discussed in Chapter Two, the NCAA found that Bush and his family received impermissible benefits. These included accepting cash, travel expenses, and a home in the San Diego area where his parents lived rent-free for more than a year and received $10,000 to furnish.

In 2010, the NCAA Division I Committee on Infractions released a report concluding that McNair "knew or should have known" that Bush and a would-be agent were violating NCAA rules. The report also found that McNair "provided false and misleading information to the enforcement staff." As a result, the NCAA issued McNair a one-year show-cause penalty and a one-year recruiting ban. *University of Southern California Public Infractions Report*, June 10, 2010.

On June 6, 2011, McNair sued the NCAA for defamation. McNair argued that the NCAA's report had the effect of impairing his ability to receive another position as a high-level coach in college football. The tort claim McNair made related to his alleged lack of knowledge about the benefits Bush received. The subsequent NCAA infractions allegedly constituted defamation because they damaged McNair's reputation based on false claims.

When the case went to trial in May, 2019, a jury in Los Angeles ruled in favor of the NCAA. But trial judge Frederick Shaller issued an order for a new trial based on his view that there was insufficient evidence to support the verdict. And a California appellate court affirmed Shaller's ruling in February, 2021.

The NCAA's conclusion that McNair knew about Bush's rules violations centered around the testimony of Lloyd Lake, a convicted felon, and his associate, Michael Michaels, who had his own sports marketing firm. At issue was a 2-minute 32-second phone call between Lake and McNair at 1:34 a.m. on January 8, 2006. Lake testified that he phoned McNair to help him convince Bush to follow through with his promise to sign with Michaels' agency. McNair testified that he did not remember the call.

The NCAA also pointed to McNair and Lake's mutual friendship with comedian Faizon Love, as evidence that McNair knew about the benefits paid to Bush. But the appellate court did not see those relationships as dispositive to the question of McNair's knowledge. It explained, "That the two men may have spoken, may have had a celebrity friend in common, and posed for the same photograph are manifestly not evidence that McNair had knowledge of the agency and improper benefits, which is the only way his denials would violate NCAA rules." *McNair v. NCAA*, 2021 WL 405876 (Cal. Ct. App. 2021).

Rather than trying the case again, the parties settled the lawsuit in June, 2021.

4.   COACHES BEHAVING BADLY

University headaches with respect to college coaches sometimes relate more to conduct than contracts. While there are numerous examples of coaches making poor decisions on the field, here is a sampling of coaches making really bad decisions off the field.

In 2002, Mike Price concluded a successful career as the head coach of Washington State, leading the Cougars to a second Rose Bowl appearance and a second consecutive ten-win season. The University of Alabama hired Price as its head coach beginning with the 2003 season by signing him to a seven year, $10 million contract. Price, however, never coached a game for the Crimson Tide.

While participating in a pro-am golf tournament in Pensacola, Florida on April 16–17, 2003, Price spent a wild night partying at a strip club, Arety's Angels. Reports in Alabama newspapers said he bought drinks for an exotic dancer named Destiny Stahl and paid for private dances at a strip club, spending several hundred dollars on a night of heavy drinking and tipping. Price also allegedly solicited the services of a prostitute that evening.

The next morning, Price awakened in his hotel room, fully clothed but unable to explain the presence of or remember the name of a woman in the room with him, according to Mac Bledsoe, a friend of Price's. The woman later ordered $1,000 in room service, requesting one of each item on the hotel menu, news reports said.

Alabama's new president, Robert E. Witt, in just his second month on the job, fired Price on May 4, 2003.

George O'Leary, the longtime successful head football coach at Georgia Tech, had a similarly short-lived tenure at Notre Dame. In 2001, O'Leary left Georgia Tech to take the job as head football coach at Notre Dame. A week after Notre Dame hired O'Leary, the media discovered inaccuracies in his published biographical sketch. The biography, which had remained the same for two decades, stated that O'Leary had earned three letters in football at the University of New Hampshire. The Manchester newspaper, the Union Leader, called the University of New Hampshire in order to research a feature story on O'Leary. The newspaper discovered that O'Leary had never played a game for New Hampshire.

O'Leary immediately offered to resign, but Notre Dame athletic director did not accept, thinking it was one minor mistake. But then O'Leary admitted to other fabrications in his biography. He admitted that he had not earned a master's degree from "NYU-Stony Brook University." That institution did not exist. O'Leary had fabricated this school, naming it after two separate schools over fifty miles apart. He had taken only two courses at Stony Brook, and never graduated. When this additional inaccuracy came to light, Notre Dame promptly forced O'Leary to resign.

Bobby Petrino was a star coach at the University of Louisville, leading the Cardinals to eleven wins in 2004 and twelve wins in 2006, and building them into a national power. On July 13, 2006, Petrino signed a ten year, $25.6 million contact with Louisville, but less than six months later accepted the head coaching position with the NFL's Atlanta Falcons.

Atlanta hired Petrino with the idea that he would help develop star quarterback Michael Vick. Vick, however, received a suspension for the 2007 season when it emerged that Vick had bankrolled an illegal dog fighting operation in Newport News, Virginia. Petrino struggled in his one season as the Falcons coach, abruptly resigning thirteen games into the season, one of the shortest non-interim NFL coaching stints ever.

Petrino then became the head coach of the Arkansas Razorbacks. By 2012, Petrino had again achieved success on the field, leading Arkansas to ten wins in 2010 and eleven wins in 2011. On April 1, 2012, Petrino was involved in a motorcycle crash on Arkansas Highway 16 near the city of Crosses. He was riding with former Arkansas All-SEC volleyball player Jessica Dorrell, whom he had hired on March 28 as student-athlete development coordinator for the football program. Dorrell had previously served as a fundraiser in the Razorback Foundation.

Petrino initially said he was alone on the motorcycle. Several days later, however, just minutes before the release of the police report from the accident, Petrino admitted that Dorrell was not only a passenger, but also that he had been conducting an adulterous relationship with her.

On April 10, Arkansas athletic director Jeff Long fired Petrino. Long discovered that Petrino and Dorrell's relationship was an open secret in the football office. Petrino frequently sent Dorrell gifts, including a previously undisclosed $20,000 cash gift as a Christmas present. Dorrell used the money to help buy a new car. Dorrell allegedly had received preferential treatment, with Petrino ignoring the university's affirmative action guidelines. He hired her after fifteen days for a position required to remain open for thirty days. And Dorrell was the only candidate with no previous experience in a football program, as well as the only candidate without a master's degree.

Ole Miss fired its similarly successful football coach Hugh Freeze under similar circumstances— the discovery of indiscretions. Freeze had back-to-back strong seasons at Ole Miss, including beating Alabama in consecutive seasons. While on recruiting trips, Freeze had, on more than one occasion, used a university-provided cell phone to place calls to escort services.

An NCAA investigation into the Ole Miss program led to a lawsuit against the university. The university's response to the NCAA's notice of allegations had angered former coach Houston Nutt, who believed that the university was inappropriately trying to blame him for sanctions in contravention of his settlement agreement at his termination form Ole Miss. In the discovery phase of that lawsuit, Nutt's counsel discovered Freeze's phone records. He reported those documents to athletic director Ross Bjork, and the university fired Freeze for cause.

Freeze has since resuscitated his career, enjoying a successful stint as the head coach of Liberty University. Auburn University hired him as its head coach beginning in the 2023 season.

5. COACH PRIME, LANE TRAIN, AND THE TRANSFER PORTAL

Colorado's Head Coach, Deion Sanders, has had a profound impact on the Colorado Buffaloes football program in a short period of time. Sanders accepted the job after a brief stint as the head coach at Jackson State University, where he led them to two bowl appearances and the first undefeated season in school history. The NFL Hall of Famer has brought a new level of excitement and energy to the program, and he has quickly turned the Buffaloes into one of the most talked-about teams in college football. The Buffaloes routinely feature prominent celebrities and athletes along their sidelines and in the stands.

Sanders' impact has been both on and off the field. On the field, the Buffaloes have improved dramatically under Sanders' leadership. They went from being one of the worst teams in the Pac-12 in 2022, boasting an abysmal 1–11 record, to being a bowl-eligible team in 2023. Sanders has helped to develop several young players into stars, including his son, quarterback Shedeur Sanders and wide receiver/defensive star Travis Hunter.

Off the field, Sanders has brought a new level of enthusiasm to the Colorado football program. He has helped to boost ticket sales and merchandise sales, and he has also helped to improve the team's relationship with the Boulder community. Sanders is also a strong advocate for HBCU football, and he has been using his platform at Colorado to raise awareness of the importance of HBCUs. Sanders convinced the top ranked cornerbacks in back-to-back recruiting classes, Cormani McClain and Travis Hunter, to follow him to Colorado after they were previously committed to other schools. His players consistently praise his work ethic and dedication.

Part of the secret of Sanders' early success is willingness to use the transfer portal. His roster at Colorado included an almost complete overhaul from the prior year. His professional career has provided a clear understanding and affinity for the free-agent like portal.

Another coach who is at the forefront of leveraging the transfer portal is Lane Kiffin. The "Lane Train" is a master of utilizing social media offering the clarion call for top athletes to "Come to the 'Sip." Like Sanders, Kiffin's extensive experience in the NFL, as the son of a longtime defensive coordinator as well as being the head coach of the Raiders, has provided him with a level of savvy concerning the transfer portal that has allowed him to succeed at Ole Miss. In his four seasons in Oxford, Kiffin has become the first coach in school history to have multiple ten win seasons. In the new NIL era, successfully navigating the transfer portal seems to be essential to having success in college football.

CHAPTER NINE
THE ROLE OF TITLE IX

The adoption of Title IX in 1972 ushered in an era of women's intercollegiate athletics. Over the past fifty years, women's sports have continued to grow and expand both in participation and popularity. The 2024 NCAA Basketball Tournament marked a new era in women's sports, with the women's tournament receiving more viewers than the men's tournament.

This chapter explores the basics of Title IX and its requirements before exploring its possible role in future models of college sports.

1.   TITLE IX'S REQUIREMENTS

Title IX is a federal law that prohibits gender discrimination in federally funded educational programs. The text states that

> No person . . . shall, on the basis of sex, be excluded from participation in, be denied the benefit of, or be subjected to discrimination under any education program or activity receiving federal financial assistance.

20 U.S.C. § 1681 (1972). While Congress passed the statute in 1972, the Senate did not really consider its application to college athletics until two years later when Senator John Tower of Texas proposed an NCAA-backed amendment that would have excluded revenue-generating college sports from Title IX. Congress rejected the Tower Amendment and instead adopted an amendment proposed by Senator

Jacob Javits of New York. The Javits Amendment required the Department of Health, Education, and Welfare ("HEW") to issue regulations containing "reasonable provisions considering the nature of particular sports." P.L. 93–380, Title VIII, Part D, § 844, 88 Stat. 612 (1974).

A decade later, however, the Supreme Court decided a case that seemed to achieve the result Senator Tower sought. The Court interpreted Title IX narrowly, finding that it applied only to the specific college programs receiving federal financial aid, not athletic departments more generally. *Grove City College v. Bell*, 465 U.S. 555 (1984). Congress subsequently passed the Civil Rights Restoration Act of 1987, which extended Title IX to all of the operations of educational institutions receiving federal aid. 20 U.S.C.A. § 1681, et seq. (1988). This law meant that all college athletic departments had to follow the requirements of Title IX.

The Office of Civil Rights ("OCR") of the HEW promulgated regulations to delineate the scope of Title IX. The OCR made clear that the test for equality did not relate to "aggregate expenditures" for individuals or teams, which could remain unequal. 34 C.F.R. § 106.41(c). Rather, the test for compliance related to whether athletes of each gender received "equal opportunity" to participate in intercollegiate athletics.

This equal athletic opportunity considers the following program factors: (1) Whether the selection of sports and levels of competition effectively accommodate the interests and abilities of members of both sexes; (2) Provision of equipment and supplies; (3) Scheduling of games and practice time; (4) Travel and per diem allowance; (5) Opportunity to receive coaching and academic tutoring; (6) Assignment and compensation of coaches and tutors; (7) Provision of locker rooms, practice and competitive facilities; (8) Provision of medical training services; (9) Provision of housing and dining facilities and services; (10) Publicity. 34 C.F.R. § 106.41(c).

To measure whether institutions are in compliance, the OCR issued a three-prong test. The answer to one or more of the following must be yes:

(1)   Whether intercollegiate level participation opportunities for male and female students are provided in numbers substantially proportionate to their respective enrollments; or

(2)   Where the members of one sex have been and are underrepresented among intercollegiate athletes, whether the institution can show a history and continuing practice of program expansion which is demonstrably responsive to the developing interest and abilities of the members of that sex; or

(3)   Where the members of one sex are underrepresented among intercollegiate athletes, and the institution cannot show a continuing practice of program expansion such as that cited above, whether it can be demonstrated that the interests and abilities of the members of that sex have been fully and

effectively accommodated by the present program.

34 C.F.R. § 106.41(c).

Thus, university athletic departments must satisfy one of the three safe harbors. If the university is out of compliance, the OCR can require the department to remedy its non-compliance by adding women's athletic teams or eliminating men's teams.

This approach has survived a number of legal challenges. Most notably, Brown University challenged the OCR's interpretation of Title IX. In 1993, Brown volleyball and gymnastics team members sued the university under Title IX, winning a preliminary injunction against Brown's attempt to eliminate those varsity teams. At the time, Brown had 48% women in its student body, but only 37% (328) of its athletes were women. The First Circuit Court of Appeals found that Brown had violated Title IX. It affirmed the injunction against Brown's dissolution of its women's volleyball and gymnastics teams.

A subsequent lawsuit by all of Brown's female athletes, including all present and future female students who might want to participate in intercollegiate sports, resulted in another finding in 1996 that Brown was violating Title IX. While the percentage of female athletes had increased from 37% to 38%, the percentage of female students at Brown had increased from 48% to 51%. This left a 13% gap in terms of proportionality between female students and female athletes.

Brown attempted to argue the third safe harbor—that its athletics program had satisfied all of the female interest in playing sports at Brown. In order to satisfy this standard, Brown had to show that it had met *all* existing female student interests and abilities in every potential varsity sport. The court rejected this argument—it found that the reduced number of women's scholarships was the product of past discrimination, not a lack of interest. In particular, the university had demoted the championship gymnastics team from varsity status and refused to promote the highly successful club ski team.

Brown further argued that, to the extent Title IX required Brown to add women's sports teams, it constituted impermissible affirmative action. The court explained, however, that it is permissible to use affirmative action to remedy discrimination under an anti-discrimination statute. Even though it found that Brown had violated Title IX, the court did not impose any particular remedy, allowing Brown to negotiate with the OCR to determine how to remedy its non-compliance. It rejected the remedial order requiring the upgrade of existing women's teams to university-funded varsity status, leaving open the option of cutting men's teams instead.

Subsequent cases have added clarity to the application of Title IX to college athletics. In *Boucher v. Syracuse University*, 164 F.3d 113 (2d Cir. 1999), plaintiffs sued the university under Title IX in an attempt to raise the club lacrosse and club softball teams to varsity status. The university acquiesced to the demands of the athletes, adding a varsity lacrosse team prior to the adjudication of the lawsuit and subsequently adding a softball team. While the gap between the percentage of female athletes (34%) and the female students (50%) were not proportional, the court rejected the possibility of a more general Title IX claim at the time, finding that Syracuse fell under the second safe harbor because of its steady and continued addition of women's varsity sports.

An extreme example of Title IX non-compliance occurred in *Pederson v. Louisiana State University*, 201 F.3d 388 (5th Cir. 2000). LSU was out of compliance with Title IX, but seemingly oblivious to these requirements. The court found intentional discrimination on the part of LSU. It explained, "The proper test is not whether it knew of or is responsible for the actions of others, but is whether Appellees intended to treat women differently on the basis of their sex by providing them unequal athletic opportunity, and, as we noted above, we are convinced that they did. Our review of the record convinces us that an intent to discriminate, albeit one motivated by chauvinist notions as opposed to one fueled by enmity, drove LSU's decisions regarding athletic opportunities for its female students."

2. CHEERLEADING AND DANCE

The NCAA currently does not recognize competitive cheer teams and competitive dance teams as sports. This is despite the extensive time and effort involved for the athletes participating in these activities and despite the competitive nature of

each of these respective activities. While both cheer
and dance were historically spirit squads whose sole
function was to enhance crowd participation in
college football and basketball games, the modern
evolution of cheer and dance focuses on competitions
first and providing support to other sports second at
many institutions. This shift from being a part of the
marching band to becoming part of the athletics
department at many universities underscores this
change. Further, the popularity of these sports
continues to grow exponentially. And the demand for
viewing the annual competitions has increased as
well.

Universal Cheer Association (UCA) and Universal
Dance Association (UDA) put on regional and
national competitions each year, working with
Varsity. These competitions are lucrative and even
involve Varsity's own television network. University
athletic departments, the conferences, and the NCAA
continue to miss an excellent opportunity to generate
revenue and address proportionality gaps under Title
IX.

In 2012, the U.S. Court of Appeals for the Second
Circuit addressed the question of whether
cheerleading was a sport in the context of Title IX
litigation. In 2010, Quinnipiac University decided to
replace its volleyball program with competitive
cheer. Stephanie Biediger and her volleyball
teammates sued to block Quinnipiac, arguing that
the dismissal of the volleyball team violated Title IX.

At the core of the lawsuit was the question of
whether Quinnipiac was in violation of Title IX in

light of the 3.62% disparity between the percentage of scholarships available to females (58.22%) and the percentage of female undergraduate students at the university (61.87%). In particular, Quinnipiac argued that the court should count the thirty members of the competitive cheer team toward their total of female varsity athletes.

In other words, the court had to decide whether cheerleading was a sport, at least for purposes of Title IX. The court noted that while cheerleading traditionally involved crowd entertainment and encouragement, competitive cheer teams engaged in real competition against each other. While the court found that the cheer team shared many characteristics with other varsity sports at Quinnipiac, the court found that several facts distinguished this activity. In particular, the court noted the lack of on campus recruiting, the lack of uniform competition rules, and the absence of a progressive post-season set of competitions. The court found that these were dispositive in establishing that cheer was not a sport for purposes of Title IX, despite the "strength, agility, and grace" required to participate. The court noted that cheer one day might reach the status of a varsity sport, but had not yet established as much.

The tension here is interesting because it pits one women's team—volleyball—against another—cheer. The question, then, is not just whether cheer is a sport. It is whether courts should recognize cheer as a sport given that the consequence of doing so is to allow the university to eliminate the more traditional sport of volleyball.

A second important part of the *Biediger* holding relates to its finding that Quinnipiac was out of compliance with Title IX. In part because cheerleading did not count as a sport for Title IX purposes, a 3.62% disparity existed, which the court found was enough to violate Title IX. Allowing such a de minimis level of disparity to rise to the level of Title IX proportionality violation suggests that the OCR and the courts take this requirement very seriously. Even a small percentage gap is enough to prevent the university from eliminating women's teams like Quinnipiac tried to do with its volleyball team.

One wonders, a decade later, whether cheer teams and its corollary competition—dance teams—have reached the status of being a sport for purposes of Title IX. The distinguishing factors the court relied on in *Biediger* seem a vestige of the past or are easily curable. Recruiting happens extensively in both dance and cheer, multiple levels and leagues of competition exist, and rules have become increasingly uniform.

The failure of the NCAA to designate dance and cheer as an emerging sports seems to be a gross oversight. The NCAA and its members have ignored the lucrative nature of these events with their extensive fan following of past and current dancers and cheerleaders. Private companies like Varsity and their corporate partners have enjoyed record profits as a result. Even so, both sports continue to grow and

one imagines that they will one day become NCAA
sports.

On the one hand, allowing cheer and dance teams
to be sports for purpose of Title IX has the advantage
of offering a counter-weight to the eighty-five
scholarships taken up by the football team. On the
other hand, doing so may enable universities to
eliminate other more traditional women's sports
without violating Title IX.

3.   TITLE IX AND THE NCAA

Title IX does not apply to the NCAA. A lawsuit
involving volleyball player Renee M. Smith explored
this question. *NCAA v. Smith*, 525 U.S. 459 (1999).
Smith played volleyball for two seasons at St.
Bonaventure University. After graduating, she
enrolled in graduate programs at Hofstra University
and the University of Pittsburgh. The NCAA barred
Smith from playing volleyball at either school based
on its Postbaccalaureate Bylaw, a rule that limited
athletics participation by graduate students to the
institution awarding their undergraduate degree.
1993–94 NCAA Division I Manual, Bylaw 14.1.8.2.

Smith sued the NCAA and argued that the NCAA's
rule violated Title IX and that the NCAA was subject
to Title IX because it received dues from federally
funded institutions—colleges and universities. The
Supreme Court held 9–0 in the NCAA's favor, finding
that Title IX did not apply to the NCAA. The Court
distinguished entities that receive federal assistance
directly (which are subject to Title IX) from entities

that only benefit economically from federal assistance (which are not subject to Title IX).

One wonders whether similar reasoning would apply to athletic conferences. If athletes challenged conference rules under Title IX, it is possible they might face similar problems. In the same way that the NCAA does not receive direct funding from the federal government, athletic conferences do not receive direct funding. To the extent that conferences benefit from federal funding, it is from dues from federally funded institutions, just like the NCAA. And *Smith* makes clear that Title IX does not apply in such circumstances.

The reason that *Smith* and its potential application matter relates to the potential of the NCAA or the conferences entering into employment relationships with athletes. If athletes formed employment relationships with the NCAA or athletic conferences, then Title IX would not place limits on the distribution of such revenue. That means that, in such a situation, the NCAA or conference could pay the athlete a share of the television revenue without having to compensate non-revenue athletes. And such an approach would allow the traditional student-athlete model to persist.

When the NCAA and its member institutions adopt a revenue sharing model pursuant to the *House* settlement, it is not clear the degree to which Title IX would mandate equal sharing of revenue in the same way that it demands equal scholarships.

Given the guidance of the OCR, providing equal revenue shares might be akin to providing equal opportunity to each gender. But the application is not clear and would require guidance from the OCR. The question might ultimately be one of statutory interpretation for courts to resolve.

4. PRIVATIZATION AS AN ALTERNATIVE TO TITLE IX?

While most in intercollegiate athletics extol Title IX and the progress it has generated for female participation in intercollegiate athletics, it is possible athletic programs will seek to devalue women's sports in a world where college football recruiting takes place in a free market. The case for redistributing football income could dissipate, as universities and their boosters seek to win at all costs in football. It is also possible that women's sports could generate increased revenue, as demonstrated by women's college basketball.

But, as discussed, Title IX will not allow for disproportionate offerings of male and female scholarships, even if it does allow wide disparities in actual revenue spent on men's and women's teams, even in the same sport. As such, Title IX would protect women's non-revenue sports, at least to the extent that those sports provided the proportional number of scholarships to balance football and perhaps men's basketball.

A model in which some or all of the college sports becomes private might render Title IX irrelevant, at least in terms of promoting gender equity in the provision of scholarships. The kind of private entity chosen would impact the degree to which it could escape the reach of Title IX. If the new private entity that employed athletes was a private collective, then Title IX would not apply to the collective. If the new entity that employed the athletes was the university foundation, then Title IX might apply depending on the degree to which the foundation and the university overlap in their operations. If the university exerts some measure of control over an athletic foundation that employs athletes, then the foundation might be standing in the shoes in such a way as to implicate Title IX. As discussed, Title IX applies to institutions that receive federal funding. If the university commingles its finances with foundation gifts, or alternatively uses the two sources of funds together to achieve the purposes of the university, a nexus might exist leading a court to find that Title IX applies to the athletic foundation.

The analysis here would be similar to state actor analysis discussed in Chapter Two in the *Tarkanian* and *Brentwood Academy* cases. The test would be slightly different, but the idea would be the same.

5.   CONFERENCE EMPLOYMENT AS AN ALTERNATIVE TO TITLE IX?

Another possible way to evade Title IX relates to a different kind of private employment model. Instead of a foundation or collective employing the athletes, the athletes could be employees of the conferences. Such an approach would successfully avoid Title IX, at least with respect to the remuneration paid to athletes. As discussed in *Smith*, the Court has held that Title IX does not apply to the NCAA as a private association. The same would be true with respect to the conference, albeit on a much smaller scale.

A further wrinkle could be a hybrid model, where athletes are amateurs with respect to their universities, but employees with respect to the conferences. Such an approach would allow Title IX to persist and promote gender equity with respect to scholarships. At the same time, it would allow the conferences to pay athletes based on their market value, without regard to gender equity.

6.   TRANSGENDER ATHLETES AND TITLE IX

One final topic concerning Title IX relates to the NCAA rules concerning transgender athletes. In January, 2022, the NCAA adopted an updated transgender student-athlete participation policy. The NCAA's policy attempts to align with the policy of the Olympic Movement. The idea is to use a sport-by-sport approach with the goal of preserving the opportunity for transgender athletes to participate while balancing fairness, inclusion, and safety for all who compete.

As a result, the NCAA determines the policy for each sports by following the policy of the national governing body (NGB) of that sport. If there is no NGB policy for a sport, then the NCAA will follow the policy of that sport's international federation (IF). And if there is no NGB and no IF, then the NCAA policy will follow the policy criteria established by the

International Olympic Committee (IOC). The NCAA Committee on Competitive Safeguards and Medical Aspects of Sports will conduct an ongoing review of such policies and recommend alterations to the Board of Governors if needed.

The NCAA implemented this policy in three stages, with full implementation for the 2024–25 regular season and championships.

In March, 2024, however, Riley Gaines and fifteen other female athletes filed a lawsuit against the NCAA for allowing transgender women to compete in college sports and use women's locker rooms at events. The plaintiffs include current and former college swimmers as well as representatives from track, volleyball, and tennis, and seek class action status.

Part of the impetus of the lawsuit concerns Penn swimmer Lia Thomas, who became the first openly transgender athlete to win a Division I title in any sport. Thomas won the 500 freestyle event at the 2022 championships, defeating three Olympic medalists by more than a second-and-a-half. Plaintiffs argue that competing with Thomas, whom their complaint calls "a biologically male student-athlete," is both unfair and illegal.

Specifically, the plaintiffs allege violations of Title IX, the Equal Protection clause, and the right to bodily privacy. Core to the legal argument made by Gaines and her co-plaintiffs is that allowing transgender female athletes deprives other female athletes an equal opportunity to compete as required by Title IX. The plaintiffs also claim violations of equal protection of the law, alleging the NCAA's policy treats women unfairly. Finally, the plaintiffs objected to the use of locker room facilities by transgender athletes.

The defendants will answer the complaint and seek its dismissal. The NCAA will likely argue that its transgender eligibility policy reflects international consensus and is consistent with the law. The NCAA will also challenge the application of Title IX, which requires federal funding as decided in *Smith*.

Gaines v. NCAA follows earlier litigation involving the eligibility of transgender athletes. Another ongoing case, *Soule v. Connecticut Interscholastic Athletic Conference*, 90 F.4th. 34 (2d Cir. 2023), concerns a challenge to Connecticut's state athletic association's rule allowing transgender athletes to compete.

As of 2024, twenty-four states have adopted bans of transgender students from participating in sports consistent with their gender identity (as opposed to their gender at birth). Despite the many competing views on the issue, it appears that only a tiny percentage of NCAA athletes are transgender. In 2023, U.S. representative Bobby Scott calculated that out of approximately 480,000 athletes playing college sports, only thirty-two were transgender.

The question of transgender athlete participation in intercollegiate sports remains unsettled.

CHAPTER TEN
GAMBLING AND CONCUSSIONS

Over the last nine chapters, this Nutshell has demonstrated the connection from advertising to the generation of billion dollars of annual revenue for the revenue sports. Part of the attention, perhaps a growing amount, relates not to interest of fans in their team winning or losing. Rather, it relates to the rise of sports gambling and daily sports betting.

A significant percentage of sports fans now focus more on gambling than the game itself. Once the province of the Super Bowl and March Madness, sports betting on college football and basketball games has become very common. Fantasy sports have evolved into daily fantasy sports which have evolved to daily prop bets, where the opportunities for risking money and sports gambling seem endless.

And the NCAA and its member institutions have increasingly pursued opportunities to partner with gaming companies. This recent phenomenon has spread from professional sports to college sports. The professional leagues, the NCAA, and individual universities now understand that gambling on their games drives interest, attendance, and television ratings. In many ways, sports gambling is becoming the edifice upon which the entire NCAA model rests.

To be sure, college sports gambling is not new. Historically, illegal gambling has been prevalent with respect to college sports. In the pre-Internet era, local bookies thrived in underground gambling rings, many of which ensnared college students. Legal sports gambling thrived in Las Vegas, the destination of choice for many who wanted to gamble on the March Madness basketball tournament.

College sports gambling, however, has become ubiquitous in the past several years, thanks in large part to the Supreme Court's decision in *Murphy v. NCAA* in 2017. As explored below, *Murphy* removed the federal law barrier to states passing their own sports gaming laws.

1.   MURPHY V. NCAA

In 1992, Congress passed the Professional and Amateur Sports Protection Act (PASPA), 28 U.S.C. §§ 3701–3704, to prohibit state-sanctioned sports gambling. Included in PASPA are exceptions for state-sponsored sports wagering in Nevada and sports lotteries in Oregon and Delaware. The law also included an exception for New Jersey, provided that New Jersey enact a sports gambling scheme within one year of PASPA's passage. New Jersey never passed such a law, and as a result, became subject to PASPA's bar on state-sanctioned sports gambling.

The law had significant reach. PASPA provides for a cause of action for any sports league whose games are or will be the subject of sports gambling to enjoin the gambling. In 2011, New Jersey began to regret its decision not to seize the PASPA exemption.

In 2011, the New Jersey Legislature held a referendum asking voters whether it should permit sports gambling. Sixty-four percent of New Jersey citizens voted in favor of a state constitutional amendment that would permit sports gambling. Partially in response to the enthusiasm of Governor Chris Christie, the legislature then drafted and received voter approval of a sports-wagering constitutional amendment. In 2012, the New Jersey legislature enacted the Sports Wagering Act (2012 Act). This law authorized certain regulated sports wagering at New Jersey casinos and racetracks. It also implemented a comprehensive regulatory scheme for licensing casinos and sporting events for wagering.

Five sports leagues sued under PASPA to enjoin the New Jersey law. The state argued that PASPA was unconstitutional under the Supreme Court's anti-commandeering doctrine. This doctrine bars Congress, as a matter of federalism, from commanding that a state legislature to act in a particular way or requiring it to pass particular legislation. It is worth noting that Congress can condition the receipt of certain federal benefits on state participation in a federal scheme without violating this anti-commandeering rule.

The district court rejected New Jersey's constitutional argument and enjoined the 2012 Act. The New Jersey legislature responded by passing a second law in 2014 (2014 Act). This law purported to repeal the regulatory scheme for licensing casinos and sporting events, effectively providing tacit authorization of them. The leagues again sued to enjoin the 2014 Law. The district court granted summary judgment in favor of the leagues and issued a permanent injunction against the governor and other state agencies. A divided panel of the Third Circuit affirmed, and upon rehearing, the Third Circuit *en banc* (the entire court) affirmed the majority opinion of the panel.

The Supreme Court, however, reversed in a 6–3 decision. *Murphy v. NCAA*, 584 U.S. 453 (2018). In an opinion authored by Justice Alito, the Court found that PASPA's provision prohibiting state authorization of sports gambling schemes violated the anticommandeering doctrine under the 10th Amendment to the Constitution as interpreted under *New York v. United States*, 505 U.S. 144 (1992) and *Printz v. United States*, 521 U.S. 898 (1997). As a result, "Congress may not simply 'commandeer the legislative process of the States by directly compelling them to enact and enforce a federal regulatory program.'"

The Court understood the repeal of the old laws barring sports gambling as an affirmative decision to authorize sports gambling. Because PASPA prevented New Jersey from acting to repeal its statute, this statute was commandeering the state not to pass a particular kind of legislation (legislation that legalized sports gambling). Again, the commandeering principle does not allow Congress to mandate what the New Jersey legislature can and cannot do. The Court stated that complying with the anticommandeering rule is important because it serves as one of the Constitution's structural safeguards of liberty, advances political accountability, and prevents Congress from shifting regulatory costs to the states.

The state response to the *Murphy* decision was swift. Some states, like Mississippi, had sports betting bills waiting and passed them within a few weeks. As of 2024, thirty-eight states allow sports betting, with mobile sports betting legal in thirty states.

2.   A HISTORY OF POINT SHAVING

The growth of sports gambling has positive economic consequences for states, universities, conferences, and the NCAA. The worry about promoting gambling addictions and ruining individuals by making such risk-taking widely available appears to have moved to the background, much like a warning label on a widely used but dangerous product.

It is worth remembering, however, the long history of college athletes colluding with gamblers to change the outcomes of games, or alternatively, shave points. The practice of point shaving occurs when athletes try to win, but not by an amount more than the betting line.

Perhaps the most notorious of college gambling scandals happened in 1951 and involved the basketball teams at the City College of New York (City College) and the University of Kentucky (Kentucky). In 1950, City College won both the National Invitation Tournament (NIT) and NCAA tournaments. During the 1950 NCAA Tournament,

City College handed Kentucky coach Adolph Rupp the worst defeat of his career, 89–50 in a game where the racist coach forbade his all white team from shaking hands with the integrated City College team before the game.

Within a year, New York District Attorney Frank Hogan had indicted players from City College and three other New York schools: Manhattan College, New York University and Long Island University. This scandal reached seven schools and thirty-two players who fixed eighty-six games between 1947 and 1950.

The point-shaving began, however, in summer games in the Catskills in 1949. A popular resort area at the time, the Catskills recruited many college kids to work for the summer. Many of the top basketball players in the country, including Wilt Chamberlain, played there in summer games. Seeking to make some money over the summer, Salvatore Sollazzo managed wagers on the summer games by setting lines for the games. Sollazzo then befriended basketball player Eddie Gard. Sollazzo would pay Gard and any teammates willing to participate to shave points by winning the game by fewer points than the betting line.

This arrangement continued into the 1949–50 season. Gard played for LIU and ultimately convinced his teammate and LIU leading scorer Sherman White to help. From there, point shaving spread to other schools in New York and then throughout the country.

In early 1951, a series of arrests in the scandal threatened the future of college basketball. First, the state of New York arrested two Manhattan players, Henry Poppe and Jack Byrnes, along with three fixers—Cornelious Kelleher and brothers Benjamin and Irving Schwartzberg on January 17, 1951. Poppe had met with junior center Junius Kellogg, a 6'8" star who was the first black man to play on the Manhattan team. Poppe had offered Kellogg $1,000 to help point shave. Kellogg reported Poppe to the coach, Ken Norton, who endorsed the idea of going to the police. Kellogg pretended to accept Poppe's offer, and his additional instructions provided enough evidence to arrest him.

On February 18, 1951, police arrested City College players Ed Warner, Ed Roman, and Al Roth at Penn Station as they were returning from Philadelphia, having defeated Temple 95–71. They arrested Gard and Sallazzo that same evening. Two days later, police arrested Sherman White, LeRoy Smith, and Adolph Bigos of LIU. *The Sporting News* had just named White the Player of the Year.

A month later, the police arrested the last of the participating City College players—Irwin Dambrot, Norm Mager, and Herb Cohen. Other arrests continued throughout the summer in the New York area, mostly focused on fixers, but also implicating players at Toledo and Bradley.

In October, 1951, police arrested Kentucky basketball players Ralph Beard, Alex Groza, and Dale Barnstable for accepting $500 bribes to shave points in an NIT game against Loyola Chicago in

Madison Square Garden in 1949. Finally, Kentucky suspended All-American Center Bill Spivey in March, 1952. A leading player on Kentucky's 1951 national championship team, Spivey denied point shaving, but received an indictment for perjury in 1953. After a mistrial, the state subsequently dismissed the charge, but the NBA refused to admit Spivey.

Most of the players received suspended sentences, and in some cases, the state dropped the charges. Ed Warner, Sherman White, and Eddie Gard served jail time of less than a year. Many of the fixers served significant time in state prison.

The basketball programs themselves had particularly serious consequences. The NCAA suspended the Kentucky basketball program for the 1952–53 season. City College deemphasized its athletic program and dropped down to Division III. LIU closed its entire athletic program from 1951–57, and did not return to Division I until the 1980s.

A point shaving scandal at Boston College followed The City College scandal twenty years later. In the 1978–79 season, informant Henry Hill accused three Boston College (BC) players, leading scorer Ernie Cobb, forward Richard Kuhn, and point guard Jim Sweeney, of participating in a point-shaving scheme. Kuhn acknowledged his role and was convicted. Cobb admitted to accepting $1,000 and Sweeney said he took $500. But both denied willingly participating on the court. Cobb was indicted, but acquitted. Sweeney was never charged.

Thanks to Hill's testimony, Pittsburgh gamblers Paul Mazzei, brothers Anthony and Rocco Perla, and New York mobster Jimmy Burke were convicted. Interestingly, the stories of the gamblers and the players differ as to the arrangement and the degree of participation.

The scheme began with the December 6, 1978 game between BC and Providence. BC was a five-point favorite, but won 83–64, resulting in the gamblers losing money. They redoubled their efforts for the December 16, 1978 Harvard game, recruiting Cobb. BC was a twelve-point favorite and won by three points, 86–83. The scheme carried on for six more games, but with inconsistent results. The gamblers went big for one last game, a February 10, 1979 game with Holy Cross. BC was a three-point underdog and the instruction was to lose by more than three points. Unsure about how to handle the situation, Sweeney later admitted that he intentionally fouled out of the game early in the second half. BC rallied at lost by two, 98–96, crushing the gamblers.

In 1981, the scandal became public and went to trial. Burke, Mazzei, Kuhn, and the Perla brothers were convicted of conspiracy, conspiracy to commit sports bribery, and interstate travel with the intent to commit bribery. Burke received a twelve year sentence, Mazzei and Tony Perla received a ten year sentence, and Rocco Perla received a four year sentence. Kuhn received a ten year sentence, later reduced to twenty-eight months. Cobb was acquitted.

On a lighter note, the gamblers served as the inspiration for the mob characters in the 1990 film Goodfellas, during which one of the characters refers to bets on Boston College games. ESPN named its *30 for 30* documentary on the scandal "Playing for the Mob," which Goodfellas star Ray Liotta narrated.

In 1985, another point shaving scandal occurred at Tulane University in New Orleans. This scandal, initiated by fraternity members at Tulane, involved both payments and cocaine. Gary Kranz, a student and cocaine dealer on campus, offered senior forward Clyde Eads a payment of cash and drugs to shave points in a game against Southern Mississippi.

Eads asked several teammates, including star center John "Hot Rod" Williams, to help keep the game close. Kranz and his fraternity brothers bet on the game and paid participating players between $400 and $800. After an attempt to fix a game against Virginia Tech failed, the students focused on fixing a game against Memphis State, who would later advance to the Final Four in the 1985 NCAA tournament. Tulane was a seven point underdog at home. Even so, they led at halftime, despite Williams getting himself in foul trouble on purpose. Memphis State pulled away in the second half, winning by eleven points to cover the spread. Five Tulane players earned $13,500 for fixing the Memphis State game, including $5,000 to Williams.

Ned Kohnke, a Tulane alum and New Orleans lawyer heard rumors about the Memphis State game and reported them to New Orleans district attorney Harry Connick, Sr. Kranz pled guilty to ten counts of sports bribery and two counts of conspiracy in exchange for dismissal of ten cocaine charges. He received a twelve year suspended sentence and a $10,000 fine. Fraternity brothers Mark Olensky and David Rothenberg received smaller fines and two year suspended sentences.

Eads and forward Jon Johnson received immunity from prosecution for cooperating in the investigation. Senior Tulane point guard Bobby Thompson received a two-year suspended sentence. Hot Rod Williams had a mistrial and was subsequently acquitted, before being drafted by the Cleveland Cavaliers.

Tulane closed its men's basketball program in 1985 as a result of the scandal. It reinstated the program at the start of the 1989–90 season.

Another scandal occurred at Arizona State University (ASU) during the 1993–94 season. Under coach Bill Frieder, ASU had one of the stronger teams in the Pac-10 that season. The leading scorer and point guard for ASU, Stevin "Hedake" Smith, was an unsuccessful sports bettor. Smith owed over $10,000 in gambling debts to Tempe bookie Benny Silman for bets on college football and NFL games. Silman tipped off Joe Gagliano, a bond trader from Chicago, about the possibility of getting Smith to engage in point shaving as a way to erase his gambling debt.

Gagliano paid Silman $20,000 per game to fix two conference games against Oregon and Oregon State. Gagliano flew to Las Vegas with $500,000 and banked over $2 million betting on the fixed games.

Others eventually started to discover what was happening, as Gagliano's bets started affecting the Vegas lines for the games. A local bookie named Big Red found out about the point shaving and threatened to expose Smith if he did not shave points in the Washington game. As rumors continued that the fix was in for the Washington game, bettors drove to Las Vegas and placed bets. The line opened with Arizona State as twelve point favorites, but dropped to seven points (where Gagliano bet) and ultimately three points. The unusual activity led the Nevada Gaming Commission to flag the game and notify the FBI.

With his team trailing at halftime, coach Frieder told his team that the FBI was watching. The players panicked, abandoned the point shaving scheme, and won the game by eighteen points.

Smith, Silman, and Gagliano were ultimately caught and served time in prison.

In 1994–95, Northwestern basketball players engaged in point shaving. Northwestern was an unusual target, given their historical struggles in basketball. Their team posted only two winning seasons between 1970 and 1994, and were among the worst teams in the Big Ten during that era. The 1994–95 team was no different, going 5–22 and finishing in last place.

In 1994, Northwestern suspended basketball player Dion Lee for six games at the start of the season for placing bets on college football games. Kevin Pendergast, a football player at Notre Dame, convinced Lee to shave points in basketball games against Wisconsin, Penn State, and Michigan. He saw the point shaving scheme as a quick way to cover his gambling debts.

Pendergast offered Lee $4,000 to fix the Penn State game. Penn State was favored by fourteen points and won by twenty, with Lee scoring just two points. Lee also solicited teammates Dewey Williams and Matt Purdy to help. Lee and Williams had a combined scoring average of 20.1 points per game, but together averaged 6.3 points in the three fixed games.

The scheme, however, became quickly discovered with Pendergast, Lee, and Williams receiving indictments, along with bettor Brian Irving. Purdy received immunity as the government's key witness. Pendergast was sentenced to two months in prison, with Lee, Williams, and Irving receiving one month sentences.

3. RECENT TRENDS IN COLLEGE ATHLETICS INVOLVEMENT IN GAMBLING

With the legalization of sports gambling in an increasing number of states, a pressing dilemma has emerged for the NCAA, primarily because of the growing trend of gambling among student-athletes. It compromises not only the personal and financial well-being of the students but also endangers the integrity of college sports. Jon Duncan, the NCAA's vice president of enforcement, has highlighted a worrying trend with NCAA infractions cases on sports wagering growing.

Supporting Duncan's observations, several studies have shown a growing prevalence of sports wagering among college students. About fifty-eight percent of students have admitted to sports betting, a number that rises to sixty-seven percent among those living on campus. The pervasive presence of gambling advertisements targeting college environments encourages such participation, with sixty-three percent of on-campus students recalling seeing betting ads. Notably, sixteen percent of students have engaged in high-risk gambling behaviors, with six percent suffering substantial financial losses in a single day. The misconception among these risky gamblers that frequent gambling can lead to consistent monetary gains aggravates the issue, reflecting a grave misapprehension of the odds and risks in sports betting.

This growth in sports gambling is not escaping college athletes. The NCAA, with its stringent regulations, forbids any form of sports betting by athletes. Prohibited wagers include fantasy leagues, March Madness brackets, Super Bowl squares, sports pools, online sports bets, sports betting apps, parlay and prop bets, live in-game betting, and single game sports bets. If a college athlete violates these rules, they can face suspension and removal from their team as well as lose their eligibility.

The current legal and regulated landscape of sports wagering has streamlined NCAA's investigations into gambling cases. Online betting leaves digital trails that provide indisputable evidence of such activities, aiding in the identification and penalization of offenders.

The NCAA's approach is clear. Sports wagering undermines the integrity of sports contests and jeopardizes athlete well-being. Educational initiatives like posters and guidelines are widespread in college athletic departments to discourage gambling. Its approach makes its current courting of gaming companies curious, as well as its long history promoting a basketball tournament whose audience wagered heavily long before *Murphy* allowed non-exempted states to legalize sports gambling.

Recognizing the changing landscape, the NCAA has revised its penalty structure, introducing more refined guidelines that consider the amount wagered and the nature of the betting activity. Further, gambling on collegiate sports not only carries legal and regulatory consequences but also poses ethical concerns. It threatens the very essence of sportsmanship, converting the focus from fair competition to monetary gain. This shift demeans the competition and contradicts the values central to athletic competition.

A critical question arises in the context of sports wagering concerning whether NCAA penalties should punish the involved individual or their institution more. The question relates to whether deterrence really works or whether the result of punishing an institution is really to punish non-participants in the infraction.

In 2023, a sports betting scandal arose involving multiple athletes from Iowa State University and the University of Iowa. Originating in Des Moines, this inquiry has involved both current and former student-athletes from these universities, with fifteen student-athletes and two student managers accused of engaging in unlawful sports betting. These allegations, emerging in August 2023, uncovered an intricate pattern of illegal and underage gambling on college sports, including matches in which the accused student-athletes themselves were involved.

Central to this controversy were Iowa State quarterback Hunter Dekkers, wrestler Paniro Johnson, offensive lineman Dodge Sauser, former Cyclone football player Eyioma Uwazurike, and University of Iowa baseball player Gehrig Christensen. Additionally, Hawkeye kicker Aaron Blom and former Iowa basketball player Ahron Ulis, who transferred to Nebraska, have been involved.

These athletes engaged in concealed gambling activities, often using the identities of others to place bets. Notably, Dekkers, Johnson, and Sauser utilized the names of relatives' names to bet through platforms like DraftKings and FanDuel. Their betting was extensive. Johnson placed 1,283 wagers and Dekkers placed nearly 370. More importantly, however, the athletes also included wagers on their own university's sports events, violating NCAA rules and state laws. Uwazurike, who played for the Cyclones from 2016 to 2022 and has been suspended from the NFL, placed bets on ISU events, including games in which he played.

The implications for the athletes are severe. Under Iowa law, tampering with records is an aggravated misdemeanor, potentially leading to two years in prison and substantial fines. Furthermore, the NCAA's stringent new guidelines for sports betting violations, effective from May 2023, pose a significant threat to the collegiate careers of the athletes. These guidelines stipulate that betting on one's own games or providing inside information for betting purposes could result in permanent ineligibility in collegiate sports. Given that the betting totals for each athlete exceed the threshold of $800, the severe NCAA penalties, including permanent bans, seem likely. These student-athletes face potential penalties that range from a deferred judgment to a maximum sentence of up to two years in prison and a fine ranging from $855 to $8,540.

This case involving sports wagering at Iowa and Iowa State sheds light on multifaceted challenges in regulating betting in collegiate athletics. The situation underscores the stringent prohibitions against such activities in college sports and the severe consequences for breaking these rules.

The scandal also highlights the challenges in enforcing NCAA rules regarding sports betting, particularly in a time when gambling has become increasingly prevalent and accepted in society. The Iowa Division of Criminal Investigation's probe did more than just expose NCAA regulation breaches; it also unearthed potential illegal activities, underscoring serious concerns about the effectiveness of NCAA policies and the broader enforcement of gambling laws. While NCAA guidelines unequivocally ban athletes from betting on sports at any NCAA championship level, this situation has ignited a wider conversation about the role of state regulatory bodies in enforcing NCAA rules apparent discrepancies in the application of these rules across various states and universities.

Furthermore, the revelation that athletes from two universities were gambling raises questions about selective enforcement. It prompts inquiries about whether similar practices might be occurring undetected at other institutions.

Another recent gambling scandal involved the former head coach of Air Force men's golf team. Processed via the NCAA's negotiated resolution method, this case exposed the coach's unauthorized involvement in sports wagering, including placing bets on Air Force football games. *United States Air Force Academy, Negotiated Resolution*, Case No. 020232, September 28, 2023.

Concealing his identity, the former golf coach set up an online betting account using his girlfriend's biographical information. In a span of four months, he made bets worth a total $9,259, spread over 253 bets, out of which 107 were on NCAA events and six on Air Force football. This action not only breached NCAA's standards of honesty and fair play but also demonstrated a failure to foster a compliant environment, contravening the NCAA's head coach responsibility rules. As a consequence, the negotiated resolution imposed several penalties. The Air Force Academy received an extended probation period until

September 2027, along with a $5,000 fine. The NCAA also imposed a five year show-cause order on the golf coach.

In April 2023, investigators discovered that a former University of Alabama baseball coach had engaged in a prohibited gambling scheme. At the center of the controversy were Bert Eugene Neff Jr., a former youth-league baseball coach, and Brad Bohannon, the former head coach of the Alabama Crimson Tide baseball team.

The scandal surfaced when Neff attempted to place a wager of over $100,000 on a college baseball game between Alabama and LSU at the BetMGM Sportsbook in Cincinnati's Great American Ballpark. This raised immediate suspicion because of the significant amount of the bet and the low gambling traffic for the game. Neff, reportedly in communication with Bohannon via encrypted messaging, had inside information. Alabama would not be starting its ace pitcher, Luke Holman, because of back tightness, and would be replacing him with Hagan Banks who had not started a game since mid-March.

Surveillance cameras at the sportsbook captured evidence of Neff's communication with Bohannon. This alleged exchange of inside information led to immediate action by BetMGM, through the U.S. Integrity wagering integrity firm. They reported the suspicious bet to regulatory bodies, including the Ohio Casino Control Commission and the Southeastern Conference. Consequently, Alabama swiftly fired Bohannon, citing violations of university policies against providing sports-related information to gamblers and engaging in betting.

The ramifications of this scandal extend to the personal careers of Neff and Bohannon. For Bohannon, the potential consequences include criminal charges and a likely end to his career in NCAA baseball. Under the negotiated resolution, the NCAA imposed a fifteen-year show cause penalty. *University of Alabama, Negotiated Resolution*, Case No. 020261, February 1, 2024. As for Neff, his involvement raises questions about the integrity of collegiate sports, especially considering his extensive network in recruiting circles and his son's position as a pitcher for the University of Cincinnati.

This incident has also implicated the University of Cincinnati and Xavier University because of their connections to Neff. Cincinnati fired two baseball staff members, and the school's head coach resigned, though it is unclear the relationship of these actions to the gambling scandal. Xavier University, too, finds itself under NCAA investigation, though the school has not confirmed any details.

This case underscores the necessity for strict regulatory measures and proactive monitoring by sportsbooks and integrity organizations to avert similar situations. The prompt actions taken by BetMGM and U.S. Integrity serve as a model for the kind of proactive steps required to maintain the integrity of sports betting.

Like similar scandals before, the Alabama baseball betting controversy stands as a stark warning about the risks of insider betting and the potential for corruption in collegiate sports. It serves as a potent reminder of the ethical obligations of those involved in sports and highlights the need for comprehensive regulatory frameworks to ensure the integrity of athletic competitions.

4.   THE CONCUSSION CASES: GEE V. NCAA

In 2016, the NCAA settled a class-action concussion lawsuit. It paid $70 million to monitor former college athletes' medical conditions, as well as contributed $5 million toward medical research and payments of up to $5,000 to individual players claiming injuries. *In re: National Collegiate Athletic Association Student-Athlete Concussion Injury Litigation*, 314 F.R.D. 580 (N.D. Ill. 2016). This settlement, however, did not foreclose other lawsuits by injured athletes.

In 2022, Alana Gee, the widow of former University of Southern California (USC) linebacker Matthew Gee, filed a $55 million negligence and wrongful death lawsuit against the NCAA. Gee alleged that the NCAA did not provide sufficient protection to athletes from concussion risks. Gee was a linebacker on USC's 1990 Rose Bowl team. Between 1988 and 1992, Matthew Gee took over 6,000 hits while playing for USC, resulting in irreversible brain damage. Following his death in 2018, Gee's family sent his brain to Boston University's Chronic Traumatic Encephalopathy Center, where researchers found evidence of chronic traumatic encephalopathy (CTE).

This lawsuit highlighted the enduring effects of concussions on college football athletes and underscored the responsibility of organizations like the NCAA in ensuring their medical well-being. Gee contended that the NCAA was aware of concussion risks but did little to protect players. She further claimed that the NCAA fostered a culture that downplayed concussions and discouraged athletes from reporting injuries.

Even so, the jury in *Gee v. NCAA* concluded that the NCAA was not responsible for Matthew Gee's death. Gee's long history of health problems, as well as his history of substance abuse certainly complicated the picture, and explains in part the jury's decision. Notably, this case was the first CTE-related lawsuit against the NCAA decided by a jury.

The Gee lawsuit is among numerous cases aimed at the NCAA, asserting its failure to sufficiently educate and protect student-athletes from concussion risks. This lawsuit spotlighted the NCAA's duty to safeguard athletes. A win for the plaintiffs could have compelled the NCAA to revise its policies, bolster athlete protections, and potentially face extensive financial repercussions.

In response, the NCAA refuted the claims, emphasizing that players like Matthew Gee opted to engage in a full-contact sport, fully aware of the risks. The NCAA further argued that they had implemented policies both to inform players of potential dangers and to shield them. Given the verdict, the NCAA is likely to reference it in defense against numerous ongoing CTE-related lawsuits, making it tougher for future plaintiffs to litigate against the organization.

The Gee case is just one of many tort cases pending against the NCAA for head injuries suffered by former college football players. Researchers have linked the repeated head trauma from playing football to later health problems ranging from headaches to depression and, sometimes, early onset Parkinson's or Alzheimer's disease.

CONCLUDING THOUGHTS AND ACKNOWLEDGEMENTS

Part of the joy and challenge of studying, teaching, and practicing college sports law is that it continually changes. Indeed, the past five years have brought about astounding changes to college athletics. And because of a combination of litigation and market factors, such change is likely to continue in the near future.

This Nutshell aspires to provide a coherent, clear discussion of the current issues, how the past informs them, and a preview of where the future might head. Whether involved in college athletics as an athlete, coach, or administrator, the study of sports law as a law student, business student, or instructor, or the practicing of college sports law as an agent, attorney, or general counsel, we hope that you find our book useful.

The fast changing nature of this area means that subsequent editions will likely soon follow. In the meantime, we will cover major changes in college sports law on Professor Lust's podcast *Conduct Detrimental: The Sports Law Podcast, and accompanying website,* https://www.conduct detrimental.com/.

We would like to thank West Academic, particularly Danny Buteyn and Jon Harkness, for their help in getting this project off the ground. We would also like to thank the law students who contributed to this manuscript, Brandon Blumer, Duncan Hubbard, Ben Radisch, Rob Ricigliano, and

Ethan Zucker. And finally, we would like to thank our families for their patience and support while we were putting together the manuscript.

All in all, it is a joy to be teaching sports law in this season of rapid change. Please let us know if there are areas that deserve more coverage in future editions. Thank you for reading our book.

William W. Berry III, Oxford, MS
Daniel E. Lust, New York, NY
May 2024

INDEX

References are to Pages

———

12th Man+ Fund, 142, 157

30 for 30, 300

AAA, see Arkansas Activities Association

AAC, see American Athletic Conference

ABC, see American Broadcasting Companies

Abdul-Jabbar, Kareem, 9

Abruzzo, Jennifer, 239

ACC, see Atlantic Coast Conference

Adams, Mike, 49

Adidas, 56, 103, 123, 155–56, 187

Affordable Care Act, 163

Agnew, Joseph, 27, 94

Air Force, see United States Air Force Academy

Air Raid, 264

Alabama 87, 109

Alabama, University of, 55–57, 60, 63–64, 66, 124–25, 131, 138, 230, 251, 258, 268–69, 271, 309–10

Alaska, 166–67

Alaska Anchorage, University of, 199

Alaska School Activities Association, 167

Alcindor, Lew, see Kareem Abdul-Jabbar

Alexander, Shaun, 110

Allen, Dede, 199

ALS Association, 189

Alston, Shawne, 99

Amateurism, 2–3, 8–10, 12–13, 20, 39, 46, 59, 75–77, 85, 90, 93, 96–98, 100–01, 103, 107, 111–12, 114, 145, 154, 167–69, 208–09, 224–26, 229, 232, 236, 243, 249

American Athletic Conference, 89

American Broadcasting Companies, 78, 86–87, 89

American Tobacco Company, 7

Anderson, Jacob, 71

Anderson, Robert, 70

Anthony, Carmelo, 110

Anthony, Cole, 181

Arizona State University, 97, 111, 124, 150, 215, 247, 255, 301–02

Arizona, University of, 247, 254

Arkansas, 157, 167

Arkansas Activities Association, 167

Arkansas, University of, 49, 205, 245, 270–71

ASAA, see Alaska School Activities Association

ASU, see Arizona State University

Atlanta 90, 109

Atlanta Falcons, 262, 270

Atlantic Coast Conference, 12, 56, 86–90, 245–47, 249–55

Auburn 83, 109

Auburn University, 50–51, 146, 272

Avatar, 97, 108, 110–11

Avoli, 155–56

Baker, Charlie, 158–61, 229

Banks, Braxston, 91–94

Banks, Hagan, 309

Barnstable, Dale, 297

Baseball, 25, 28, 95, 104, 192, 207, 256, 306, 309–10

Basketball, high school, 103, 177, 181

Basketball, men's, 3–4, 9, 15–16, 19–20, 22–25, 28, 30, 36, 40, 48–50, 53–56, 59, 65, 76, 89, 95–97, 99–100, 102–04, 110–12, 123, 158, 161–63, 177, 192, 204–05, 209, 212, 214–19, 223, 240–43, 246, 248, 256–59, 262, 275, 281, 286, 291–92, 295–98, 301–03, 305–06

Basketball, women's, 61, 120, 149, 161, 184, 219, 223, 248, 275, 281, 286

Baton Rouge 87, 109

Battle, Eugene, 31

Battle's End, The, 142

Baylor University, 70–73

BC, see Boston College

BCS, see Bowl Championship Series

Beard, Ralph, 297

Bears, Chicago, see Chicago Bears

Beats by Dre, 186–87

Bech, Jack, 188

Bennett IV, Stetson, 189
Berger, Gillian, 231
BetMGM Sportsbook, 309–10
Bewley, Matthew, 177–78
Bewley, Ryan, 177–78
Biediger, Stephanie, 281, 283
Big 8 Conference, 79, 245
Big 12 Conference, 12, 89–90, 245–47, 250, 255
Big East Conference, 86, 245–46, 250
Big League Advance, 124
Big Red, 302
Big Ten Conference, 12, 60–61, 86–87, 89–90, 237, 245–47, 249–
    51, 253–55, 302
Bigos, Adolph, 297
Bill of Rights, 39, 42
Bill Walsh College Football, 108–09
Bjork, Ross, 59, 272
Bledsoe, Hon. Louis A., 253
Bledsoe, Mac, 268
Blom, Aaron, 306
Bloom, Jeremy, 1–3, 20, 177
Boeheim, Jim, 53
Bohannon, Brad, 309–10
Bohannon, Jordan, 28
Boost Mobile, 120
Booster, 3, 35, 46, 52–54, 58, 62–64, 76, 105, 116, 121–22, 131,
    136, 138–40, 144–52, 154, 175, 180, 210, 215, 225–26, 228,
    248, 261, 286
Boston College, 68, 88, 245, 298–300
Boston University, 311
Bowen, Brian, 56
Bowl Championship Series, 51, 88, 96
Bradford, Steven, 113
Bradley University, 297
Brandr group, The, 120, 164–65
Brentwood Academy, 43–44, 287
Briles, Art, 72
Broncos, Denver, see Denver Broncos
Brown University, 161–62, 219, 238, 278–79
Buckeyes, see Ohio State University

Burke, Jimmy, 299

Bush, Reggie, 47–48, 110, 266–67

Butler, Touré, 18

Byers, Walter, 8–9

Cadwalader Report, 24

California, 97, 107, 111, 113–14, 125–28, 166, 168, 254, 267

California-Berkeley, see California, University of (Berkeley)

California, Los Angeles, University of, 9, 40, 48, 96–97, 111, 181, 246, 249, 255

California, University of (Berkeley), 88, 247, 255

Calipari, John, 205

Camp, Walter, 7

Cardinals, see Louisville, University of

Carlyle, Kanaan, 178

Castro-Walker, Marcus, 150

Catskills, 296

Cavaliers, Cleveland, see Cleveland Cavaliers

Cavinder, Haley, 120, 149

Cavinder, Hannah, 120, 149

CBPA, see College Basketball Players Association

CBS, see Columbia Broadcasting System

Centenary College, 15

CFA, see College Football Association

CFP, see College Football Playoff

Chamberlain, Wilt, 296

Champions Circle, 136, 142

Chapman, Neils, 31

Cheerleading, 280–83

Cheney, John, 16

Chicago Bears, 124

Chicago, Illinois, 236, 301

Chicago State University, 177–78

Choh, Tamenang, 161–62, 219

Christensen, Gehrig, 306

Christie, Chris, 293

Chronic traumatic encephalopathy, 311

Cigarette Racing, 149

Cincinnati, Ohio, 309

Cincinnati, University of, 310

City College of New York, 295–98

Clarett, Maurice, 49, 104–06

Clark, Kihei, 28

Class action, 99, 111, 161, 215, 219, 258, 289

Classic City Collective, 142

CLC, see Collegiate Licensing Company

Clemson 81, 109

Clemson University, 88, 249, 251, 253

Cleveland Cavaliers, 301

Coach Prime, see Sanders, Deion

Cobb, Ernie, 298–99

Code, Merl, 102

Cohen, Herb, 297

Cole, Emily, 185

Cole, Tony, 48

Collective Association, The, 141–42, 144

Collectives, 66, 121–22, 124–25, 131, 136–44, 147, 150, 152, 154,
    156–57, 162–63, 169, 175, 181, 211–15, 225, 287

College Athletes Players Association, 236

College Basketball Players Association, 239

College Football Association, 78–79, 86–87

College Football Players Association, 165

College Football Playoff, 60, 85, 88–90, 109, 247–49, 252

Collegiate Athlete Fair Pay Act, 130

Collegiate Licensing Company, 110–11

Colorado, 2, 20, 134–35, 166, 193, 221

Colorado, University of, 1–3, 20, 135, 177, 187, 198, 247, 254–55,
    272–73

Columbia Broadcasting System, 78

Columbia University, 219, 238

Columbus 79, 109

Conard, Kevin, 33

Conference USA, 89

Connick, Sr., Harry, 300

Cooke, Alexa, 233

Corman, Jake, 69

Cornell University, 219

Corum, Blake, 188

Courtney, Patrick, 94

Craft, Aaron, 50

Creighton University, 22–23

Crimson Collective, The, 143
Crimson Tide, see Alabama, University of
CTE, see Chronic traumatic encephalopathy
Cureton, Tai Kwan, 16–17
Curley, Tim, 66
Cyclones, see Iowa State University
Dambrot, Irwin, 297
Daniels, DaVaris, 55
Dartmouth College, 162–63, 214, 219, 240–43
Dartmouth Peak Performance, 242
Dawkins, Christian, 102
Dawson, Lamar, 232–33
Death penalty, 62–64, 66
Dekkers, Hunter, 306
Delaware, 292
Dennison, Ray, 8–9
Denver Broncos, 106
Department of Health, Education, and Welfare, 276
Deppe, Peter, 95
Dexter, Gervon, 124
Dillingham, Rob, 178
DiNardo, Gerry, 260–61
District of Columbia, 166
Division Street, 136
Dorrell, Jessica, 270–71
DraftKings, 306
Drake University, 30
Due Process Clause, 39, 41–42, 265
Duke University, 185, 209, 220
Duncan, Jon, 303–04
Duncan, Tim, 110
Dunne, Olivia, 181
Durant, Kevin, 110
EA Sports, see Electronic Arts
Eads, Clyde, 300–01
Eagles, Philadelphia, see Philadelphia Eagles
Electronic Arts, 108–09, 162, 165
Elliott, Tevin, 71
Emmert, Mark, 67–68, 158
Equal Protection Clause, 15, 289–90

ESPN, 50, 86–89, 109–10, 251, 253–54, 264, 300
Evers, Nick, 188
Exit fee, 249–53
Faculty Athletics Representative (FAR), 39
Fair Labor Standards Act, 163, 230–34, 242
Fair Pay to Play Act, 113, 125–27
Falcons, see Atlanta Falcons
FanDuel, 306
FBI, see Federal Bureau of Investigation
FBS, see Football Bowl Subdivision
Federal Bureau of Investigation, 56, 67, 102, 302
Fencing, 59
Fields, Jaiden, 185
Fiesta Bowl, 105, 109
Final Four, 40, 51, 262, 300
Financial aid, 11, 22, 27, 33, 127, 162, 164, 173, 221, 237, 276
Fisher, Jimbo, 138, 260
Fitzgerald, Larry, 110
Fitzgerald, Pat, 240
Florida, 107, 114, 120, 123–25, 127–28, 130, 151, 252–54, 268
Florida Atlantic University, 134
Florida State University, 61–62, 88, 108, 139–40, 142, 153, 188, 227, 245, 251–54
Florida, University of, 123–24, 150–53
Florida Victorious, 152
FLSA, see Fair Labor Standards Act
Football, 1–2, 4, 7–9, 13, 18, 20, 24–25, 28–33, 43, 47, 49, 51–56, 58–72, 75–79, 81–89, 92–97, 99–100, 103–05, 108–12, 120, 122, 125, 138–41, 143, 150, 153, 164–65, 177, 180–81, 184, 187–89, 192, 198, 204, 212, 216–18, 223, 227, 232, 236–37, 239–40, 245–49, 251–52, 256–57, 259–62, 264, 266, 269–74, 281, 284, 286, 291, 301–02, 306, 308, 312–13
Football Bowl Subdivision, 47
Fort Lewis A&M, 8
Fox Sports, 87, 89
Francis, Steve, 110
Frazier, Tommie, 109
Freeh Report, 67
Freeh, Richard, 67
Freeze, Hugh, 57–59, 259, 271–72

Fresno State University, 120, 149
Frieder, Bill, 301–02
FSU, see Florida State University
FTW360, 143
Fudzie, Vincent, 33
Fulmer, Philip, 64
Gagliano, Joe, 301–02
Gaines, Brad, 94
Gaines, Riley, 289–90
Gainesville, Florida, 151
Gamecocks, see South Carolina, University of
Ganden, Chad, 18
Gard, Eddie, 296–98
Gardner, Andrea, 16
Gator Collective, 124, 150, 152
Gatorade, 187
Gatto, James, 56, 102–03, 123, 227
Gee, Alana, 311–12
Gee, Matthew, 311–13
Geiger, Andy, 263
General Catalyst Partners, 159
Georgetown University, 16, 220
Georgia, 130, 177
Georgia 80, 109
Georgia Institute of Technology, 47, 109, 261–62, 269
Georgia Tech Athletic Association, 261–62
Georgia Tech, see Georgia Institute of Technology
Georgia, University of, 48, 79, 82–84, 124, 136, 142, 151, 185, 189
Gibbons, Dillan, 188
Glatt test, 234–35
GoFundMe, 188
Golf, men's, 308–09
Golf, women's, 59
Golson, Everett, 55
Goodfellas, 300
Grant-in-aid, 31, 95, 99, 111–12, 114, 117, 240
Great American Ballpark, 309
Griffin, Blake, 110
Group of Five conferences, 89–90
Grove Collective, The, 136, 142

Groza, Alex, 297
Gymnastics, 278–79
Happy Valley United, 142
Harbaugh, Jim, 60–61
Hardy, Eilar, 55
Harrick, Jr., Jim, 48–49
Harrick, Sr., Jim, 48
Harrington, Joey, 110
Hart, Ryan, 111
Harvard Pilgrim Health Care, 158
Harvard University, 158, 219, 299
Hathcock, Hugh, 150–51
Hawaii Bowl, 63
HBCUs, see Historically Black Colleges and Universities
Heisman Trophy, 47–48, 79–80, 109, 186, 266
Hennig, Taylor, 231
Herron, Daniel, 49
HEW, see Department of Health, Education, and Welfare
Hill, Henry, 298
Historically Black Colleges and Universities, 187, 273
Hockey, 95, 104, 192
Hofstra University, 284
Hogan, Frank, 296
Hogan, James, 7
Holman, Luke, 309
Holy Cross University, 299
Home rule, 14
House, Grant, 215
House of Victory, 142
Howard, Desmond, 110
Hsu, Michael, 239–40
Hunter, Travis, 272–73
Hysaw, Vernon, 31
IAAUS, see Intercollegiate Athletic Association of the United
    States
Iamaleava, Nico, 122, 227
IARP, see Independent Accountability Resolution Process
IHSA, see Illinois High School Association
Illinois, 114, 166, 168, 178, 193, 221
Illinois High School Association, 168

Illinois, University of, 215
Independent Accountability Resolution Process, 36, 103
Independent Commission on College Basketball, 103
Instagram, 180–82
Intercollegiate Athletic Association of the United States, 7, 75
International Olympic Committee, 289
IOC, see International Olympic Committee
Iowa, 114, 166, 307
Iowa Division of Criminal Investigation, 307
Iowa State University, 306–07
Iowa, University of, 28, 95, 124–25, 188, 306–07
Irving, Brian, 303
Islamorada Beer Company, 134
ISU, see Iowa State University
Ivy League, 7, 11, 161–62, 219–21, 240
Jackson State University, 187, 272
Jackson, Terrell, 30–31
James, Adam, 264
James, Bronny, 171, 181
James, Craig, 264
James, Don, 33
James, LeBron, 125, 181
Javits, Jacob, 276
Jefferson Pilot, 87
Johnson, Jon, 301
Johnson, Paniro, 306
Johnson, Ralph "Trey", 233
Kansas, 166
Kansas University, 102
Kelleher, Cornelious, 297
Kellogg, Junius, 297
Kelly, Chip, 51
Kent State University, 202–03
Kentucky, 19, 114
Kentucky, University of, 205, 295–98
Kerkeles, Stephanie, 233
Kiffin, Lane, 138, 198, 273
Kirk, Grace, 161, 219
Knight Commission, 247
Knight, Phil, 146

Kocian, Madison, 181
Kohnke, Ned, 300
Kramer, Roy, 64
Kranz, Gary, 300
Kuhn, Richard, 298–99
Labella, Nicholas, 233
Labor law, 105, 162, 213–14, 230–31, 235, 239–40
Lake, Lloyd, 267
Lane Train, see Kiffin, Lane
Langham, Antonio, 63
Las Vegas, Nevada, 292, 301–02
Lasege, Muhammed, 19–21
Leach, Mike, 261, 264–65
Lederman, Doug, 47
Lee, Dion, 302
Lewis, Leo, 57–58
LHSAA, see Louisiana High School Athletic Association
Liberty University, 272
LifeWallet, 149
Linderbaum, Tyler, 188
Liotta, Ray, 300
LIU, see Long Island University
Long Beach State University, 40
Long Island University, 296–98
Long, Jeff, 271
Longhorn Foundation, 157
Louisiana, 114, 166, 168
Louisiana High School Athletic Association, 168
Louisiana State University, 58, 181, 188, 260–61, 280, 309
Louisville, University of, 19–20, 55–56, 88, 102, 123, 246, 269–70
Love, Faizon, 267
Loyola Chicago University, 297
LSU, see Louisiana State University
Lyles, Will, 51
Madden, John, 108
Madison Square Garden, 298
Mager, Norm, 297
Manchester Union Leader, 269
Manhattan College, 296
Manning, Arch, 171

March Madness, see NCAA Basketball Tournament
Marino, Dan, 79
Maryland, 114, 166, 169
Maryland, University of, 88, 246, 249–50
Massachusetts, 158, 166
MaximBet, 134–35
Mazzei, Paul, 299
McAndrews, Sean, 199
McCaw, Ian, 72
McClain, Cormani, 273
McCord, Rob, 69
McGee, Andre, 55–56
McNair, Todd, 261, 266–67
Means, Albert, 64
Meier, Katie, 149
Memphis, 63–64
Memphis State, see Memphis, University of
Memphis, University of, 300
Mercedes-Benz, 187
Miami 91, 109
Miami, University of, 61, 64–66, 88, 123, 148–51, 227, 245
Michaels, Michael, 267
Michigan, 130
Michigan 85, 109
Michigan State University, 18, 69–70, 73
Michigan, University of, 49, 60–61, 70, 73, 124, 136, 142, 188, 303
Mid-American Conference, 89
Miller, Harry, 188
Minnesota, 166
Minnesota, University of, 249
Mirando, Angel, 52
Mississippi, 114
Mississippi State University, 24–26, 35, 52, 57–58, 249, 265, 295
Mississippi, University of, 56–59, 136, 138, 142, 198, 259, 271, 273
Missouri, 169
Missouri High School Activities Association, 169
Missouri, University of, 25–26, 53–54, 87, 246
MLB Players Association, 180
Moody, Ashley, 253

Moore, Kendall, 55
Mountain West Conference, 89, 256
MSHSAA, see Missouri High School Activities Association
MSP Recovery, 149
Murray, Harper, 155–56
Nakos, Pete, 186
Name, image, and likeness, 1–2, 4–5, 10, 21, 46–47, 61–62, 66,
    77, 97–99, 102–04, 107–61, 164–89, 209–11, 215–18, 225–29,
    254, 273
Napier, Billy, 150, 152
Nassar, Larry, 69–70
National Basketball Association, 4, 103–04, 180–81, 263, 298
National Broadcasting Company, 79, 86
National Collegiate Athletic Association, 1–3, 7–28, 35–79, 82–
    85, 90–105, 107–17, 119–23, 126, 131, 136, 138–43, 146–60,
    163–64, 166, 177–79, 184, 191–204, 207–10, 212–19, 221–29,
    231–34, 236–39, 243, 247–48, 258–59, 263–64, 266–67, 271,
    275, 280–81, 283–86, 288–95, 298, 300, 303–13
National Governing Body, 288
National Invitation Tournament, 295
National Labor Relations Act, 105, 213, 230, 237, 239–40, 243
National Labor Relations Board, 162, 236–40, 242
NBA, see National Basketball Association
NBC, see National Broadcasting Company
NCAA, see National Collegiate Athletic Association
NCAA Basketball Tournament, 22, 40, 48, 56, 89, 184, 243, 275,
    291–92, 295, 300, 304–05
NCAA Board of Governors, 160, 289
NCAA Transformation Committee, 163
N.C. State, see North Carolina State University
Nebraska, 166
Nebraska 83, 109
Nebraska, University of, 97, 109, 155–56, 246, 306
Neff, Jr., Bert Eugene, 309–10
Nevada, 41–42, 44–46, 159, 166, 292
Nevada Gaming Commission, 302
Nevada-Las Vegas, University of, 40–41, 43–44
New Era Pinstripe Bowl, 68
New Hampshire, 166
New Hampshire, University of, 269

New Jersey, 166, 292–94

New Mexico, 114, 167

New Orleans, 300

New York, 102, 167, 193, 221, 276, 296–97, 299

New York University, 296

Newport News, Virginia, 270

Newsom, Gavin, 125

NFL, see National Football League

NFL Players Association, 180

NGB, see National Governing Body

NIL, see Name, image, and likeness

NIT, see National Invitation Tournament

Nkemdeche, Robert, 56

NLRA, see National Labor Relations Act

NLRB, see National Labor Relations Board

No-Agent Rule, 91–92, 104

No-Draft Rule, 91, 94, 104

Non-statutory labor exemption, 105, 213–14

North Carolina, 167, 193, 221, 250–51, 253

North Carolina A&T University, 94

North Carolina Central University, 202

North Carolina State University, 102

North Carolina, University of (Chapel Hill), 23–24, 120, 202–03, 249

Northern Illinois University, 95

Northwestern University, 236–37, 239–40, 302

Notre Dame, University of, 54–55, 79, 86, 88, 90–91, 220, 246–47, 249, 269, 302

Nourse, Nicole, 185

Nutt, Houston, 57, 59, 271

O'Bannon, Ed, 96–97, 111

O'Brien, Jim, 261–64

O'Leary, George, 269

Oakland Raiders, 108, 273

Oakman, Shawn, 71

OCR, see Office of Civil Rights

Office of Civil Rights, 276

Ohio, 114, 193, 203, 221, 228, 263

Ohio Casino Control Commission, 309

Ohio State University, The, 47, 49–50, 59, 61, 104–05, 120, 188, 262–64
Oklahoma, 157, 167, 169
Oklahoma State University, 52–53
Oklahoma, University of, 47, 79–80, 82–84, 87, 188, 246, 249–50
Ole Miss, see Mississippi, University of
Olensky, Mark, 301
Oliver, Tymir, 215
OneTeam, 164–65
Orange Bowl, 79, 109
Orange Pride, 52–53
Oregon, 114, 167, 292
Oregon State University, 90, 247, 255–56, 301
Oregon, University of, 51, 136, 146, 247, 301
OSU, see Oklahoma State University
Overtime Elite Academy, 177–78
Pac-10/Pac-12 Conference, 12, 86, 232–33, 239, 245–47, 254–55, 272, 301
Palmer, Carson, 115
Parish, Robert, 15–16
PASPA, see Professional and Amateur Sports Protection Act
Paterno, Joe, 67–69
Pearl, Bruce, 50
Pell grant, 173
Pendergast, Kevin, 302–03
Penn, see Pennsylvania, University of
Penn State, see Pennsylvania State University
Penn Station, 297
Pennsylvania, 68–69, 167, 170, 174–76
Pennsylvania Interscholastic Athletic Association, 174–76
Pennsylvania State University, 61, 66–70, 73, 142, 245, 303
Pennsylvania, University of, 20, 77–78, 219, 231–32, 289
Pensacola, Florida, 269
Pepper Hamilton, 71
Per se antitrust violation, 80–81, 90, 220
Perla, Anthony, 299
Perla, Rocco, 299
Perry, Katy, 57
Perry, N'Kosi, 57
Petrino, Bobby, 269–71

Phi Delta Theta, 71
Philadelphia, 297
Philadelphia Eagles, 3, 51
PIAA, see Pennsylvania Interscholastic Athletic Association
Pitino, Rick, 55–56
Pittsburgh, 299
Pittsburgh 80, 109
Pittsburgh Steelers, 3
Pittsburgh, University of, 79, 88, 246, 284
Point shaving, 295–98, 300–03
PointsBet, 135
Poppe, Henry, 297
Posey, DeVier, 49
Power conferences, 11–12, 28, 47, 88–89, 136, 142, 160, 180–81, 210, 216, 246–48, 254, 260
Price, Mike, 268
Prince, Sedona, 215
Princeton University, 219
Principle of Amateurism, 2–3, 12–13
Pro-competitive justifications, 81, 83–84, 92, 95, 98, 100, 217, 220–21, 224, 228–29, 259
Proctor, Kadyn, 124
Professional and Amateur Sports Protection Act, 292–94
Proposition 16, 16–17
Proposition 48, 15–16
Providence University, 299
Provo 84, 109
Pryor, Terrelle, 49
Purdy, Matt, 303
Quinnipiac University, 281–83
Radojević, Aleksandar, 262–63
Raiders, Oakland, see Oakland Raiders
Ram 1500 Big Horn Trucks, 143
Rane, Jimmy, 146
Raptors, Toronto see Toronto Raptors
Rashada, Jaden, 123–24, 150–53
Razorback Foundation, 270
Razorbacks, see Arkansas, University of
Rebel Rags, 58
Residency rule, 191–92

Restraint of trade, 80–83, 92, 95, 97–98, 100, 105, 112, 207–09, 213, 217, 220, 222–23, 228–29, 259
Rhode Island, 167, 170
Rice, Condoleezza, 103
Rice University, 94, 220
Rodgers, Franklin C. "Pepper", 261–62
Roman, Ed, 297
Roosevelt, Theodore, 7
Rose Bowl, 60, 109, 268, 311
Ross, Kevin, 22–23
Roth, Al, 297
Rothenberg, David, 301
Ruiz, Claudia, 233
Ruiz, John, 149
Rule of reason, 80–84, 92–93, 98, 208, 220, 223
Russell, KeiVarae, 55
Rutgers University, 111, 246, 250
Saban, Nick, 125, 138, 257–58, 261
Sacks, Laura, 240
SACS, see Southern Association of Colleges and Schools
Safe harbors, 278
Saint Bonaventure University, 284
Salt Lake City, 1
San Diego, 266
Sanders, Deion, 187, 198, 272
Sanders, Sarah Huckabee, 167
Sanders, Shedeur, 187, 272
Sandusky, Jerry, 66–68
Sanity Code, 8, 75
Sauser, Dodge, 306
SC 79, 109
Schultz, Gary, 66
Schwartzberg, Benjamin, 297
Schwartzberg, Irving, 297
Schwarz, Andy, 113
Scott, Bobby, 290
SEC, see Southeastern Conference
Self, Bill, 257
Shapiro, Nevin, 64–65
Shaw, Leatrice, 17

Sherman Antitrust Act, 79–82, 84–85, 92–93, 95–96, 100–01, 104–05, 111, 116, 193, 209–10, 213, 216, 219, 222, 258

Show cause order, 41, 48, 50–52, 60, 62, 310

Silman, Benny, 301–02

Sims, Billy, 80

Skinner, Nancy, 113

Smith, LeRoy, 297

Smith, Renee M., 284–85

Smith, Stevin "Hedake", 301–02

SMU, see Southern Methodist University

Sollazzo, Salvatore, 296

South Bend 88, 109

South Carolina, 114

South Carolina, University of, 120, 245

Southeastern Conference, 12, 50, 64, 79, 86–87, 89–90, 236, 245–47, 249–51, 253–54, 270, 309

Southern Association of Colleges and Schools, 24

Southern California, University of, 47, 142, 185–87, 232, 239, 246, 249, 255, 266, 311

Southern Methodist University, 62–63, 88, 93, 247

Southern Mississippi, University of, 300

Sovereign immunity, 250, 253, 265

Spanier, Graham, 66

Spivey, Bill, 298

Sports Wagering Act, 293

SportsCenter, 185

Spyre Sports Group, 142

Stahl, Destiny, 268

Stalions, Connor, 61

Stanford University, 88, 108, 212, 220, 247, 255

Starr, Ken, 72

State College 86, 109

Steelers, Pittsburgh, see Pittsburgh Steelers

Strip club, 268

Strippers, 55

Student-athlete, 1–4, 8–9, 12–14, 24, 54–55, 72, 76–77, 85, 90, 92, 94, 99, 101, 116, 118–19, 130–33, 135, 142, 144–45, 153, 156, 160–63, 166, 168–70, 172, 179–80, 197, 200, 204, 207–08, 215–16, 226, 232, 239–40, 248, 270, 285, 288, 303, 306–07, 311–12

Sugar Bowl, 49, 57, 63, 79, 109

Sun Belt Conference, 89
Sun Devils, see Arizona State University
Super Bowl, 108, 291, 304
Sweeney, Jim, 298–99
Switzer, Barry, 80
Syracuse University, 53, 88, 246, 279–80
Tallahassee 87, 108–09
Tarkanian, Jerry, 39–44
Taylor, Gregg, 29–30
TCA, see Collective Association, The
TCU, see Texas Christian University
Tempe, 301
Temple University, 16, 297
Tennessee, 43–44, 62, 114, 122, 167, 193, 221, 227
Tennessee 85, 109
Tennessee Secondary School Athletic Association, 43–44
Tennessee, University of, 47, 50–51, 64, 122, 142, 153, 227
Tennis, 289
Texas, 71, 142, 157, 214, 230, 265, 275
Texas 81, 109
Texas A&M University, 87, 136, 138, 142, 144, 157, 246, 260, 265
Texas Christian University, 230
Texas Tech University, 264–65
Texas, University of, 87, 120, 157, 212, 246, 249–51
The Shop, 125
The Sporting News, 297
Thomas, Lia, 159, 289
Thomas, Solomon, 49
Thompson, Bobby, 301
Thompson, John, 16
Tik Tok, 180
Times Square, 120
Toledo University, 297
Toronto Raptors, 263
Tower, John, 275–76
Track, 185. 231, 289
Transgender athletes, 158–59, 288–90
Treadwell, LaQuon, 56
Tressel, Jim, 49–50
TSSAA, see Tennessee Secondary School Athletic Association

Tulane University, 300–01
Tunsil, Laremy, 56–57
Twitch, 180, 182
UCA, see Universal Cheer Association
UCLA, see California, Los Angeles, University of
UDA, see Universal Dance Association
UGA, see Georgia, University of
Ukwuachu, Sam, 71
Ulis, Ahron, 306
UNC, see North Carolina, University of
Unions, 4, 162–63, 180, 213–14, 235, 239–40, 242–43
United States Air Force Academy, 308
Universal Cheer Association, 281
Universal Dance Association, 281
UNLV, see Nevada, Las Vegas, University of
USA Gymnastics, 69
USC, see Southern California, University of
Utah, 167
Utah, University of, 143, 247, 255
Utah360°, 143
Uwazurike, Eyioma, 306
Vanderbilt University, 94, 260–61
Varsity, 281, 283
Velocity Automotive Solutions, LLC, 151
Vick, Michael, 270
Virginia, 122, 167, 227, 270
Virginia Tech University, 88, 245, 300
Virginia, University of, 28
Volleyball, 155–56, 184–85, 270, 278, 281–84, 289
Waivers, 18–19, 28, 192–93, 195, 201, 222
Wake Forest University, 29–30
Waldrep, Kent, 230–31
Walk-on, 182, 195
Walker, Herschel, 79
Walker, Tez, 202
Walker, Travon, 186
Walsh, Bill, 108
Ward, Charlie, 109
Warner, Ed, 297
Washburn University, 31–32

Washington, 33, 167
Washington 91, 109
Washington State University, 90, 247, 255–56, 265, 268
Washington, University of, 18, 33, 60, 247, 254, 302
Weinke, Chris, 110
Wesby, Andrew, 16
West Virginia, 193, 221, 250
West Virginia State University, 199
West Virginia University, 47, 99
White, Sherman, 296–97
Willebeek-Lemair, Jacob, 233
Williams, Caleb, 186–88
Williams, Dewey, 303
Williams, Ishaq, 55
Williams, John "Hot Rod", 300–01
Williams, Mikey, 171
Williams, Ricky, 110
Wisconsin, 236
Wisconsin, University of, 303
Witt, Robert E., 269
Woodson, Charles, 110
Xavier University, 310
Yale University, 7, 219
Yankee Stadium, 68
Yeager, Thomas, 64
Yost, Dave, 193
Young, Logan, 64